Praise for *The Frugal Book Promoter*

"If you're going to read only one book to get other people to read your book, it should be *The Frugal Book Promoter*."
~ Tim Bete, director of Dayton University's *Erma Bombeck Writers' Workshop*

"I want to tell you how remarkably useful and efficient your *HowToDoItFrugally* Series is... Ms. Ho-Jo, you rock! Millions of thanks for the care and effort you have invested, and for your fabulous sense of organization. My media kit is all set up and being filled in. Whew!"
~ Deborah Hicks Midanek (Bailey), author

"I think all THREE *HowToDoItFrugally* books for... authors and novice publishers would make excellent, comprehensive textbooks for college courses on writing and publishing."
~ Jim Cox, Editor-in-Chief, *Midwest Book Review*

"Carolyn Howard-Johnson started me on this whole journey of book publishing with her book *The Frugal Book Promoter*. I've hit best-seller status on Amazon several times since. I'm forever grateful to her."
~ Christopher Meeks, author and writing instructor at USC and other colleges.

"At last—a solid, sensible, systematic guide to the ins and outs of promotion and publicity... Carolyn Howard-Johnson proves that she's not only an accomplished poet, essayist, and novelist, but also a marketing maestro!"
~ JayCe Crawford, *Cup of Comfort* author, copyright professional

"...until now I didn't have many other staples to recommend to new authors looking for publicity."
~ Jenna Glatzer, author of *Make a Real Living as a Freelance Author*

"[Carolyn Howard-Johnson is] an incessant promoter who develops and shares new approaches for book promotion."
~ Marilyn Ross, founder Small Publishers of North America and coauthor of *The Complete Guide to Self-Publishing*

"Interesting, informative, readable. Easy to follow quotes and technique mixed together wonderfully. An 'A-1' job. I'll have to put it under my pillow."
~ Leora Krygier, author of *First the Raven* and *When She Sleeps*

"*The Frugal Book Promoter* offers practical advice the author has gleaned from personal experience. Unlike other books and articles on the subject, this one is detailed—and it's chock full of ideas that even seasoned book promoters will not have tried."

~ Dallas Hodder Franklin, editor of SellWritingOnline.com

"Great book! My copy [of *The Frugal Book Promoter*] looks like a porcupine, so many pages are flagged with great tips to try."

~ Karin Ireland, author, motivational speaker

"Howard-Johnson has the comforting tone of a mentor and writes with the precision of a surgeon."

~ Francine Silverman, author, editor of *Book Promotion Newsletter*

"I'm thrilled with all the helpful info and I like the way you've clearly defined the various parts. Makes it much easier to use as a reference."

~ Vicki Malone, publicist

"Carolyn Howard-Johnson's advice in Frugal is like having your own private tutor, writing coach, PR person, English teacher, salesman of the year, marketing agent and, once you've talked to her, cheerleader, all rolled into one. They ought to bottle her energy and sell it. I'll take ten bottles. Uh ... Make that twenty."

~ Queen Jaw Jaw, humorist

"*The Frugal Book Promoter*! I love it. Most authors don't have deep pockets for publicity, promotion, and marketing. The chapter on perks offered by Amazon is a perfect example of the kind of practical advice offered—the kind that took me months to discover."

~ Rolf Gompertz, author, veteran publicist for NBC, and UCLA instructor

"*The Frugal Book Promoter* is excellent.... It has given me ideas that would never have occurred to me and has changed the way I think about book promotion."

~ Mark Logie, award-winning poet and short-story writer

Unsolicited Note from a Publisher

"While brainstorming marketing ideas with one of my authors, she informed me she had just purchased the book *The Frugal Book Promoter: How to Do What Your Publisher Won't* [1st Ed.]. My immediate reaction was an internal 'oh no.' Then I clicked to Amazon to order it and read up on what it was I wasn't going to be doing! When the book arrived, I devoured it. By the time I was done there was neon-highlighter everywhere and, as a fan of Post-its, I made the book look like a yellow-feathered peacock! Carolyn Howard-Johnson has been there, done that in marketing her own books and she packed all her hard-earned wisdom into this *HowToDoItFrugally* series."

~ Nancy Cleary, publisher, Wyatt-MacKenzie

The Frugal Book Promoter

How to get nearly free publicity on your own or partnering with your publisher

3rd Edition

By Carolyn Howard-Johnson

Modern History Press
Ann Arbor, MI

The Frugal Book Promoter: How to get nearly free publicity on your own or by partnering with your publisher, 3rd Edition.
Copyright © 2011, 2017, 2019 by Carolyn Howard-Johnson.
Cover design by Doug West (ZAQ Designs).
Cover photo by Kimberly Olivares, Holland America Photo Gallery photographer

All Rights Reserved. No part of this book may be reproduced or transmitted in any form or by any means, electronic or mechanical, including photocopying, recording, or by an information storage and retrieval system.

Library of Congress Cataloging-in-Publication Data
Names: Howard-Johnson, Carolyn, author.
Title: The frugal book promoter : how to get nearly free publicity on your own or partnering with your publisher / by Carolyn Howard-Johnson.
Description: 3rd edition. | Ann Arbor, MI : Modern History Press, [2019] | Series: How to do it frugally series | Includes bibliographical references and index.
Identifiers: LCCN 2019020104 (print) | LCCN 2019021793 (ebook) | ISBN 9781615994700 (kindle, ePub, PDF) | ISBN 9781615994687 (paperback : alk. paper) | ISBN 9781615994694 (hardcover : alk. paper)
Subjects: LCSH: Books--Marketing. | Advertising--Books. | Authorship--Marketing.
Classification: LCC Z283 (ebook) | LCC Z283 .H69 2019 (print) | DDC 002.068/8--dc23
LC record available at https://lccn.loc.gov/2019020104

Published by:
Modern History Press www.ModernHistorPress.com
5145 Pontiac Trail   info@ModernHistoryPress.com
Ann Arbor, MI 48105 tollfree USA/CAN 888-761-6268
USA   fax 734-663-6861

Distributed by: Ingram (USA/CAN/AU), Bertram Books (UK/EU)

Trademarks and myriad names of products, journals, and businesses used in this work are not authorized by, associated with, or sponsored by the trademark owners. No association with the corporations or names is implied or intended.

This book is available at a discount when purchased in quantity to use as premiums, sales promotions, in corporate training programs, or by schools or social organizations for educational purposes. For information, please contact us.

Dedicated to...

...my first demanding teachers and bosses in the fields of journalism and publicity, including Mary Chachas, former society editor of the *Salt Lake Tribune* and the late Eleanor Lambert of the Eleanor Lambert Agency, New York. It is also dedicated to *you*, the author-publicist of the new millennium.

In Memoriam...

Hazel McElroy Cutler

1923–2004

whose chosen career centered
on libraries, the drivers
of all things literate

and

Trudy McMurrin

1944–2009
university press director
and editor extraordinaire

Other Books in the Multi Award-Winning *HowToDoItFrugally* Series of Books and Booklets

The Frugal Editor:
Put your best book forward to avoid humiliation and ensure success

How to Get Great Book Reviews Frugally and Ethically:
The ins and outs of using free reviews to build and sustain a writing career

Great Little Last-Minute Editing Tips for Writers:
The ultimate frugal booklet for avoiding word trippers and crafting gatekeeper-perfect copy

The Great First Impression Book Proposal:
Everything you need to know to sell your book in 30 minutes or less

A Retailer's Guide to Frugal In-Store Promotions:
How to increase profits and spit in the eyes of economic downturns with thrifty events and sales techniques

Your Blog, Your Business:
A retailer's guide to garnering customer loyalty and sales online and in-store

The author's poetry and fiction may be found at
bit.ly/CarolynsAmznProfile *And* HowToDoItFrugally.com

Contents

Acknowledgements iii
Why a Third Edition of The Frugal Book Promoter? iv
Before We Get Started... v

Section I – Getting Started and Getting on with It 1

Chapter 1 – Excuse me I have to do what? 3
Chapter 2 – Marketing Basics: The Short Course......................... 13
Chapter 3 – To Hire or Not to Hire a Publicist............................. 19
Chapter 4 – Promoting Ethically 23

Section II – Plunging In: Publicity Basics Now............................ 25

Chapter 5 - The Three Ps and Your Writing Career..................... 27
Chapter 6 - Public Relations: The Granddaddy of Great Publicity 29
Chapter 7 – Free Publicity Isn't Really Free 35
Chapter 8 – Branding: Publicity's Cornerstone 37
Chapter 9 – Advertising: The Weak Partner................................ 41
Chapter 10 – Your Now and Forever PR Skills............................ 43

Section III – Do-It-Yourself and Partner Publicity........................ 63

Chapter 12 – The Media Release 69
Chapter 13 – The Rest of Your Media Kit 79
Chapter 14 – Your Query and Cover Letters 95
Chapter 15 – Your Reviews 99

Section IV – Promote Your Book by Doing What You Love 111

Chapter 16 – Loving Writing and Recycling 113
Chapter 17 – Learning to Love What You Thought You Couldn't 131
Chapter 18 – Publishing Dreams vs. Marketing Needs 145

Section V – You and the Media: What's New, Old, and In Between? 165

Chapter 19 – Radio and TV: The Ageless Pair 167
Chapter 20 – The Old Internet.. 177
Chapter 21 – Game Changers... 185
Chapter 22 – Using Social Networks 199
Chapter 23 – The Dangers of Online Promotion........................ 203

Section VI – Well Traveled, Oft Forgotten 205

    Chapter 24 – Reading Groups 207
    Chapter 25 – Catalog Sales... 209
    Chapter 26 – Corporate Sales 213
    Chapter 27 – Retail is More than Bookstores 215
    Chapter 28 – Library Saes 217
    Chapter 29 – Postcards 219
    Chapter 30 – Get Quoted 223

Section VII – Onward and Upward 225

    Chapter 31 – Success as a Motivator 227
    Chapter 32 – Book Sales Getting Musty 229

Appendices 235

    Appendix 1 – Sample Query Letters 236
    Appendix 2 – Sample Media Release 240
    Appendix 3 – Sample Blog Entry 244
    Appendix 4 – Sample Invitation for Tradeshow Appearance 247
    Appendix 5 – Sample Script for Phone Pitch 249
    Appendix 6 – Automated E-Mail Signatures 250
    Appendix 7 – Sample Tip Sheet 252
    About the Author 253
    Bibliography 255
    References 261
    Index 263

Acknowledgements

>...traditional marketers count dollars;
>guerrilla marketers count relationships.
>~ Jay Conrad Levinson, author,
>the *Guerilla Marketing* series

Oh, to remember all those who have been instrumental in the birth of a book! Once, at a writers' seminar, I overheard a well known author deride writers who include many thank-yous to mentors and helpmates in their acknowledgements. He thought the process a ridiculous name-dropping tradition. He is a wonderful writer, but he must have an inflated opinion of his own abilities if he believes he writes books by himself. He may also have no knowledge of marketing, for the nourishing elements of PR are helping *others*, accepting help from *others*, and being grateful for the growth that comes from that exchange. My thank-you list is long, but probably not long enough. My apologies to the many others who contributed to my success but are not noted.

Thanks to members of my most enduring critique group, Leora Krygier, Phyllis GeBauer (now deceased), Iris Fabrikant, and JayCe Crawford; to Emily Heebner who was made to nourish others; to my talented cover designer Chaz DeSimone; to my photographer Uriah Carr; to publicists Debra Gold and Rolf Gompertz; and to all those who cheerfully gave me permission to relate their PR successes and disasters.

Thank you, too, to Joyce Faulkner, Kristie Leigh Maguire, T.C. McMullen, and members of the writing and marketing organizations I belong to who have been generous with their time. Oh! And to my teachers.

Special thanks to my husband Lance G. Johnson, author of *What Foreigners Need to Know About America from A to Z* (bit.ly/AmericaAtoZ). He is never too busy to apply his organized and unrelenting passion for detail to editing my work. And to my new publisher, Victor Volkman, for welcoming me to his Modern History Press.

Why a Third Edition of The Frugal Book Promoter?

We all know that book promotion (and life!) has changed since *The Frugal Book Promoter* was first published in 2004 and even the subsequent *2nd Edition* in 2011. It's mostly changed in ways that have to do with the web, but in other ways, too. As an example, the publishing world in general is more open to indie publishing now than it was then. So, this update includes lots of information on ways to promote that were not around or were in their infancy a few short years ago. The *3rd Edition* still includes the basics that make you into an on-your-own publicist or a great partner for a professional publicist. That includes everything you need to know to put together the best, most effective media releases, query letters, and media kits possible.

You'll love the chapters on what I call the game changers (yeah, the digital world!). These really are game changers! There's information on using online bookstores to your benefit. And how to make your blog actually work for you. And how to save time with your blogging! And ideas for blog posts—even if you write fiction or poetry.

You'll find it loaded with resources you can use, but they're all updated. There is new information that answers questions like these:

- What do I really need to know about copyright? I get so much conflicting advice.
- What is Carolyn's simplified method for making social networks actually work—without spending too much time away from my writing?
- How can I avoid falling into scam-traps for authors?
- How can I get my book into one of those big tradeshows like BEA?
- What are the best "old-fashioned" ways to promote—the ones I shouldn't give up on entirely?
- How do I go about writing (and publishing) an award-worthy book.
- How can I use the fancy little, flowery QR codes to promote my book to mobile users? And to others?
- What are the pitfalls of using the web and how can I avoid them?
- What are the backdoor methods of getting reviews—even long after my book has been published?

Before We Get Started

> Knowing the rules of promotion is like knowing the rules for writing. When you have mastered them, you have the confidence to break them when you need to. ~ CHJ

Don't misunderstand the above quotation. I'm not suggesting that an author run willy-nilly breaking the rules of public relations (PR). That will not benefit her reputation as either an author or someone who knows how to brand herself. Many books give you PR essentials, but once you know the rules, you are better able to let your writer's imagination loose so you can promote yourself and your book with confidence. When you do that, even our rule-oriented culture will appreciate your creativity rather than criticize you for it. Rather than the tinkle of bells, your efforts will be the sound of timpani to the ears of gatekeepers—you know, folks like editors, producers, and anyone else able to help you get your message out there.

In some circles it appears to be stylish to eschew promotion as vocally as possible. However, it is a myth that authors—especially the greats—lack the ability to promote. Many famous and literate authors were very good promoters, and some did it without PR classes (or books!) to tell them how. Mark Twain is an example.

Laura Skandera Trombley, president of Pitzer College in Claremont, California, and a noted Mark Twain scholar, says the image we have of this American icon is the one we have "because that's the image [Twain himself] wanted people to have," and that Twain was a man "so gifted at marketing himself that nearly a century after his death, his name still evokes his white-haired likeness." Branding works so well that Trombley was moved to add, "And [Twain's image has] been so co-opted, it sells everything from pizza to banks to luggage. You know, Twain and Elvis, two symbols of American cultural life that are just indelible."

As important as branding is, building relationships (that might be read as networking) is even more important. Certainly networking is part of branding, but it can obscure the definition. Branding is everything you do to encourage people to think of you favorably and often.

We all know what building relationships is. The thing is, with the advent of the web the possibilities for relationships are so much greater than they once were. Relationships have become—if not a more important part of a good promotion campaign—at least more widespread. "Social networking" is the new term for some of that relationship building and I don't neglect that concept in this book. Having said that, the basic concepts and tools of public relations are still the drivers behind promoting with new media.

Marketing and all it encompasses (PR, branding, promotion, building relationships, and more!) works. And it works better if the author is proactive. A publisher's publicist can only do so much without an author's cooperation. Further, most publishers assign no publicist or, if they do, she may have access to a very slim Rolodex, an even thinner budget, and hardly any experience or none at all. It is up to you to overcome these drawbacks.

This book is for authors who want their books to soar and do not want their careers to languish. It is structured so authors can select chapters that address aspects of their marketing plan most needed at any given time.

When I refer to something I cover in depth elsewhere, I give the reader a prompt. The Index also makes it easy for authors like you to find tips for different kinds of promotions as you need them. As an example, when you look up "TV," you'll find information on how to get TV appearances, how to prepare for them, and how to utilize them in your promotion.

The Frugal Book Promoter is not a textbook. It contains opinions—some as black and white as the page you find them on. It is me talking to you, sharing with you. I had no desire to write a tome that would make my readers hearken back to their boring (and heavy!) high school texts.

I may not cover every possible promotional idea out there. In fact, I avoid anything I have not tried as a professional publicist, retailer, or in promoting my own books. You will, however, find some new (or rarely used) ways to promote that have not been scorched, stirred, and then warmed over.

What is important is that you find a path for promoting that fits *your* interests, skills, pocketbook, and your book's title. I expect you to pick and choose. Only someone who had no guidance (like me in the days right after my novel was published) would attempt to use them all. I hope that my experiences will save you time, money, and heartache.

Novelist and political powerhouse Hill Kemp and I had a conversation about how interesting it is that writers scorn something so commercial and practical as marketing, but when they sign with a fine traditional publisher (or any other publisher!) who doesn't market their books, they are most put out. That is one of the reasons the first *Frugal Book Promoter: How to do what your publisher won't* came to be and why I expanded it in the second edition and this, the third. Marketing is essential. It is also creative. Hill suggests that both nonfiction and fiction writers can help themselves overcome their aversion to promotion with this exercise:

"Pretend you are writing a novel. Create a character who lives to market something—anything. Put that character into situations you might face in promoting your own book. You'll then have in this character a mentor for furthering your writing career."

Section I –
Getting Started and Getting on with It

> The aim of marketing is to make selling superfluous. The aim is to know and understand the customer so well that the product... sells itself.
> ~ Peter Drucker, management theorist

As making a living from selling books has gotten tougher for publishers and budgets have gotten slimmer, big and small publishers alike have put a greater priority on grassroots marketing.

Even as publishers shift more of the responsibility for marketing to the authors, many authors are convinced there is something déclassé about the words "marketing" or "selling." We coyly say "submitting" our work or "shopping" our books, even though we sense we must build platforms, regardless of the words we use. We know we must submit the most professional proposal, synopsis, and chapters we can, but the idea that the image we are creating is part of a promotion plan sort of gets lost in... well, the language.

Ever-changing technology has also made authors fearful of what we must do—what we must learn—to carve a successful career.

As they say, we need to "just get over it." This first section of *The Frugal Book Promoter* helps assuage your fears. Trust me. Great marketing is merely sharing your passion with others. And it's lots of fun.

1 Excuse Me! I Have to Do What?

> No matter how authors publish—on their own or traditionally—their books may live or die at the hands of their own marketing skills. ~ CHJ

True publishing includes the marketing of a book. That means your writing (and you!) will be *exposed* to the public no matter how it is published. If you managed to find a great agent or publisher, you are probably aware your work was favored over some very good writers because your résumé (or platform) shows you write well *and* know how to market yourself and your writing. Once we authors realize how important these skills are, we understand that we must come to terms with fears that keep us grounded when we should be flying high.

Doubt and uncertainty about the publishing world are in the air. My clients and students say things like, "If I let people see my work, will it get stolen?" or "Is it safe to send my work to an agent or publisher?" or "I'm a writer, not a publicist and I'm scared."

Now just about the time we authors have finally decided to follow our dreams, we learn we must also do something most of us are not suited to or something we expected someone else would do for us. That is, we must market our books.

This is how we deal with it. Though the world of publishing is very different from our expectations, those differences will open doors for us. Just as writing has made a difference in our lives, so will the entire publishing process.

For the first time we writers can take complete charge of our own careers—or not. It's our choice. Technology lets us aim at niche markets that were once economically unfeasible. There are more ways to publish than we could have imagined a decade ago. We can reach more people with news of our book than was ever possible, and less expensively. We are living in miraculous times for writers.

Some successful authors have talent, some don't. Some talented authors have never taken their manuscripts out of a drawer. Though a few writers get lucky and soar to the bestseller lists with no effort outside having produced a manuscript, it is foolhardy to expect we will be among the fortunate few. The good news is we can have successful writing careers if we are motivated, have patience, persevere. And if we promote.

Even then, the prospect of facing the publishing world is daunting. Myths and exaggerations circulate. It is easy to be fearful. We can get over that. We can grab at success and we can do it our way. Wasn't it Roosevelt who said, "The only thing we have to fear is fear itself?" So, let's get rid of our fears so we can "just do it." Wasn't it Nike who said that?

Big Worry Number One: Plagiarism

Fear of plagiarism is a topic of discussion among the writers I meet on the web, in my critique groups, in my classes or wherever authors get together to further their careers. Some writers are so crippled by the idea that someone might read their work without paying for it or plagiarize it, they fear sending their manuscripts to publishers and agents. They fear trusting professional editors and teachers. Worst of all, they fear using proven marketing techniques like "peek-inside-features" offered by online bookstores and other methods that successful publishers have used to find readers for decades—or even centuries.

The most important part of writing, after the process itself, is to be read, to *share*. Worry about plagiarism keeps inexperienced writers from doing that and produces anxieties that interfere with their creativity.

An author must take precautions, of course, but I would rather have a million people read one of my poems in a Dear Abby column credited only as "Anonymous" than have it read not at all. Having our voices heard is more important than selling books. Having our voices heard is sharing our souls. I fervently hope more writers will come to share this view.

The kind of plagiarism that authors worry about is quite rare—that is, having an agent or someone in a writing class steal an idea. It's hard to steal an idea. For one thing, there are no truly new ideas in the world. If you don't believe me, read Joseph Campbell's works (which you should do anyway). He divides all of literature from Greek plays onward into a few categories with a few basic elements. It's unlikely that your work is so unique that it doesn't fit into one of them.

Further, ideas cannot be copyrighted. A recent court case reaffirms this notion. If it had not, much of Shakespeare's works would be considered plagiarism and, because science fiction writers often borrow theories from those who win Nobel prizes in physics, that genre could no longer exist as we know it.

Many kinds of borrowings are not plagiarism but the result of the similar way our brains function. You've probably heard the story of monkey colonies on one island who take up the same habits of monkeys on another island with no understandable way for them to have communicated.

You should know that anyone who used your idea would surely write a different book than yours. Reinforce your confidence by trying this exercise: Ask three writers to pen a piece using a very specific subject—maybe even something you've considered writing yourself. My critique group used a story about how, as a child, one of our members sneaked into a neighbor's house and ate frosted strawberries out of the Fridge. We then set a lunch date and read each work aloud. In spite of the similar plot lines, the voices, characters, themes, and details were so different we wondered why we had been concerned about a fellow writer stealing an idea. Usually, a writer won't be interested in writing someone else's stuff, anyway. Most writing, after all, is about *self*-expression.

Often when a case of plagiarism occurs among those who have the public trust, it gets lots of press. However, by the time the perpetrator is found innocent, the case has lost its news value, and we never hear about the accused's exoneration. Thus, authors feel bombarded with reports of plagiarism-that-never-happened.

Careers of a few writers have been broken into kindling when plagiarism was uncovered, but sometimes the opposite happens. Near-anonymous writers or those relegated to the obscure halls of academia become household names when they are found to have picked clean the bones of others' words. When controversy threatened to tarnish names like Stephen Ambrose and Doris Kearns Goodwin they became known among people who would never have heard of them before.

Many times plagiarism goes unnoticed because the thief is not caught or her work is so poor that even stealing cannot make it star-worthy. But think! Think! How much is written, published, put out into the world. Though computers and the internet have made plagiarism easier, the chance that your story might be *the* one stolen from that vast universe is still small.

Plagiarism is most rampant in academia. If you need proof, Google "plagiarism." Yep, a few famous cases and lots *more* stories about kids trying to make the grade at school. We cannot condone such theft, but we authors should not allow the idea of plagiarism to doom the progress of our writing careers. Generally it is only the poor young schmuck who grabbed down someone else's work who suffers—whether or not she is caught.

Another consideration. If someone should swipe a few of your words or an idea, her chances of becoming rich, famous, and envied because of them are no better than yours. If she should, that sets her up for legal action worth pursuing. If she doesn't get rich on your work, you have the satisfaction of knowing she didn't, and won't need to bother your talented head about chasing after a pauper. Or you might choose to do that chasing because publicity surrounding such a case could be the lucky stroke that makes *you* the rich, famous, and envied author. A professional publicist can make a sweet drink out of very sour fruit and a good copyright lawyer will be invaluable to that mission should you care to explore it.

That is not to say there is no such thing as mass production of knock-off books. Definitions of such a practice vary, but they seldom have much to do with writing that has an essential voice. Some use the word "content" which I think denigrates what writing is or what real writers do.

> **Note:** It helps to remember that books were Xeroxed long before computers let us download them as e-documents. Some practices deprive authors of their royalties, but they also drive word-of-mouth exposure. In any case, these borrowings are impossible to control completely no matter how you publish and never have been. It's another fear you must conquer rather than let it handicap you.

Sending a copy of your work to yourself is not the great idea it appears to be. My publisher and many others think this so-called poor man's copyright "should be debunked." The US copyright office says it is sometimes called a "poor man's copyright" and reminds us that "There is no provision in the copyright law regarding any such type of protections [the protection of manuscripts using this mail-to-yourself method], and it is not a substitute for registration." A little voice goes off in most of our heads that says, "Of course *they* would say that."

Here's the thing you should use before you let a process like this give you *misleading* confidence you are protected. Pretend it is tattooed on your forehead:

> **Writers are *already* protected in several ways at no cost—no legal fees, no postage fees, as few sleepless nights as possible—and a couple fairly frugal ways as well.**

The US copyright law was amended in 1978 to offer protections once your work is "fixed" in some way. A draft of your novel qualifies as "fixed." Even before you register it with said copyright office.

> **Note:** I am still squeamish enough to "fix" my creative work by printing, dating, filing, and sending it to myself as an attachment to an email. It's my idea of "fixed" that gives me the feeling of security I crave.

- Authors can register their work with the US copyright office easily and relatively inexpensively. Go to go copyright.gov for instructions (screenwriters go to Writers Guild of America, wga.org).
- Registration gives you the additional protection of something called a "statutory damages rule" (look it up on Wikipedia)

- The US is a signatory of the Berne Convention.
- Great copyright lawyers are ready and waiting if you need one.
- When you publish, your publisher (traditional or partner publisher) can and should register your work with the Library of Congress Cataloging-in-Publication (CIP). This is a step often neglected by self-published authors which puts them at a disadvantage if they are determined to see their books in bookstores and libraries. In addition to this benefit, it "shows quite authoritatively when a work has been 'fixed,'" according to the publisher of Modern History Press.

   that broadens your protections beyond provable and specific financial suffering caused by the plagiarism at no extra cost.

Because I am here to give you *frugal* advice, I'm telling you the above copyright precautions will probably cost you less than postage and a trip to the post office using the poor man's copyright and could *save* you a ton of money if you are one of the few who faces plagiarism-worth-pursuing first hand.

So what about the envelope-and-postage method? If you want to use it *in addition to the above precautions* because it gives you peace of mind, have at it. Whatever *else you do that makes you more comfortable* probably can't hurt. Nothing is guaranteed in life. Attorneys can't guarantee you will win even an "air tight" case. Publicists can't guarantee you great exposure. Sealed envelopes in a drawer and typing © after your title aren't guarantees. And asking an agent for a nondisclosure agreement isn't the great idea it at first appears to be because agents may hesitate to work with someone who doesn't respect the traditions of the publishing industry or appears too litigious. I am not going to shred the poems I once mailed to myself and put in an old hope chest. But neither will I eschew all the good stuff the publishing industry and some governments worldwide have put in place to help creatives.

> **Note:** If your fear of plagiarism is a hurdle that easy and inexpensive fixes listed above will not assuage, read Tonya Marie Evans and Dan Poynter's *Literary Law Guide for Authors* (bit.ly/LitLawGuide) or hire a copyright lawyer. A good attorney can be worth her pounds in sterling. Check the faculties of respected writers' conferences to get good referrals.

Many authors give away their work or barter it. They do it in trade for exposure of their names and titles, to help build their platforms (their résumés), and to encourage writers to buy their other works.

Some consider this trend unfortunate. They forget that a no-pay model has been used for decades by many of the most reputable poetry, literary, and academic anthologies and journals. Some literary entities "pay" with only a few copies of the finished book.

Some well known authors like James Patterson have updated that model. Patterson, no newbie to marketing, was the once-chairman of a major advertising agency. He made free e-copies of his old novels available to publicize his new work. He doesn't need a career boost, but marketing like this work—even for him.

I offer free content directly from howtodoitfrugally.com/free_content.htm (my website). My publisher and I offer excerpts used for educational purposes as long as the reprints include my byline and credit line (the mini bio at the end of the piece that I provide with each article). I may use Patterson's free e-copy idea when my next novel is released.

Building a platform is what all this writing and publishing and giving away your work is about. It's also about something called branding. (You'll learn more about both in Section II of this book.) For now, suffice it to say that when you have built a great platform one plank at a time and kept your branding in mind as you do it, it becomes easier to snag a great agent or publisher.

You've probably heard of the old-fashioned term, "clips." Clips are tear sheets (your work in print that is torn from a newspaper, magazine, or other printed matter) or a photocopy of that piece. They prove to a gatekeeper that you have been published. Today your "clips" may be hard copies, but they will probably also include printouts or links to your work.

Your clips are part of your branding and branding is part of the book promotion process. Every time your byline appears on subjects related to your book, you make at least some gatekeeper aware of what you do.

Every time you are published—for pay or not—you have a new clip. A credit appears beneath the published piece that tells something about you and it often links to your website, your email address, or the online Buy page for your book. Each one becomes part of your résumé, part of your media kit, part of the confidence you need to promote with your chin up and a brave smile on your face.

So, what is the worst thing that could happen if you don't get paid for something you write? Whatever that "worst thing" is, it's worse to be paralyzed by something that may never come to pass.

What can you do on your own if your work is plagiarized? We can make plagiarism by making into a win-win situation. When one of my articles for *Home Décor Buyer* showed up on a website, that magazine's lawyers didn't care to pursue the problem (probably because two hours of a lawyer's time would cost more than what they had paid me for the article). I pointed out to the offending webmasters that they had used a story this magazine had paid good money for and suggested that they give both the magazine and me a little publicity in trade. The webmasters were apologetic and happy to make amends. That's an example of good public relations, by the way. Nonconfrontational. Willing to communicate. Willing to compromise.

Big Worry Number Two: Oops! Swiping Others' Work

Plagiarizing others' work is something that should be a bigger concern for you than that *your* work might get filched. Sometimes our memories don't serve us, our minds absorb something so completely we don't remember where we first saw something, or we or our researchers don't take accurate notes. To protect yourself, research carefully, keep accurate records, and assiduously credit others.

We should also take care when we quote others, though it is legal to quote for certain purposes and in certain amounts without getting permission. Generally you may quote without permission if you write commentary, satire, criticism, academic material, or news reports. The number of words you can use without permission depends upon the size of the copyrighted work as a whole. Guidelines differ from genre to genre. Find specific guidelines at the Library of Congress website, loc.gov, or let a research librarian help you. The online bookstore division of Amazon protects itself by allowing quotations and blurbs of up to twenty-five words.

If you borrow a theme or idea from someone, read *Literary Law Guide for Authors: Copyrights, Trademarks and Contracts in Plain Language* (bit.ly/LitLawGuide) by Tonya Marie Evans, Susan Borden Evans, and Dan Poynter, or check with a lawyer familiar with literary law. Freelancers or those employed by newspapers and other publishers can look to their companies' legal departments for advice.

> **Caveat:** Sometimes getting unnecessary permission is cumbersome and counterproductive. Balance your decision-making process. If you're writing an unofficial biography (which often means the person you're writing about isn't thrilled with your project), you probably need a good lawyer. If you're writing a piece for a newspaper or academia, research their policies. In many other cases, asking permission can slow you down but also earn you friends.

Big Worry Number Three: Being Sued

Many of you worry—a lot—about legal suits. Fear of litigation can help you protect yourself, but it can also be a creativity spoiler and lead you to make counterproductive marketing choices.

To avoid lawsuits (and sometimes to avoid being in the limelight), some of you consider writing under a pseudonym. That is certainly an option. Doing so, however, will make it much harder to promote your work and won't necessarily protect you from litigation.

It surprises first-time authors to find that it is at least as important (sometimes more important) to promote the author than the title of her book. Frequently the identity of the real author becomes known very quickly anyway.

Many are familiar with Joe Klein's 1992 novel *Primary Colors* (bit.ly/JKleinsColors). He published it anonymously to great fanfare. It quickly began to die. There was no one to interview, no story, no driving personality. He may deny this motivation, but it appears the author came out of the closet to save his baby from a quick death of slow—then no—sales. Would it have come to the big screen in 1998 with John Travolta and Emma Thompson if the author had not come out? Probably not!

Pseudonyms are useful for branding a separate series or genre. If you're determined to use a *nom de plume*, study the techniques Nora Roberts used for her romances and the mysteries she wrote under the name of J. D. Robb. Both Roberts and Robb are pseudonyms, but this author has a team of marketers and lots of experience to make the juggling process easier.

Big Worry Number Four: Success or Rejection

Psychology journals are full of information about the mirror image twins, fear of success and fear of rejection. They can both be fatal to your writing. You worry that you won't be successful. Then something inside your head screams, "Gulp! What if I am?"

If you suffer from disabling fears of success or failure and want to be published, you must learn to at least mitigate them. This book gives platform-building methods that will help even the shy writer shop her book effectively and, once published, give her a chance at topping best-seller lists. She can't completely avoid the public, though. Her publisher will (at a very minimum) expect a writer to meet her adoring public on book tours and a book launch. It is true that a few reclusive authors appear to do very well, but that is mostly a myth perpetrated by the media. Louise Glück, the famous and well-respected poet, is one of those. Yes, she avoids media exposure, but she is no recluse. She teaches and teaching is an excellent way to build a following. And teaching certainly requires some crowd-pleasing skills.

A good therapist can help you with worries like these that often run deeper than the writing problem at hand. A book that addresses several of the psychological intricacies of writing is Bruce Holland Rogers' *Word Works* (bit.ly/ThrivingWriter).

Try a few exercises on your own. Affirmations and baby steps help us get over some fear because the subconscious absorbs what it is exposed to and little steps are less daunting than big ones.

Affirmations work better when you say them out loud. Here are some that may get you toddling. Look in the mirror and say them once a day:

- The universe protects the work I send out.

- The universe lets my career progress surely and comfortably.

- The universe is infinite; there is space enough in it for everyone to succeed, including me.

It helps to divide the submission process into baby steps. You dig into the bowels of your computer for something you wrote years ago the first day. Edit it the next. Find a magazine that publishes similar material the next. Once you have taken several tiny steps, you have taken a giant step. You begin to overcome your fears because good things begin to happen. All you need add is love and a pat on your own back.

Tip: Repeat these baby steps at least five times for five different submissions. It is hard to worry about any one of them with so many submissions out there working for you.

Big Worry Number Five: I'm Not Enough

If that little voice in your head keeps telling you that you don't measure up, there are remedies for that, too. Knowing you are a fine writer and have other skills required to support a writing career will help dissipate fear. Here is what you can do to build confidence.

- Take classes from a reputable college that specializes in classes for writers. Pick some classes in writing craft and some that cover the business of publishing. I chose UCLA Extension Writers' Program (UCLAExtension.edu) and taught there for nearly a decade. Maybe you can do something similar.
- Join a critique group or assemble one from members of classes you have taken. They have demonstrated an eagerness to learn more about their craft and already have experienced the delicate nature of the critique process.
- Read books. Books on editing. Books on grammar and the elements of writing. I love June Casagrande's *It was the best of sentences. It was the worst of sentences* (bit.ly/BestSentences). Read books on marketing other than this one, too. The more you know, the more you can pick up on advanced ideas. Check the Index and Appendices of this book for more good books to read. We all know good books are one of the thriftiest ways to learn.
- Utilize experienced support people. Eve Lasalle Caram (ecaram@roadrunner.net), one of my first teachers at UCLA and one of their award-winning instructors, teaches and critiques privately.
- Read Milli Thornton's book *Fear of Writing* (bit.ly/FearWriting) to help you with other mental blocks.

    Caveat: Try to find university-vetted mentors. If you must rely on the web to find seminars, editors, instructors, or other reliable experts, try to get referrals from folks who are not new at writing. Use the same research and analytical skills you would use to hire a contractor to build your dream home.

Big Worry Number Six: Fear of Marketing

The most pressing fear seems to be the fear of marketing. It's amazing that in a capitalist country where money, success, and entrepreneurship are admired, many don't value the skills that energize our economy. That cultural disapproval leads to a fear of marketing and is the most destructive fear for the future of a manuscript that's already been written. When you have finished reading this book, marketing techniques and principles will feel like old neighbors. You'll know which ones to embrace and which to avoid.

If you read this book from front to back, rather than use it as a tutorial on specific promotion basics as you need them, you may come away with a new anxiety: "How will I ever find the time to do *everything The Frugal Book Promoter* says to do?"

Just know you don't have to.

You get to pick and choose from this book what fits your pocketbook, your book's title, your personality, and the time you can give over to marketing. As you learn one skill newer ones seem to come naturally. You'll soon be an expert on book-related topics you never dreamed you would know so much about.

Just know you *can* do it.

The more you work at it, the more baby steps you take, the easier it becomes. Your fears will fall away. Plutarch said, "Go on, my friend, and fear nothing: You carry Cæsar and his fortunes in your boat." As writers, we carry a valuable cargo. We, too, should go without fear.

2

Marketing Basics: The Short Course

> In a few short years the internet changed the world of marketing, but, at its best, it still relies on understanding, caring, and passion. ~ CHJ

In Chapter One you learned you must market your book to give it its best chance for success and, I hope, you committed to learning what you must do to give your baby—your book—the best start in life. That's the hard part. The next hurdle—learning the marketing essentials—will be easy for you. I know because you're creative and have perseverance. That's what it takes to market a book.

Getting over the I-don't-want-tos is the next step. Go ahead. Have your little tizzy fit. Pick any excuse or scary marketing word from the list below. Afterward we can get to work.

- **Marketing:** I don't want to "market." It's an ugly word. Reminds me of selling pigs at a renaissance fair.

- **Promotion:** The word "promotion" gets paired with "self" way too often. I get embarrassed just thinking about it.

- **Publicity:** Give me a break. "Publicity?" What is that? Sounds expensive and I haven't figured out how it's different from "public relations."

- **Advertising:** That sounds expensive. I have big hopes for my book but no assurances my book will make any money, so how can I spend money on advertising?

- **Branding:** My book isn't published. It's too early to do any branding, much less learn what it is.

- **Platform:** Don't even mention the word. I'm a writer, not a politician.

- **Public Relations:** Oh, gosh. Does that mean I have to get out from behind my computer and relate to people?

All the misunderstandings, prejudices, and concerns expressed above are why you hold this book in your hands. You know you must do something so readers know about you and want to read your book. Indeed, to convince them they *need* your book.

Putting off your marketing is dangerous to your book's health. The arguments most destructive to the success of your book usually go something like this:

- I don't need to learn this stuff. I'll have a team behind me—everyone from an agent to the marketing department of a powerhouse publisher. My writing career will be fine.

- It's too early to begin worrying about promotion. I've got a book to write.

- I'm willing. I'm able. Maybe I don't even need this book on marketing. I'll start soon. Maybe tomorrow.

- If I need a publicist, I'll use that huge advance I'm going to get to hire one.

No, no. Please don't delay! It gives me an Excedrin headache to think of the time you are wasting by rationalizing away the need to learn to market. It gives me a migraine if you really think you can wing it. If you've even breathed these objections, it's very nearly certain you're living in the last millennium.

It's unlikely that even if you snag a big publisher they will allot much of a budget to what used to be called a midlist author. Now "midlist" merely means a new author with a publishing house—one who'd better be able to market her book to stardom on her own if she wants another book contract.

Here's why you must start using some marketing tools right now rather than later.

- When you build credibility, experience, marketing expertise and become familiar with your marketing tools the moment you decide to become a writer, you're building your platform. That platform works in your favor when you go after an agent or publisher.

- Elements of marketing, like writing query letters, taglines, and knowing how to pitch, is the power behind your entire writing career, not just your book's marketing campaign.

- To be effective, publicity must build.

- You can't possibly learn all you need to know about publicizing your book in one evening. Publicity is like practicing piano. The more you do it, the better it will play in Peoria and everywhere else.

A *Marketing Umbrella* is my gift to you.
Picture a big red umbrella with the words

"S-E-L-L-I-N-G S-T-U-F-F"

printed around the edge in pristine, white letters. It helps if you add

"E-V-E-N B-O-O-K-S."

This umbrella is your map. Each of the umbrella's ribs represents a division of marketing similar to those the marketing departments of universities and corporations use. One rib might be "market research." One might be "advertising" (something you may want to avoid—but more on that later). One is "public relations." "Publicity" is the happiest rib because—as you will learn—it's partially about getting *free* ink. There may be further divisions right down to the ever-dreadful "statistics."

"Branding" is what you do so your reader will call to mind a certain image when *you* or your writing (notice I didn't say "your book") come to mind. Hang in there. We'll talk a lot about branding.

You might hear the word "promotion," but you probably won't find a class dedicated to it in any university catalog. It's not that "promotion" won't get discussed in some classes, but authors tend to use that term inaccurately, just as the title of this book does. In its strictest sense, a promotion is an individual gimmick that businesses use to sell a product. Esteé Lauder has frequent gift-with-purchase promotions to coax women to buy their anti-aging creams. An author offers her book packaged with another author's book at a book fair. Magdalena Ball and I offered the Christmas chapbook we coauthored to our readers in quantities at a discount so they could use them as greeting cards. (bit.ly/BloomingRed).I'll probably use the word "promotion" incorrectly in this book again—for convenience's sake. "Promotion"—the way we use it—is important for authors, so we're going to designate one of our umbrella ribs to it whether academics or marketing professionals like it or not.

You'll also hear the word "campaign." A campaign is all the promotions and other marketing ribs that a business carefully crafts into an overall plan for the success of a product. McDonald's began offering coupons or apps to get free cups of latté to promote its McCafé line when it was new. Later it did the same thing for its real fruit smoothies. Those promotions, combined with others, fit its overall "campaign" to boost its image as a cool place with more healthful food choices. No matter that we prefer not to think about it, authors are in business. We need to work on a plan for the progress of our writing careers.

The publishing world has sort of co-opted the word "platform" in the sense of résumé. Even though business people need to build platforms to get jobs just as authors must, the word "platform" did not come up at the PR class I took at USC's Marshall School of Business. Still, authors must be business people. We start building our platforms in high school when we begin to collect tangible evidence that we're motivated, talented, and persistent. All that good stuff. We start building a platform for our writing with the first article or story that comes out in print or on the web. We also build platforms when we show in verifiable ways that we know how to market. Publishers have always needed their authors to be good marketers, but authors need those skills now more than ever.

One of the most important ribs in our marketing umbrella for building platforms (or careers) is "public relations." "PR" is short for public relations or your relations with the public and the media. You know. That free ink or exposure you need to get your book read.

"Public relations" is neither advertising nor free ink. It is the part of your marketing that builds the right relationships between you and your readers *and* those folks who can give your career a boost. It is, in part, dissemination of information that sets a standard for how you would like to be perceived. First and foremost, your public relations must be undertaken with the highest ethical standards.

Public relations advances your career and, done well, keeps you from putting out brushfires. You avoid ticking people off (readers, editors, radio hosts, your providers, and a host of other folks associated with your career) by using great PR. When you do, you have more time and energy to market your book.

To have great relations with the public, you must never assume the worst about any situation. Think of yourself as the best coach in any league. You rally support. You *know* that people want what's best for you. That means no chips on shoulders, no low esteem for yourself or others, no thoughtlessly flying off the handle. It means viewing every challenge that arises as an opportunity.

When it comes to the aspect of marketing that is best for your writing career, we're playing Pickup Sticks. Sometimes the sticks intersect. Sometimes they mess with each other. "Branding" and public relations are a little like those two sticks that can't be pried apart without jiggling the other. What you do to create an image for yourself as an author and for your books can be ruined in an instant if your public relations goes awry. What you do to better your public relations (like remembering the thank-you notes your mother taught you to write) contribute to both your branding *and* your public relations.

You've been practicing PR most of your life. Getting along with family. Impressing a new boss or teacher. Choosing an outfit to wear to an interview. You've been a customer and know why you like some products and businesses better than others. All it takes is some examination of the processes that influence you to get a grip on public relations—even on marketing as a whole. You may have lots to learn in terms of your book but you will begin to understand the basics so you can go forward. It's mostly about the golden rule.

Branding, publicity, and PR are thriftier and more effective than most other means of selling, with an emphasis on publicity. Other aspects of marketing are important, but all the above divisions are the essential freebies. This is one time we don't have to give up quality to save money.

You now have the definitions down and will soon have all the essentials you need to carve out a writing career for yourself and a niche among those most likely to read what you have written. Now it is time to think about hiring a publicist—or not.

3 To Hire or Not to Hire A Publicist

> A publicist, like an artist, must have the proper brushes, paints, and thinners to do her work. For your PR person, the credentials you have built and the contacts you make are the palette from which she works. ~ CHJ

You may be asking why you need to know marketing and promotion stuff if you're going to hire a publicist or if your top-flight publisher will be assigning one to you. That you, the author, must still work your marketing campaign diligently—even if you have a publicist—is part of what makes the decision to hire one so difficult. If you still must face your fears and toil like a worker bee on a hot day—even after spending thousands of dollars on a publicist—what is the point?

I'm inserting a disclaimer here. I worked as a publicist. I hired one for my novel *This Is the Place*. You would think that makes me an unbiased giver of advice because I've seen it from both sides. It doesn't.

Even with journalism, marketing, and publicity backgrounds, my experience with a publicist did not go so well. That made me wonder how well it will go for an author who doesn't have any marketing- or journalism-related experience. That's why I wrote this book on publishing industry-specific marketing. It will help authors do it themselves or be a better partner for their publicist. Here is what a publicity partner can do for you.

- You'll have a partner to share the work.
- You'll have her expertise so you can learn even more PR stuff.
- You'll have access to her contacts.
- You'll have a credible voice other than your own to laud your talents.
- You'll benefit from the prestige of having your releases and other marketing essentials go out under the letterhead of a professional.

Some publicists specialize and some are full service. Some have tiered levels of service and charge only for what you want or need, and some expect that to reap the benefits of their profession you must give them the freedom to run in whatever direction they feel is best for your book. Find out exactly what the publicist you are considering will do and what she won't. Here are some services offered by publicists.

- Most publicists disseminate media releases and query letters *en masse*. They may have no knowledge of your local media possibilities outside of your city's daily newspaper.
- They probably have lists for libraries, bookstores, editors, producers, and charity and professional organizations, but you must provide your list of personal and local contacts.
- A publicist who specializes in representing authors may produce a catalog or newsletter for a targeted group of bookstores (usually independent stores) or editors.
- Some publicists concentrate on getting book-signing tours at bookstores, blog tours (an online version of book tours), print, or TV or radio appearances.
- Some larger publicity firms have many associates. Ask who you'll be working with.

Hint: A mailing service that collates, stuffs, manages lists, and has a close working relationship with an excellent printer can be a reasonably priced partner for some of your direct-mail promotions.

Only you can decide whether or not to hire a publicist. It will depend on:

- If your publisher has assigned a publicist to you, and, if so, her expertise and workload.
- The budget your publisher assigns to promoting your book. Remember, what *seems* like a big budget may not cover much. Ask what she will *do* with that budget.
- The time you can give over to marketing.
- The calorie quotient of your wallet. How fat is it? How willing are you to spend your own money or use your advance to publicize your book?
- How you feel about the skills and projects outlined in this book, especially those of traveling and speaking. If your fear limits your publicist too severely, she won't be able to do as much for you. Catch 22. If you are eager to hit the campaign trail, you might be less likely to need a publicist.
- If you can, find a publicist who is familiar with books. Nay, not just books but the kind of book you have written.

- Find a publicist who already has contacts. If she doesn't, her query letters and releases will be hardly more effective than if frugal you sent them out yourself.

Even if you hire a publicist, you need to know marketing basics. When *Publishers Weekly* writer Judith Rosen interviewed Lissa Warren about publicity efforts for her book, the seasoned publicist and author emphasized that, at a very minimum, the author needs to be "actively involved—even proactively involved."

You should be prepared to do those tasks that only the author can do. Your book benefits if you determine to do the jobs that, no matter how savvy your publicist, you can do better. Here is a quick run-down of where your publicist (or your publisher's publicist) will need *your* expertise:

- She'll need your personal mailing list and the list of contacts you've made with editors and producers. See Chapter Eleven on building contact lists.

- She'll need you to be willing to speak, to workshop, to travel, and to back up her efforts at organizing events.

- She'll need your input on current news that relates to your book so she can work on coverage apart from other aspects of your campaign like getting reviews and pitching acquisition librarians.

- She'll want the media kit this book helps you put together (see Chapter Eleven). If you've hired your own publicist, having that kit will save you money. If you don't have a kit ready to go, your publicist will ask you to provide a bio and a sample interview page or FAQ suggestions and more. She can't manufacture information out of the air so you'll end up doing lots of the work anyway.

Hint: Publicists familiar with the book business are not easy to find, and most authors are reluctant to recommend them because they are acutely aware that the publicist who worked their book well might not work for yours. Contact university public relations departments and PR organizations for recommendations. Ask for references. Ask why they liked that publicist. Their expectations may differ from yours.

Caveat: Don't be surprised if hiring a good publicist feels like a reprise of what you experienced finding a good agent. You may be required to submit a marketing proposal and a copy of your book. Also beware the sticker shock. If a publicist is reasonably priced, the scope of her services or experience might be limited.

Maybe above all, you and your publicist must operate a scrupulously ethical campaign Keep reading for what that means and how it applies to publishing in way you might not have expected.

You may be tempted to skip the next chapter now you are practically a PR expert, but please don't. Certain kinds of mistakes can, at a minimum, put a damper on your whole marketing campaign. And avoiding those errors can improve your chances at success incrementally. Making ethical decisions is more difficult for those unfamiliar with an industry and the publishing industry is full of lots of new authors (And publicists! And agents! And publishers! You get the idea!) who may not have the experience to anticipate the downsides of new marketing promotions.

4 Promoting Ethically

> It's easy to get roped into unethical behavior when we're the new kid on the block. We're naïve, and everyone else professes to know what they're doing. ~ CHJ

Promoting ethically online or off is a must. Authors often get tricked into buying (and participating in) all kinds of promotional services that are unethical, don't sell many books, and aren't useful as lasting marketing practices. I could mention them, but I don't want to give them any traction. As they say, "Buyer beware." Now you know they are rampant you'll be more likely to know 'em when you see 'em.

Review-and-opinion sites, online bookstores, and online popularity contests like the annual one run by *Preditors and Editors*, attract unethical practices. Often these involve getting bestseller status for one's book. Mind you, there is nothing wrong with coordinating a launch or promotion to try to propel your book to a top ranking, but much depends on how it is done. There is a difference between buying up a slew of your own books to skew numbers versus working a joint viral promotion campaign with an expert like Denise Cassino (bestsellerservices.com/), just as there is a difference between asking for a review of your book and telling the reviewer how to rate it. If it smells fishy, it probably is.

> **Note:** For more on getting reviews and fully utilizing them to market your book, read *How to Get Great Book Reviews Frugally and Ethically: The ins and outs of using free reviews to build and sustain a writing career* (bit.ly/GreatBkReviews), the third in this *HowToDoItFrugally* Series of books for writers. Getting reviews is my favorite way to promote. It took a whole book to tell you what you need to know to power a long-lasting book campaign.

When authors participate in unscrupulous behavior, they often do a disservice to the publishing industry as a whole. I've seen benefits offered by websites like Amazon.com disappear after authors abused them.

Occasionally people react to these abuses by appointing themselves watchdogs for these sites. Vigilante groups often go overboard and these folks are no exception. Authors caught in the in this cycle find themselves at the brunt of a campaign against them. Sometimes the fight against unethical behavior becomes as destructive as the practices they were meant to curtail.

Be alert to anything that feels manipulative. If your book is going nowhere, do something positive for it. Take a writing or promotion class or buy a book to learn more about the publishing industry. Learn the time-honored publicity techniques outlined in the next few chapters of this book. Your career will soar—ethically.

Section II –
Plunging In: Publicity Basics Now

Publicity is a not a sprint but a marathon. As any coach knows, you start training slowly and build up steam. ~ CHJ

Maybe your book isn't written yet. Or you haven't decided how to publish the one you've written. Makes no difference. Now's the time to start promoting. I believe in the Five Ps. They are: Prior Planning Prevents Poor Performance.

My father quoted those five Ps, often in situations when the damage had already been done, always with a twinkle—make that a glint—in his eye. For emphasis, I added another P. It's a four-letter P-word, so close your eyes for the next two lines if you're sensitive to them. It goes, "Prior Planning Prevents Piss-Poor Performance." Sometimes the unexpected, even the unacceptable, is the best teacher.

The Six-P maxim is the one that makes me a nag. The more organized you are, the more you know early on, the earlier you start to practice promotion and publicity magic, the more good it will do for your book. The more you learn the easier it is. And that leads me to the three most important Ps for marketing books. Platform, Publicity, Public Relations.

5 The Three Ps and Your Writing Career

> Publicity is a surprise package. We think we know what's in the box but don't. Surprise! Publicity, platforms, and the rest are not about book sales. They are about career building. ~ CHJ

If you decide to publish your own book, you must know how to market it. You also should know how to market if you hire someone to do most of your publicity for you or if your publisher assigns you a publicist armed with a decent budget. You *need* to know the basics early on for the good of your writing career.

Too often an author elects to write a book and then sits back and hopes—never turns a hand to market it, not before the book comes out, not at its release, not after. Here is what might happen to an author who dodges a publicity campaign:

- Unless the universe is truly smiling on her, she will neither sell many books, nor will her publisher be endeared to her.

- The author's book—perhaps years of work—will be out of print in short order. She may see it again, trashed on the remainder pile in discount book stores.

- If the author is self- or subsidy-published, the book will be available but will languish.

- If a talented author refuses to participate, she may have trouble retaining or finding an agent for her next book. Ditto if her book sales are dismal.

So, the first step to great marketing is to know the essentials, the parts that make you the little writing engine that could. Those are the Three Ps. When you work on Publicity and Public Relations, the Platform comes chugging along as the caboose. You need only know it's there, that it's the backup container for all the marketing you do. When it comes time to show someone what you've been up to—in the writing of a résumé, book proposal, query or cover letter, and media kit—your successes are waiting in the caboose for you to use.

You'll learn something about branding in this section, too. Branding is the track your marketing train runs on. Keep it always in mind and in good repair and your publicity train will run smoothly indeed.

When authors first start working on publicity they may get discouraged. Publicity is not a quantifiable or predictable science. Professional marketers may talk about statistics and try to convince us otherwise, but lots of times they're fooling themselves. If their tools are so perfect, why did the world's best marketer get in trouble with its "New Coke" introduction and have to backtrack with the "Classic" brand, the one they had (the one we loved!) all along. And there's no good reason to bring up Ford's Edsel fiasco, now is there?

The practice of publicity requires a positive attitude and perseverance because it is difficult if not impossible to trace a direct line from your promotional efforts to the sale of a book. Of course, it's possible for an author to snag an interview on "Today" and see her book sales bounce, but generally if she measures the success of her publicity efforts by the number of books she sells, she will soon consider her efforts unsuccessful.

On the other hand, if an author thinks of her efforts as a process toward branding—that is, long-term image-making for herself and her writing career—her efforts toward building relationships with publishing and media professionals will eventually be rewarded in significant ways. And she won't be tempted to give up just before her efforts start reaping benefits. Publicity, Public Relations, and your Platform are career builders. You're going to hate this. Forget the big *S*. Sales eventually come, but only if we stay focused on the essential Three *P*s.

J. W. Marriott, founder of the famous hotel chain, once said something like the emphasis of any company shouldn't be on dollars but on service and performance. I would add that great service and performance are the batteries that energize great promotion and publicity.

6   Public Relations: The Granddaddy of Great Publicity

> Without publicity there can be no public support.
> ~ Disraeli

The basics of public relations and publicity are much like the golden rule. Good PR, of course, is carefully targeted. But mostly PR is connecting with people in a way that makes them feel cared for, and those connections are made—with love and expertise—over and over again. Those are the essentials and they work. Done this way, great publicity becomes great public relations and vice versa.

Beyond the golden rule, I have some commandments—eighteen of them—for getting free ink. But they'll do lots more than get free exposure for you. They will build your career, starting now.

Eighteen Publicity Commandments

1. Thou Shalt Educate Thyself

Hooray for the web. There are lots of freebie ways to learn more about book marketing. And books are an inexpensive way to learn more.

- Learn to write a great media release. A release is one of the best tools for getting the publicity you want. Use the instructions in this book in Chapter Twelve and the samples in the Appendix. Find more samples at howtodoitfrugally.com/recent_releases.htm.

- Subscribe to free writing-oriented e-letters and other aids from fellow authors like L. Lynn Goodwin at writeradvice.com, Shelley Hitz and Heather Hart at trainingauthors.com/newsletter/, or my blog at SharingwithWriters.blogspot.com or newsletter at bit.ly/SWWNewsletter.

- Join groups of folks interested in the subject of your book and organizations of like-minded authors.

- Dana Lynn Smith keeps her free eBook guides for online promotion updated. See bookmarketingmaven.typepad.com/

- Check out *The Guerilla Marketing* series by Jay Conrad Levinson from Houghton Mifflin, bit.ly/GuerillaMktg. Levinson's advice is not specifically for the marketing of books, but you may pick up some radical ideas that can be adapted to your own marketing ethically.

- Borrow ideas from other industries that suit your personality and titles. With that advice in mind, see my books for retailers at howtodoitfrugally.com/retailers_books.htm.

- For the concept of "free," including information specifically related to book marketing, get *Free: The Future of a Radical Price* by Chris Anderson on Amazon in audio, paperback (bit.ly/RadicalPrice), or at your library.

- Read more than one book on marketing. You're reading this one. Try Patricia Fry's *Promote Your Book, Over 250 Proven, Low-Cost Tips and Techniques for the Enterprising Author* (bit.ly/250PromoTips). Writers needn't be competitors. Together we can help more writers.

2. Thou Shalt Not Be Snooty

Read everything. Your newspaper, your e-zines (online magazines or newsletters), your rubbish (and that includes spam) can be geese that lay golden eggs. My daughter found a flier from the local library stuffed between grocery coupons in the Sunday paper. It mentioned a local merchant's display in a window at our city library. I asked the library personnel if I could decorate a display window using my book. They were glad to have me help. People who frequent libraries borrow books. Borrowers are readers and tend to recommend books to other readers.

3. Know Thyself, Know Thy Book

Reread your book. Pretend you didn't write it so it feels fresh. Look at its themes to find angles you can exploit when you're talking to editors. What's different about your book? How does its plot or subject matter fit with what's currently in the news? What different demographics does it appeal to? What's happening in the publishing industry and the world that you can connect it to with your queries? A romance website might like my novel, *This Is the Place*, but so would a literary one. That it is set in Salt Lake City where the Olympic Games were played in 2002 was an unexpected publicity bonus. I found sports and feature editors open to it as winter games fervor grew because of its setting and because there is a cute-meet on the slopes of Alta, famous for its powder. They were interested as it waned, too, because they still needed news and had used all the closely related material they had access to. Millie Szerman wrote a how-to book on working from home offices back in the 80s and was soon seen working from her bubble bath on the cover of a national business trade magazine.

4. Thou Shalt Cull Contacts

When you add a new file of media contacts to your computer's database, you need to develop new habits. If you find the name of a new editor and wait to record it, that name may get lost forever. The website gebbieinc.com sells targeted lists of media contacts. Some partial directories on the web are free (check John Kremer's bookmarket.com). Ask for help from your librarian. A good research librarian is like a shark. She'll keep biting until she's got exactly what she wants. Still, the best contacts of all are your own. But with great networking you can make a helpmate of almost any expert. You'll learn more about how to build lists and put them to good use later in this book.

5. Though Shalt Write Notes

Send thank-you notes and small gifts to contacts after they've featured you or your book. Editors pay attention to your next idea, because people they work with rarely remember their manners. Once you've made a good impression on a gatekeeper, stay in contact. The more pleasant you make it for others to help you market, the more likely they'll be there for you.

6. Walk Not Alone

Partnering with others is essential, especially your publisher. It's okay to ask them for what you need like a sample media release or image of your bookcover. Showing your associates you are willing to work with them may spur them to do more. As an example, give your publisher or agent a good reason to feature your book more prominently on their websites. What will benefit their visitors? Suggest that you write a feature story for them, a poem on the joys of writing, or an article on how to query a publisher.

7. Publicize Thyself

You needn't be humble, just caring. Approach the gatekeepers who could use your ideas so it is evident you are concerned about their audience, not just about making a big splash for yourself.

Think about your own life and career. Hundreds of thousands of books are released each year so the release of a book is no longer newsworthy; what else about you will interest an audience? Utilize the fame you may have accrued in your day job. Several editors liked the idea that I wrote my first book at an age when most are thinking of retiring; they saw me as an example that it is never too late to follow a dream, an idea that might inspire the huge Boomer demographic.

My local newspaper publishes pictures of residents holding copies of their newspaper as they stand proudly before a tourist attraction during their travels to China or Key West. Maybe yours does, too. Your son gets engaged, married, has a baby. You're elected secretary of Kiwanis. You hit a hole in one. Some media don't use these kinds of things but some TV stations and small papers sure do, and the fact that you are also a published author makes you more newsworthy. Here are five things that may interest your local newspaper:

- You are asked to teach at your local college.
- A publisher asks you to act as an advisor or ombudsman. Mine did, and I didn't think of it as something that might interest a business editor until later.
- You are asked to be a panelist at a book fair.
- A national journal publishes an excerpt from your book.
- You win an award. (See Chapter Eleven on the importance of awards and how to use them.)

You can see what seems mundane to you may be newsworthy to local papers, and what seems like the biggest news of your life may not interest some media at all. It's all in who you present your news to—and how.

8. Use Thy Creativity

Develop new activities to publicize and manufacture reasons to send out releases.

- Utah novelist Marilyn Brown sponsors an annual writers' award in her name through a writers' organization. Nora Roberts' foundation funds a course in writing at McDaniel College in Westminster, MD. I once did a free contest as part of my *Back to Literature* column at MyShelf.com. I now see why contests must ask for a reading fee or have a financial sponsor.
- Some colleges and writers' organizations encourage people to sponsor scholarships in their names. Giving to the community makes you feel good and you can tie the scholarship to writing in some way. The media will cover the story when you fund the scholarship, when you name judges, when you submit names and pictures of the contestants, and when you hold a gala to honor winners. Use your imagination for a spectacular inauguration for your award. Involve a local dignitary. Get a charity involved.
- Throw a party for reasons other than a book launch—perhaps a salon where artists of all kinds pool their lists to provide a stimulating day for their friends and for the press.

9. Thou Shalt Listen to Thy Readers

Did your book, poem, or story inspire a reader to start a new career? Suggest that story to an editor. Human interest angles like this make you a hero to your reader and to columnists looking for content. Your book's title may get mentioned in the story she writes.

10. Do Good Turns When They Are Needed Most

Do a good turn during a crisis. Donate your books for earthquake or tornado victims to read while they are waiting for permanent shelters or to those who are giving their time to help.

11. Thou Shalt Make Thyself Helpful

When you make a reporter's work easier, you become her preferred resource. When you give her a way to visualize your idea or event, she can imagine how to use your story more easily. When you supply contacts for opposing opinions, she's more likely to use your story idea. When you thank her, she's surprised and appreciative because so few do it.

12. Thou Shalt Make Thyself Evident

Frequency counts. The editor who ignores your first release may pay more attention to your second or twenty-fifth. She will come to view you as an expert and call you when she needs a quotation. Both nonfiction writers and novelists may qualify as experts.

13. Time Thy Contacts

Put yourself in editors' shoes. Time your contacts with them. Asking for exposure in a slick, print magazine's Christmas gift guide in November is futile. Magazine editors work four to six months in advance. Contacting editors of morning newspapers late in the afternoon as they are going to press is not a good idea. Nagging is also a no-no. Wait a decent amount of time to check on correspondence or offer a new idea.

14. Thou Shalt Follow Up

After you send a media release, follow up with a call. Voice contact builds relationships better than other means of communication. Follow up on a breaking news story related to your book immediately.

15. Thou Shalt Keep Clippings

Professional publicists keep clippings for their clients. Mindy P. Lawrence who contributes a regular column to my *Sharingwith Writers* newsletter keeps a database of the clips she gets for hers. The clip file you maintain will be both a record of resources and a visual of how well you are doing.

16. Thou Shalt Evaluate

One year after your book's release, add up your column inches. Measure the number of free inches in any paper that published anything about you or your book. Include headlines and pictures. If the piece is three columns wide and each column of your story is six inches long, that is eighteen column inches. How much does that newspaper charge per inch for their ads? *The New York Times* charges a one-time rate of about $1,000 per column inch! Multiply the column inches by that rate to know what the piece is worth in advertising dollars. Add fifty percent for the additional trust readers put in editorial material over paid advertising.

17. Thou Shalt Set Publicity Goals

You now have a total of what your year's efforts have reaped. New publicist/authors should set a goal to increase that amount by 100 percent the next year. If you already have a track record, aim for twenty percent.

18. Thou Shalt Observe Progress

Publicity is like planting bulbs. It proliferates even when you aren't trying very hard. By watching for unintended results, you learn how to make them happen again in the future. So, don't stop working at it, even at your busiest, most creative times.

Keep reading for a short chapter about all this "free" stuff, what it really costs you and how to manage it.

7
Free Publicity Isn't Really Free

> There may be no free lunch, but publicity is better than a mere lunch and about as free as anything gets. ~ CHJ

I don't want to lead you astray with my frugal approach to marketing. "Free" publicity costs, whether you hire a publicist or do it yourself.

Rolf Gompertz, an author and thirty-year veteran of NBC's public relations department and a one-time instructor for UCLA, once said, "If I had to pay me, I couldn't afford my services." That seems to be the ultimate reminder of how important it is for an author to know something about promotion, and it dispels the notion that getting publicity is scot-free. Time is money, too.

Gompertz reminded me that review copies add up in real dollars, too. So, do supplies and expenses like media kit folders; postage; a new computer; and gas for runs you make to the post office, Office Depot, and to onsite speaking engagements.

The skills you build for getting publicity are well worth your time despite these hidden expenses. Publicity—the art of interesting the media in ourselves or our books enough to result in no-cost ink or airtime—is economical compared to advertising. Never fear, later in this book I'll give you tons of ideas that truly cost you nothing but time.

It's that time thing that will be the most chafing part of marketing your book. It must be managed and balanced. May I suggest goal-setting and time-management expert Deborah Eckerling, an author who consults on those topics and often runs free training on Twitter and YouTube. Find her on Twitter @WriteOnOnline.

Hint: For more day-to-day publicity ideas, subscribe to Joan Stewart's e-letter, *The Publicity Hound*, publicityhound.com.

Next up, branding—the marketing you have been doing since you first learned to dress yourself and didn't know it. Pat yourself on the back and determine how to apply that brilliance to making your writing career sizzle in the next chapter.

8 Branding: Publicity's Cornerstone

> Branding is not advertising, nor publicity, not even general exposure. It is the result of all your efforts working together and how they coalesce into the public's perception of who you are, what you do. ~ CHJ

Back in 2003 when I was still laboring under the misconception that big presses give big marketing budgets to new writers, *Poets & Writers* reported writer ZZ Packer's publisher, Riverhead Press, "Bank[ed] on... name recognition" when they sent her on a ten-city tour, something that her publisher's publicist maintained was a rare occurrence for a first-time author. That implied that if Packer hadn't already built a platform of her own, Riverhead wouldn't have bothered spending that kind of money on her or her book.

We've talked about the importance of your platform before. But the idea that without one a publisher might not give you every opportunity possible to make money for them was astounding and still is! Unless you are already well known in a field and are writing a nonfiction book allied with it or you've been diligent about publicity for some time, it is unlikely you will have built the kind of brand Packer had. That is why *now* is better than later for beginning a publicity juggernaut firmly rooted in branding yourself. That's why your publicity efforts should *not* be aimed at your *book* early in the game, but rather at *who* you are, including your other writing.

Even with a general background in PR and journalism I fell into a pothole or two. For one, I put my book—my passion—first. One day I realized I should be branding me instead of my book. I was designing a business card on vistaprint.com. I wasn't very computer savvy and I couldn't get the cover of my first book to load. I had seen business cards for real estate professionals that used thumbnail photos, so I loaded my photo instead. Then I muttered to myself, "Well, it's okay because I won't have to do much redesigning when and if I complete another book." Another book! Of course! When we think of books, it is the author's name we think of first and, if she's written quite a few, we probably can't name them all.

Even after this burst of clarity, I continued to use the name of my book because "This Is the Place" is a metaphor at several levels. It is, of course, Utah, my beloved home where I was born and raised. "Place" also refers to the farm where my protagonist goes to learn about her history and to that singular spot inside each of us where we must go to find the courage to follow our passion. That's when I realized I wouldn't have to change the name of my website. It, too, was a place—*the* place in fact—for learning more about me and my books. Since the *HowToDoItFrugally Series* for writers (the book you are holding is the first in that series) became popular, I was forced to change to HowToDoItFrugally.com because the tail had begun to wag the dog and wasn't doing a very good job of it.

The world's savvy marketers like Coca-Cola use several related approaches to branding. (Coke Is It! The real thing!—More than 50 of them since 1904.) Branding is not necessarily an all-or-nothing proposition. If I work fervently to promote tolerance, "The Place" in *This Is the Place* will be like Coke's "It" or "Thing." The public will subconsciously assign a meaning to it—the spot inside each of us that is similar or identical to that place in every other person in the world regardless of race, religion, or gender.

It just worked out that my next book was a collection of creative nonfiction. I'm glad I didn't brand myself too narrowly because stationery or business cards that say "novelist" would no longer fit nor would they have fit the *HowToDoItFrugally Series*. My next book was a chapbook of poetry. Again, "novelist" is wrong, and "writer" seems too broad because it encompasses everything from someone who pens letters to a journalist. Since then, I've been forced to do some sub-branding. Usually branding works better when different segments can be made to fit under one big umbrella.

That one big umbrella is almost always the author. One logo. One website. Related colors for each separate product or genre. In my case, my nonfiction for writers and retailers are one thing, my creative work another. And there are divisions within these categories. Even horror guy Stephen King wrote *On Writing* (bit.ly/SteveOnWriting) and that had to make life lots harder on his publicist. From a marketing standpoint, you'll be lucky if your writing is more or less homogenous, but authors shouldn't usually let the marketing of their books determine their career paths unless their reason for writing is to further another profession or career. This may sound nitpicky, but one word can be important.

Some writers use *nom de plumes* to keep their branding efforts from mucking up one another, but using pseudonyms is usually counterproductive. The author misses crossover sales, however small that percentage may be.

Here are some aspects of branding to consider:
- Decide what you want your brand to say. What might you write in the future? If you choose a red-hot image for your

romance and decide to write a literary book, you will have chosen your brand unwisely.

- If your pre-book experience is associated with the subject of your book, consider ways to tie your branding to that expertise.
- Select color, style, font, and artwork for your website with branding in mind. Coke is always red and white. Its sub-brands like Sprite and orange juice have their own colors.
- Coordinate a look for your stationery, cards, invoices, website, and bookmarks. Do it for your voicemail greeting, your email signature, and the look of your instant messaging.

Hint: Once you or your publisher has firmed up your title, think about banners and a logo for your online efforts. If you are not graphics-savvy, try Doug West facebook.com/pg/zaqdesigns. Keep in mind that bookcovers and logos require a different skill set than the illustrator of your children's books or your aunt who paints murals for your state capitol building.

Caveat: Wait until just before your book is released to print your media kits and other promotion material. You'll want to include your bookcover image in as many places as possible.

- Make yourself into an expert based on something related to your book. The author of a series of mysteries might be a forensics expert.
- When you're making publishing decisions, follow your star. It is easier to pursue a subject for which you are passionate. Readers will be attracted to your passion.
- Don't be afraid to widen your path. A literary author's expertise could include grammar or communication. You are building a reputation. You wouldn't want to be known only as honest among dozens of other traits you aspire to.

Hint: When your book is about to be published, marketing leans a bit from branding the author toward what's exciting about the book and how it will benefit its audience. Notice I said "a bit," not a 180 degree turn.

Dress the part when you are in public. So what if you hate cocktail dresses or tuxedoes! So what if you hate costume parties. What *do* you like? Use the parts of *you* that are real to forge a visual identity. Whatever that is will likely fit in with what you write, too. What you write cannot fall very far from your essential self. One of my poetry mentors, Suzanne Lummis, wears berets. She often wears one when she teaches her poetry classes. A photograph of a bereted Suzanne appeared on the cover of a popular writers' magazine. That beret suits her Leslie Caron-type features as well as her poet-self. We love that Steve Jobs wasn't an IBM type, and we sense that his jeans and turtlenecks were part of his brand—intentionally or not.

I mentioned Mark Twain earlier. People like Twain, Jobs, and Lummis are individuals. They would be wearing their Levi's, Panama hats, and berets in any case, because that's what they like. But their own look is affecting. They will be remembered both for their public presentation and for being exactly who they are.

Here's a final shot on branding. When corporations choose a brand too narrowly, we see them struggle to present a new image when they diversify. That is bad enough for corporations with big budgets. It can be deadly for writers on smaller or nonexistent budgets.

I love the "dos and don'ts" in this chapter. But Chapter Nine covers a strong "do not"—with a caveat—that can save an author from one of the most budget-treacherous potholes of all. If you have a big budget to spend on marketing, you'll want to read it. If you don't have much to spend and no idea how many copies your first book will sell, you really *need* to read it!

9 Advertising: The Weak Partner

> Advertising works, we just don't know how, why, or where it works best.
> ~ Paraphrased from the founder of a large chain of retail stores

Advertising and publicity live under the umbrella of marketing. Though the two work well in a well-planned marketing campaign, advertising's mysterious cousin, publicity, works better alone than advertising. It is the more reliable relative because the public—your readers—trust an editor chose it for its value, not because it was paid for. In other words, it carries the cachet of an editor's approval. It is also surrounded by the ever-magic word "free."

I don't advise an author to use her budget—large or small—to advertise. It is nearly impossible for anything but the largest advertising expenditure to penetrate any given market. I use the word "market" to mean the media most likely to reach the audience interested in a particular title, genre, or topic and therefore the most likely to buy it.

Having said that, if the publisher of a book decides on an advertising campaign, the author should assume (or at least hope!) the publisher has allotted a sufficient budget to make those advertising dollars work. Even then, it wouldn't hurt for the author to ask about their advertising plans and their expectations for them. An author might even suggest that publicity might be a better use of their publishers' advertising budget.

Sometimes it is helpful (but certainly not necessary) to advertise. Occasionally the author or her publisher runs across what appears to be an especially fortuitous advertising opportunity for a particular title.

In that case, you should know that when advertising and publicity walk hand-in-hand they can appear to be unethical or worse. In an effort to be impartial, the editors of the best media outlets don't allow their advertising department to influence their editorial staff.

Still, some media reserve the right to use advertisers' stories editorially if they deem them newsworthy. That's when authors might use that relationship to their advantage: If a particular media plays to the audience you would like to see standing in line for your book, paid-for exposure may become an entrée to the editorial decision-makers (a term for all the people in charge of the space that *isn't* paid-for advertising).

Your contact in the advertising department may be willing to put your media release and book on the desk of an editor for her consideration. She should not promise you results, but her efforts might help.

If you decide to go the advertising route on your own, choose a small media outlet—perhaps a local weekly, an arty quarterly, or a website that focuses specifically on your audience. That way the dollars you spend have a better chance to be influential. And don't run the ad only once. The amount of exposure is always important, but frequency is less important in publicity than advertising.

Sometimes a magazine or newspaper runs a special promotion called advertorial. These are sections where you pay for space to cover the story you want told. This paid-for article may be "free" with the purchase of an ad or you may purchase the advertorial outright. Advertorials carry some of the prestige of editorial copy because its copycat character can lead the general reader to assume the article has been chosen only on its merits. The writer or editor you work with on a project like this can be more effectively approached when you have something exceptional you want to submit to the editor (the media decision makers) as honest-to-goodness news.

Advertorial is generally only a little more frugal than advertising. If "free" sounds as if it will serve your needs better than "paid," do your own publicity. If you have money available for your marketing campaign, hiring a book publicist or help with your do-it-yourself publicity projects is a better way to spend it than advertising. Either way, the Eighteen Publicity Commandments in Chapter Six the now-and-the forever-publicity skills in Chapter Ten will help you avoid making booboos you will regret.

10 Your Now and Forever PR Skills

> Marketing skills are essential to success in every business, every profession. They are so basic marketing should be a compulsory subject in schools everywhere along with math and history. ~ CHJ

The *HowToDoItFrugally* method of marketing includes using our time and skills well, er... frugally. It's about the proven essentials that worked in the past and will continue to work. It's about making everything we do build while we avoid reinventing the wheel.

In his run for the presidency, Bill Clinton had a Keep-It-Simple-Stupid (KISS) philosophy. The five p's (maybe six p's—but only if you prefer!) maxim I talked about in an earlier chapter is a keep-it-simple promotion philosophy. You'll see many ways to simplify in this book, from recycling articles to integrating your online presence. Yep, practical, frugal me. My brand. Along with, I hope, the words "accepting" and "caring."

As an example, I make building a media kit (which we discuss in Chapter Eleven) a double-process tool; you use a kit to plan and record your progress rather than merely as a marketing device. It is one of the now-and-forever PR skills that will stand you in good stead. When you collect information for your media kit from the first time the idea of a book enters that creative little brain of yours, the process of building it helps you get confident. A record of your progress is evidence of how well you're doing—in black and white—so you can't forget or deny it.

This build-a-kit-as-you-go also helps you remember all the stuff that needs to go into your kit before the next step in your writing career pushes it out of your memory banks. And your mock kit will make it easier (and faster!) to whip your real media kit into final shape when the time comes.

I call this method "The Great Book Promotion Planning Media Kit" and it has become one of my most popular seminar topics at writers' conferences.

Hint: I store several iterations of my media kit in my computer. One focuses on my teaching and speaking, another on my retail books, another on my poetry. You will probably do something similar, depending on how your career grows.

So, what are the basic, multi-use PR skills, specifically? The ones that help you do just about everything you're doing in the world of business now (that includes publishing!), and everything you're going to do later.

Your Credits, Taglines or Mini Biographies

These identify you as the person who wrote a certain piece. It gives the entire work credibility because it mentions your expertise, not least of which is that you are the author of a book on a related subject. Your credit or tagline becomes the caboose on almost everything you publish. It is as important to you as a well-tied elk hair mayfly is to a fly fisherman. Without one he may have difficulty reeling in his limit.

You know which media use credits and what styles editors prefer because you read their submission guidelines and pay attention to their design and style choices. You save your editor the trouble of writing one (and maintain better control of your own branding) by submitting your material with your credit already attached.

Caveat: Editors often ask you to put no identification on contest submissions, but once you win, they will need your tagline or bio information.

Your credit or tagline goes into your media kit, too, so gatekeepers can easily paste it at the end of the essays, op-ed pieces, stories, or articles they accept from you.

In your credit line, include at least your name, the URL or address of your website, the name of your book, and a little about you. It's a nice extra to include an email address your readers can use to give you feedback.

Hint: Rarely seen in taglines is a hook (perhaps that mayfly a fisherman uses?) to encourage the reader to visit your website. It might be an offer for a free eBook, a contest, or an intriguing bit of information that will pique the reader's curiosity enough to act.

You may also need a longer biography. You'll need it for your media kit, for your website, and possibly for the flap of the dustcover for your hardcover book. Check the backmatter of this book for my biography, an example of a really long one.

Here are two other variations, the first a mini bio, the second a shorter tagline. The longer one might be a credit used with an article on a website where length is not as important. Note how this author tailors her tagline to fit the audience for one of her nonfiction articles. She could write a similar one for a different audience featuring only her literary achievements.

Example of a long tagline or mini bio:

> Leora Krygier is the author of *First the Raven* and *When She Sleeps*. She was a finalist in the Ernest Hemingway First Novel Competition, the James Fellowship, and the William Faulkner Writing Competition. Lauded for her "linguistic spell" and "poetic prose," Leora is also the author of *Juvenile Court: A Guide for Young Offenders and Their Parents*. She is a referee with the Superior Court of Los Angeles and has been profiled in the *L.A. Times* for her innovative use of essay writing in juvenile dispositions. She lives in Los Angeles with her husband and has a growing brood of grandchildren.

Example of a short tagline:

> Leora G. Krygier is a juvenile court referee and contributor to magazines for young adults. Reach her at xxxx@aol.com.

Humor and a personal touch can work very well in your credits or biographies.

Caveat: Editors have style preferences and space limitations, but if you include it in the copy you submit, they often publish it exactly that way. When they publish an article you offer at no charge, they should definitely publish a tagline, too. If not, politely request they use one. If they refuse, offer your material elsewhere.

You'll add to your assortment of taglines and subtract from them as you accrue experience or as your focus changes. Keep examples in a special folder in your computer or in your dual-purpose media kit so you won't need to rewrite every time you use one.

I include several versions of my biography in my media kit—a two-line tagline, a mini bio, and a longer About-the-Author biography. Doing so gives me more control over my brand, and it makes it easy for an editor to use whatever version suits her needs.

Use Your Bylines

Bylines are like mini credits, but they can go beyond your name preceded with the word "by." They might include an "author of..." or an "excerpted from..." addition to the usual attribution. When you submit your writing, it is a courtesy to include your byline under the title. Type it in as you'd like to see it. Your editor may change it, but having it there gives you more control, let's your editor know what you consider important, and may save her time.

Endorsements, Testimonials, and Blurbs

Call them what you will—the business of blurbs has become nearly biblical, probably because the giver of such praise gets as much as she gives. They are a basic marketing tool because endorsements can be used across the board in every aspect of your marketing.

Well-known book marketer Penny C. Sansevieri says, "As powerful a tool as a celebrity endorsement can be, it is the most overlooked marketing aspect of an author's campaign. In fact, most authors I work with—even those who have spent years in the business—never give any thought to celebrity endorsements."

Blurbs may be so neglected because no one knows quite what to call them. I've heard "endorsements," "testimonials," "praise," "quotes," "blurbs," and sometimes "bullets" because they are frequently printed on the back cover of books set off by little BB-sized dots. When my husband solicited blurbs from VIPs in the Asian community for his book *What Foreigners Need to Know About America From A to Z* (bit.ly/AmericaAtoZ) he came up with a few other... ahem!... choice words for blurbs because getting them from celebrities is so difficult.

I use "blurb" in this book because most publishers use it. When you hang out at a bookstore, notice readers unfamiliar with a work trust blurbs from readers whose names they don't recognize as well as celebrities to help them make a decision. Many books list quotations on the first page or two under the header "Praise for this Book," too.

When my *SharingwithWriters* newsletter subscribers ask me questions, I sometimes publish them in the style of the much-loved *Dear Abby* columns. A published author who was determined to promote her second book better than her first sent this one to me:

> **Author:** "Do you know how traditionally published books get the advanced blurbs from famous authors? Does the publisher go after them, or the author, or both? Do the famous get paid to read the manuscript and write a blurb?"
>
> **My Answer:** A distant relative of mine works as an editor for a fine literary press. To get blurbs for her authors' books, she calls in favors using her power-packed Rolodex. She is known as the pit bull in her office; few of her fellow editors take the time or have the tact and persistence to do this for their authors. Like just about everything else in the world of publishing, it is best if the author chases blurbs down for herself.
>
> Though you may need to give a book or a manuscript to whomever you ask for a blurb, the famous don't get paid; that would invalidate the authenticity of the process. The famous do it because they are charity minded toward emerging authors, because they owe the publisher a favor, or because they feel the exposure will help their own cause in some way. Many of the most famous won't do it at all—it's too time-consuming, and they fear putting their names on something without thoroughly investigating it.

Try these resources to contact celebrities for the endorsements you covet:

- The Screen Actors Guild at sag.org.

- To find well known authors, go to the list at Authors Guild at authorsregistry.org.
- Use a search engine to find writers' websites. Once found, use their guestbooks or the contact information you find there to submit your request. You can also write to their publishers or agents who should pass along your appeal.
- Get a 30-day free trial professional account at pro.imdb.com

As difficult as it is to get endorsements from well known authors or experts, it is not impossible. Here are the secrets:

- Ask for endorsements with a query letter. (See the Appendix in this book for sample query letters.) Get other tips straight from the mouths of picky (but helpful!) agents in my *The Frugal Editor* (bit.ly/FrugalEditor).
- Shoot for the stars, but shoot for the moon, too. In fact, go star-shooting first. Follow up with requests to earth-bound teachers and fellow writing students.
- Your contact may ask for more information than you sent in your query letter. They may want a synopsis, an outline, or a copy of the manuscript. Accommodate such a request promptly before your celebrity forgets or has a change of heart.
- A written query carries more clout than one sent by email. Send it by USPS and include a self-addressed, stamped envelope (SASE) or your personal email address to make responding easy.

Hint: Many organizations and institutions block mail with attachments. Many public figures won't open email with attachments or the attachments themselves for fear of viruses. If you *must* send your query by email, *offer* your attachment upon request.

- If someone chooses one of your prewritten blurbs, remove it from the query letters you send to others in the future.
- Don't get discouraged.
    - When your request is ignored or denied, a phone call may be all it takes to clinch the deal.
    - You might try again once you have snagged another celebrity's endorsement. A good blurb is like honey. Spread the early ones you get around in your future requests and they may attract someone else who is impressed by the sweet stuff you're offering.

- When you read, watch TV, and open your mail, watch for new blurb-getting possibilities.

Hint: People who write endorsements tend to be more reserved with their tributes than those who spontaneously compliment your work. To collect passionate blurbs, watch for mini raves in your casual correspondence. Drop the person a note asking if you might use what they said in future promotions. Opportunities like these increase once your book is in print because you will receive congratulations, even fan mail. Yes, you will! And you can still collect endorsements after your book is published. For your next book, for your website, for your media kit.

Here's what to do with blurbs:

- Those who endorse your book have done you a favor. Credit them, but choose what it is about their expertise that will most benefit *them—and* will most impress your reader. "Joy V. Smith, author," is nice. But is she an award-winning author? Could you include the title of her most famous book? Does she teach for a well known writers' program?

- Once someone has complied with your request, you may use the whole statement or fragment from the quote. If you omit words, use ellipses to indicate the omission. If you substitute, say, a noun for a pronoun, or add a word to help understanding, put it in those little squared-off [] parentheses to indicate that those precise words were not part of the original quote.

- Send thank-you notes. Send copies of your newly-released book to your beneficiaries.

Put your blurbs to good use:

- Put your new endorsement on the Praise page in your media kit. See Chapter Eleven for building your media kit segment by segment.

- Use them in your email signature lines.

- Some make good teasers in mini biographies.

- Garnish query letters (or the footer on your printed stationery) with a suitable blurb.

- Use a blurb on your promotional postcard, just above the bookcover art.

- Use blurbs on business cards.

- Use blurbs on your signs. (Kinko's/FedEx is a good place to get posters made and laminated. Research floor- and table-standing retractable canvas banners and other display goodies online and locally. Some are expensive but worth it if you choose book fairs and tradeshows as one of your major promotions. Try www.ElcoColor.Net for poster printing.)

Ask for blurbs with confidence. You can see that the author who puts blurbs to good use is doing a marketing favor for those who contributed them.

> **Hint:** Once you are an established writer, remember what it was like to be a newbie. Try to accommodate requests for blurbs when you can. Being quoted as an expert will benefit your own branding, too.

Say it with Soundbites

Soundbites are the little sayings that set your promotion apart from the pack. They are clever metaphors, similes, or phrases someone says on TV or radio that grab attention. They appear off-the-cuff, but someone probably wrote them and the celebrity, newscaster, or author who says them probably memorized them and rehearsed them.

You're a writer. You can do it. Your soundbites should be about seven seconds long or twenty to twenty-five words. With practice you can toss these memorable and clever phrases into your interviews, your titles and headlines, and your pitches.

Often soundbites that fit your needs come to you as you market. Interviewers or hosts sometimes use great ones. Jot them down. Memorize them. Use them again. One might become your motto. The best soundbites become part of your brand. Someone may have tossed off "It's the real thing" in a conversation about Coke. Soundbites are marketing gold.

Pitch it Like You Mean it

Your pitches are worrisome tools. You've seen films about the movie business. A screenwriter sits across the desk from a big producer and pitches her screenplay. She is scared and miserable. Her job is to convince this gatekeeper that her script is the best thing since baked Alaska. We shudder. We think that pitches are pushy at best, desperate and seedy at worst. In our real world, authors need to know how to make pitches that don't feel like that.

Sales are the cogs that make our capitalist society work. Pitches are what make sales. Simply put, if you have a distaste for selling, you need to get over it fast. The best way to do that is to be so passionate about your book you know you aren't selling something to someone who doesn't want it, and certainly not to someone who won't benefit from it.

Pitches come in two flavors. Let's call them the "benefits" and the "beejeebees." First, we'll talk about those two categories which are as different from one another as licorice ice cream is from French vanilla bean. Then we'll talk about how to write them and then how to use each of them when addressing different audiences—the publishing industry, the media, and your prospective readers.

Two kinds of pitches must be stowed in your bag of now-and-forever PR skills. Most of us are aware that our sales pitches make audiences aware of the benefits of the product we offer—in this case our books, our expertise, or our personal entertainment value. We know how to list what readers will get from our books. Entertainment. A thrill. A little romance in their lives. Important information. The trouble is, many times those things don't seem much different from what they would get by reading any other book of the same genre. So, we may need to examine the advantages of pitching consequences (what will happen if a reader *doesn't* read your book).

Using consequences instead of benefits is espoused by Dan Seidman in *The Death of 20th Century Selling* (bit.ly/Deathof20th). As unfortunate as it may sound, consequences can be more powerful arguments than benefits. Our politicians know this. They use consequences against the public all the time—quite effectively.

When I owned retail stores, I told my new sales associates that people shop because they want to buy something. I was surprised that I had to give them this lecture, but experience told me it was necessary. "Shopping makes them happy," I'd say. "When we shop, our friends may ask, 'How did you do?' They know you 'did well' if you found something to buy. If the shopper didn't find something she loves, she is disappointed. Her shopping companion is disappointed. The sales associate who was trying to help her is disappointed, too."

We almost always sold the benefits of a product but sometimes consequences were implicit. As an example, when people bought gifts for their bosses, they were often reluctant to buy less prestigious brands.

It is no different when customers are thumbing through the books at a bookstore; your book's cover is a silent sales associate. Of course, if you happen to be a presenter or are signing at an event, you shouldn't be at all silent. Your pitch must jump from print to the spoken word. You will become a walking, talking pitch from what you say, to how you say it.

Seidman's book tells readers how to turn benefits around to scare the beejeebees out of prospective readers and tell them the horrors that will befall them if they don't buy your book. You already hold *The Frugal Book Promoter* in your hands but, if I were trying to sell you using consequences, I would tell you:

- That booksellers send one-third of all books published traditionally each year back to their publishers. Those publishers ship them off to be used on remainder (discounted) tables. When they're returned a second time, they're often shredded.

- If you don't promote yourself and your book early, the same thing (or something like it) could happen to your book.
- This book is the best place to learn to promote because it gives you marketing basics and ideas from someone who used them herself and because books are the most frugal way to find credible experts on any given subject.

The first two are "beejeebees bullets." The third bullet gives a benefit. You can see how they may be used in conjunction with one another for greater effectiveness and to soften the beejeebees part.

Paul Hartunian, the author of *How to Find the Love of Your Life in 90 Days or Less* (bit.ly/LoveofLife), used a twist on the consequence approach in one of his media releases. He used a short list of "Don'ts" and included: "The worst place to go on a first date—go here and you'll probably never get a second date." He tormented the editors by not giving them the answer to the question he posed in his query letters. The recipient of such a release is not only curious but also aware that his audience will be, too. It's a sure bet that Hartunian's release was effective.

Though it is easier for writers of nonfiction to use consequences, fiction writers can use them, too. In 2002, I might have told prospective readers that their enjoyment of the Olympics would be severely impaired if they didn't read *This Is the Place* so they would understand the history and culture of the city in which the games were set or why they would have difficulty getting a Rum Bacardi with their dinner in that state.

> **Hint:** Select benefit, consequence, or both when they fit the occasion, not when they feel forced.

Finding Your Perfect Pitch

Crafting a pitch may be easier if you reread your book to find possibilities for pitches within it. As you read:

- Identify the aspects of your book that will interest any demographic (age, profession, etc.).
- Turn these features into statements that show how readers benefit. For this book, I might use: "*The Frugal Book Promoter* is a super coach for your book's marketing campaign." On the back cover of my book *Your Blog, Your Business: A retailer's guide to garnering customer loyalty and sales online and in-store* (bit.ly/RetailersBlog), I tease future readers with ways to:
    o Build a blog in five easy steps.
    o Minimize the time it takes to run a blog.
    o Find material to blog about.

- o Integrate your blog with other social networks.
- o Manage a blog frugally or free.
- A frequently-used fiction example is: "This book keeps readers turning pages late into the night." I'm sure you can do better than this because you have the details of your plot stowed in your head. Working with and learning from the screenwriters' loglines we discuss later in this chapter will help you with this project.

You *can* find possibilities in your book of fiction. My first novel, *This Is the Place*, is one of the most difficult genres to promote. I thought of it as a literary novel but found that it also fit into little bitty categories: a little bit historical, a little bit saga, a little bit romance, a little bit feminist, a little bit women's, a little bit western. There were lots of aspects of my past life and former careers that interested feature editors, too.

Don't miss the obvious pitch for your book. Brainstorm session with several readers. Assure them no idea is too silly. Nothing is to be repressed. You may be surprised at how many angles come from such a group effort.

Because we are immersed in our own writing, we don't see it clearly. Writing a pitch for someone else's book is easier than writing one for our own. Practice writing pitches for books you've read and movies you've seen.

Once you have an idea for a pitch, add a little cayenne.

- Boil down your plot or nonfiction premise into three sentences or less.
- Maintain the passion you feel for your story. It's easy to lapse into staid, business-like language.
- Use present tense. "Is" instead of "was."
- Use punchy, specific verbs. "Lobs" instead of "throws."
- Avoid adjectives and adverbs. (If your verbs are strong enough, you probably won't need them!) Find more on getting rid of unhelpful adverbs and adjectives (and turning them into metaphorical gold!) when you read my *The Frugal Editor* (bit.ly/FrugalEditor).

To learn more about writing pitches in all its forms, take a class from screenwriters at a nearby university, or join a screenwriters' forum. Throw out the topic of loglines (very short, catchy plot synopses) and watch members of the group go to town. Offer up one of your own and let them tear it apart and rebuild a thing of beauty. Search for these groups at YahooGroups.com, GoogleGroups.com, Facebook, LinkedIn, and other social networks. With any such group, it is only right for you to contribute as well as learn from others.

You can also find talented screenwriters like Jonathan Treisman, President of Flatiron Film who produced Warner Brothers' film *Pay It Forward* and then search for how-to articles on pitches those pros have written.

> **Hint:** The screenwriter's craft is fertile ground for learning marketing, structure, and dialogue skills that may be adapted to any kind of writing.

Now you have a picture-perfect pitch or two, find a place for one or more of them:

- In your media releases.
- In your fliers.
- On your business cards and other stationery.
- On your posters—the ones you use for events like fairs and book signings.
- In taglines and credits.
- In your email signature.
- On the back cover of your book.
- In your advertisements.

Stockpile your pitches in a special file in your computer so you can pick, choose, and perfect them as needed.

Now you can write pitches, let's put them to work. Pitch an agent or publisher. Pitch the media. Pitch that all-important group we call readers.

> **Note:** Your pitches to the media are indirect pitches to your readers. Their audience is your audience.

Pitching the Publishing Industry

Picture offering a taste of perfectly chilled spring water to the publisher or agent most suited to selling your book. You proffer your book's essence so that whoever drinks of it is sure to want more.

When authors offer their book, they generally don't use the term "pitch." They use the silly euphemism, "shopping a book." Many are averse to the term "sales." You will know you are a pro when you realize you are selling... selling your passion.

Even if authors don't know or won't confess to what they are doing, most already have experience as pitch writers. That's because they have been writing query letters, a basic skill we discuss in Chapter Fourteen. Some of you have already used pitches to get an agent, to get published, to get reviews. You may have woven pitches into media releases and book proposals.

A book proposal is, in fact, a very long pitch. Some fiction writers need to know how to write them but proposal writing is essential for writers of nonfiction. Learn more about when to write a proposal and how to write one with my booklet *The Great First Impression Book Proposal: Everything you need to know to sell your book in 30 minutes or less* (bit.ly/BookProposals).

Pitching Your Readers

This pitch is like sending them a love letter. It may be commercially packaged, but it must be delivered with passion for your book and the needs of your reader.

Early on you pitch readers in writing; later you'll pitch both friends and strangers verbally. In an elevator or a restaurant, at a book signing, and when you're being interviewed by an editor or radio or TV host.

When a reader (anyone really) says, "What is your book about?" you need to tell her quickly (in the time it takes her to get to her floor in an elevator) why she will benefit from reading your book or give her a synopsis of your fiction that makes her want to read it.

When you see a tease like this on a movie poster, they call it a logline but it's also a mini pitch. It goes something like this: "When... (fill in the blanks here), then... (fill in the blanks here)." Here's an example of a pitch that uses conflict just as all good fiction does:

> "When an earthquake rocks Carrie's world, she faces the consequences with a pickax, stored water, and the talents of her two young sons."

Nonfiction authors should try to find conflict in their books, too. They'll find that just being aware of it helps many aspects of their marketing effort.

Pitching the Media

To pitch the media requires both courage and knowledge. It helps to know that the likes of journalists, hosts, and bloggers need you as much as you need them. Without content (that's where you come in!) they have no reviews, no stories, no interviews.

Think of yourself as building relationships when you approach the media. You present yourself as someone who can help a feature editor, business editor, fashion editor etc. do her job. You present your book or expertise as something that will interest her audience. To do that, your pitch might include:

- Information that is brand new to a gatekeeper's audience.
- Something that will solve a problem for her or for her audience.

- Something that will entertain her audience.
- Something that will involve the audience emotionally (a human-interest story).
- An idea how she might use your message or skills in a regular feature that appears in her magazine or an idea for an article for her blog.

The time or space you have available to catch a prospect's attention is limited. The journalist / editor / host / producer needs to know what you can offer that will make her job easier. In the sample Tip Sheet I give you in Appendix Seven of this book are twelve publicity "No-Nos." One of those no-nos tells you that editors you are pitching do not exist to give you free publicity because you want or need it. They are on deadlines and overworked. It is your job to make this editor's job really, really, *really* easy for her. Make it clear that you are there to help and that you have all your ducks quacking in unison.

Start your pitch quickly. Make the media person aware of a problem that you can solve for her, then—just as rapidly—outline how information about you or your book is the solution to that problem. She won't want your life's story or a synopsis of your book until she's convinced that she *needs* you.

Here are some ways *you*—not necessarily your book—might be interesting to the media gatekeepers:

- Hometown reporters want to know they have a published author living in their town.
- Journals for seniors are interested if you are over fifty-five, but almost all publications will be interested if you are very young.
- Perhaps you've changed careers midstream. That might interest editors of newspaper business sections or business magazines.
- You might have a women's or men's angle that will work for gender-related periodicals.
- You are a vegetarian or practice yoga and that affects your creative process. Many magazines and bloggers specialize in narrowly focused topics like this and when your lifestyle (or the topic of your book) is a fit, it's a fit!
- You have a controversial philosophy. Some say there is no such thing as bad publicity. The exposure and sales of Richard Clarke's book, *Against All Enemies: Inside America's War on Terror* (bit.ly/AllEnemies) was helped considerably by controversy *and* its well-timed release.

Here's how your *book* might fill a reporter's need:

- Some editors like novels set in their locale.
- Does your book have a premise or theme related to current news? An example: Editors looked for books that exposed the corrosive nature of intolerance after 9/11.

Is there a literary interest? Did you write in cross-genre or experiment in some other way? Unusual concepts may be news for some media.

Is there a strong similarity in your work to a film or book that everyone is talking about? Sometimes reporters tie one book to another, and some reviewers pack reviews of two or more similar books into one critique or essay.

When we are squeamish about meeting the media face-to-face or by phone, we often rely on mail, email, and faxes. We shouldn't. In-person contacts bring a caring attitude to your association with editors. Aesop said, "Do you, while receiving benefits from me and resting under my shade, dare to describe me as useless and unprofitable?" He knew that those with whom you've built a relationship are more likely to do you a favor and more reluctant to be negative about you to others.

Hint: Scripting a pitch can help. In fact, when you make contact by phone, you can use your script as crib notes to guide the conversation. Well known publicist and author Raleigh Pinskey graciously allowed me to use her scripted pitch in Appendix Five of this book. I encourage you to learn from her example.

Why do publishers put the pictures of authors on the flaps of dustcovers? Because human beings relate to faces. Although editors try to be impartial, they are human; they relate best on a one-to-one basis just like readers or anyone else. You will have more success if you get to know your media contacts at close range. When that's impossible, include your photograph in your media kit or add a link to a video of you on the web or, second best, a podcast of your voice.

If this feels scary to you, make your first contact a fact-finding mission so the editor is aware you want to make her job easier. You might even arrange to see her in her office. Let's pretend you're working on your first, big event—your book launch. This contact will require your short pitch to be as close to letter perfect as you can make it. It will include one or two sentences about your book and then a sentence about the launch you are planning. Then ask her questions like these:

- "How can I help with pre-event coverage?" Word this so that the benefits of covering your event before it occurs rather than after are visible to her.
- "May I give you photos to accompany your stories or would you prefer to have your photographers cover them?" I wrote to ask for a copy of a picture the head photographer of my local paper had taken of me, complimented her on it, and

- copied that praise to her superior. All sincere. They didn't charge me for a copy of the photo.

- "How do you prefer photos be submitted? Electronically? By mailing slick copies? Color or black or white?"

- "Would you be interested in a feature story about (you fill in the blank about one of the remarkable people associated with your launch)?" Be prepared with specifics about your story idea. When editors use your idea, she usually refers to you and your event.

"I would love to have you attend as an honored guest. May I send you a parking pass?" If the editor accepts, formally introduce her to the audience during your presentation.

Caveat: Match the editor to the kind of coverage you're seeking. Study the newspaper's roster to learn what each editor covers. Call TV and radio stations and ask the receptionist to direct you to editors interested in different kinds of stories. Check websites. Pronounce names correctly. You may want to contact more than one editor for a given event. Here are some possibilities for newspaper editors who specialize:

- Calendar Editor.
- Feature Editor.
- Weekend Editor.
- Book Review Editor.
- Assignment Editor (usually TV).
- City Editor.
- Beat Reporters. (These can range from business to arts and entertainment.)

When you approach the media, you need more than one pitch. You need one for what your book is about. That can be wrapped in a pitch about how your story benefits a specific audience and you need a pitch about *you*!

Your Photo and Your Brand

Your photo is another element of your marketing campaign. It gets used so often it defines your brand (who you are as a writer). Because it is so ubiquitous, it is important you get it right.

The photo that most authors get wrong is the headshot or what the trade calls a "glossy," a term left over from the days when pictures were printed on shiny black and white Kodak stock. Today they can be transmitted digitally. Your headshot appears on the dustcover, cover, or last page of your book. It appears on your website, your blog, your business card, and your media kit. It gets sent to about anyone in the media you work with. You need not be picture-perfect, but your headshot must be. Even though many authors know how to use Photoshop, think twice about doing it yourself.

"The best" photo does *not* come from the studio photographer in town who does prom portraits—no matter how expensive and artistic he or she is. It is not the one your Aunt Minnie offered because she took a photography class and needs a confidence boost. "The best" for your marketing campaign is a photographer skilled in taking photos for models' and actors' portfolios and websites. He captures your features and your personality. He understands lighting, has the proper equipment to achieve it, knows where your eyes should be focused, and how your head should be tilted. It may be hard for novices to see, but the finished photo tells the whole world it was done by a professional.

I used John Gibson, photographer to the stars, before the days when most everything was done digitally. He captured something that no photographer ever had, even when I was younger and had fewer flaws to conceal. John's in Hollywood, but you can find the best available in your nearest metropolitan area. Discuss your branding goals, the tone of your book, and where your photo will be used with whomever you choose.

After John took shots of me, some with my Great Dane, he provided glossies and permission to have my choices reproduced by editors. He also supplied .jpg files of these photos. If you're not techie, don't even ask what a "jpg" is—just know that pictures coded this way are the ones most editors want or can easily use. Keep them in your computer's "My Pictures" folder to send electronically.

You may need a few hard copies. I ordered five-by-seven color prints from a commercial graphics company that was equipped to put an author or actor's full name or *nom de plume* in the white margin beneath the image. To save money, order only a few more of them than the number of media kits you plan to send out via post.

Cross Promotion is Sharing

Using cross promotion helps authors reach more people in less time. Unfortunately, authors seem to be as confused as Hamlet: *Ahh, to cross promote or not to cross promote, that is the question.* If we reword this so it becomes "to share or not to share" we can see the folly in questioning its usefulness.

Sharing resources, contributing time and skills to a common cause can only help authors do what they need to do for the welfare of their careers and books. This is not a competition. We are all in this together.

Cross-promotion can even benefit your book launch. We think of launches as a time to shine on our own, but what would happen if you asked another author to read from her work at your launch? That someone would invite her readers to your party. They might become your readers. Your guests would be introduced to your cross-promoting partner. You both sell books. You both increase the size of your contact lists. You provide your guests with an even more festive event. Your spotlight doesn't fade because it is trained on a fellow author for ten minutes.

You've been promoting and studying so you know other authors. The benefits of sharing projects are:

- Sharing allows you to participate when costs would otherwise be prohibitive.
- The support offered by others gives you confidence to try new things.
- Cross-promotion can result in better trafficked events because authors share their contact lists.
- Cross-promotion draws crowds to events, that cluster of people attracts even bigger crowds.

> **Caveat:** Do not assume authors who write in your genre are competition. Authors who write cozy mysteries may be ideal cross-promotion partners for you if your book is a cozy mystery, because fans of cozy mysteries probably read many more than one book in that genre each year. It is more reasonable to be concerned (and selective!) when it comes to your partner's reliability in terms of shared costs and shared promotional efforts.

Magdalena Ball and I collaborated on our Celebration Series of chapbooks (howtodoitfrugally.com/poetry_books.htm) when we decided to contribute to a chapbook of poetry for Mother's Day and our idea grew to include little booklets for Women's Day, Valentine's Day, Christmas, Father's Day, and Earth Day.

She's an Aussie, I'm from Los Angeles. That lead to a feature story idea about the wonders of the web that we pitched to newspapers and tech magazines.

Improbable as it seemed, there we were sharing skills across hemispheres. She writes half the poems for each book and I write the other half. We critique one another's work. She publishes the eBooks and paperbacks. I edit. We both contributed marketing ideas. She found us an online florist to sell our Valentine chapbook, *Cherished Pulse,* as an add-on for traditional bouquets. I got some of our individual poems published on the web with credits and links to our Amazon sales page (bit.ly/CherishedPulse). You get the idea.

> **Note:** You can see, collaboration is a seedbed for ideas. We promoted these chapbooks as thoughtful gifts of poetry at little more than the cost of most greeting cards and held a contest for

the cover art of *Deeper into the Pond* (bit.ly/DeeperPond) as part of our pre-promotion campaign.

Here are a few other times cross-promotion works especially well for you:

- Book signings.
- Workshops and teaching gigs. University program directors may judge your effectiveness in part on the visiting lecturer you invite to address your students.
- Book fair booths.
- Anthologies and other writing projects.
- Blogs and your newsletter. When you extend the planks of your platform to others, they tell others about your services.
- Partnering at tradeshows like BookExpo America (BEA) (see bookexpoamerica.com) and writers' conferences. One person can't be at every seminar or cover every booth on a tradeshow floor. Your partner pitches your book over dinner. You talk up hers. You share notes, ideas, maybe even hotel room expenses.

Tune in to the World

Tuning in is how we know what's going on the world so that when something comes up that cries out for our expertise, we can be there! In a flash!

Tuning in is how you know where your book fits into the daily grind of news, what editors or hosts will be interested in it, and when the time is right. Spam is not the danger; censorship is. A good publicist knows that if she has a dearth of information, she and her clients will wither and die. It is your job to be a good publicist and a great partner for her.

If you are lucky enough to be assigned a great publicist, she will need (want!) your help. She knows that you know your book better than anyone. She hopes you will voraciously read everything that comes your way, analyze it, and apply that new knowledge to your publicity campaign.

When I was studying at the University of Southern California (USC), the head of the public relations department insisted on teaching all the beginning PR classes. He wanted to lobby the best and brightest students to major in public relations, students like Steelers' pro-bowl star Lynn Swan who was then a USC shining light and a student in my class. Our professor's example showed us how being involved with the universe is crucial for success.

This teacher (Let's call him Mr. Marketing!) quizzed us each day on the entire contents of the *LA Times*. I wanted to avoid the sports section.

He cut me no slack. Later, the habit he enforced helped me forecast winning streaks of our winning Lakers, Dodgers, and Pac10 teams so I could preorder shipments of Christmas ornaments emblazoned with their colors and logos. That helped our store win an award for top seasonal sales.

Use a search engine to find e-groups and chat rooms where you can ask questions, get ideas, and stay ahead of the curve. Use services like Google Alerts to learn what your competition is doing—not to sabotage them but as resources.

Subscribe to e-zines (online magazines and newsletters) and blogs. You don't even have to tear open an envelope to learn from them. Submit releases, tips, and articles to them, too.

Hint: Include a short thank-you in your online subscription requests. In the world of public relations, blank emails to individuals aren't acceptable.

Here are some newsletter starters:

- Beth Cox at MidwestBookReview.com edits a newsletter that gives insight into the process of getting book reviews.

- Marketing sage John Kremer puts out *Book Marketing Tip of the Week*. Send an email to JohnKremer@bookmarket.com to subscribe.

- Check Penny Sansevieri's AMarketingExpert.com for her email notices.

- My *SharingwithWriters* newsletter is loaded with writers' resources. Subscribers may submit articles, writing tips, and announcements of successes, along with their book's title and sales link. Send an email with SUBSCRIBE in the subject line to HoJoNews@aol.com.

When you put your tuned-in antennae on, you become aware that even unlikely messages can lead to new contacts, new promotion opportunities, even new writing ideas.

Your Mom Taught You This

Thank-you notes are not duties but gifts. Throw in notes of congratulations, sympathy, and those others your mother made you write, and you have an important component of your book's marketing campaign. Despite Carolyn See's death, her book *Making a Literary Life* (bit.ly/LiteraryLife) is a winner. She suggests writing one "generous, lovely letter a day." Notes create goodwill. Goodwill creates opportunity. Use your writing skill to make the recipient feel valued rather than a cursory note like the ones you tried to get away with when you were in the third grade.

Here are ways to let gratitude boost your promotion efforts and leave a little happiness in your wake:

- Write a sincere note to those who participate in your events and promotions. Write when your book is reviewed, online or in print. When you are interviewed. When you are mentioned or quoted in a newsletter or article. When you collect names at your presentations.

  Hint: Your most memorable note may be the one you send to a reviewer who was critical of your book. One of my least favorite reviews was written by Rebecca Brown on the site she ran then. I told her—sincerely—that I learned much from her critique and soon my essays and rants appeared regularly on her site.

- Collect land and email addresses in a special contact file. Flag some for your Top Fifty (or Top Hundred) list. Stay in touch with them. Send them postcards when you travel, cards during the holidays—communications both personal and book-related.

- Follow up. Send an email to see how that person is doing when it's appropriate. Friend them on Facebook.

Closely aligned with thank-yous are other niceties like asking editors if this is a convenient time to talk, offering collateral material to make their job easier, including alternate contact information, and anything else that brands you as caring.

- **Hint #1:** A snapshot taken at an event that includes poses of the person you're thanking is a thoughtful addition to your note. Something too costly may smack of bribery.

- **Hint #2:** Send congratulatory notes when media friends receive awards, redesign their web pages, write a great feature story, or are assigned a new column.

Personal notes build relationships. When we have relationships, we don't have to *sell* ourselves or our books. Friends want to be there for their friends.

So far, you've learned (or been reminded of) a lot. But wait! The next section covers techniques you need to approach the media world like a pro!

Section III –
Do-It-Yourself and Partner Publicity

> A good contractor builds a home with a strong foundation and sturdy studs. They support his vision no matter what else he takes on. ~ CHJ

You want to boot your book up to the bestseller lists and keep it there. You want to earn back your advance and draw down even more in royalties. You can't count on your publisher. Publishers focus on their next big profit maker when sales of your book dwindles. Besides, no one knows your book as well as you do. No one can be the passionate advocate for it that you can.

When it comes to marketing your book, your advance or budget only goes so far. If you hire a publicist, you may find your schedule will limit the time you can spend with her and your budget will limit the time you can afford to have her spend on your book. The answer is forging a money- and time-saving partnership. Or going the do-it-yourself route. You can see it is smart to learn to do for yourself what you can do better than anyone else, regardless of the path you choose.

This will be easy for you. You *are* a writer. Lots of publicity *is* writing. This section is where you learn the skills you need to advance your entire writing career.

11   Media Kit Preparation Now

A media kit is a tool box for editors or producers who open it. It should provide any gizmo they need to get a story out fast and easy. ~ CHJ

A well designed media kit assures your contact that you are qualified. It is a resource and a sales tool that makes it easy for a gatekeeper to write the news, review your book, conduct an interview, or write a feature story. Today's editors have more responsibility than they ever had. It is only natural that they favor news that is supported so well it nearly writes itself. Your kit serves you in many ways. Mostly it lets you be the go-to resource for gatekeepers who can make a difference for your book and writing career.

We'll build the skeleton of your media kit so you can begin to construct it right now. As you add tendons and muscles to your credentials, you'll have a place to store the information so you don't forget whatever might occur in the here and now. This kit then requires only a little grooming before your publicity campaign starts in earnest. Having the bones in place early helps you visualize the progress of your career and helps you select the promotions that best suit your needs.

Make a new major folder in your computer titled MEDIA KIT GENERAL. In caps. So you can find it quickly! It will contain subfolders labeled in lower case for different sections in the kit. The word "general" lets you identify it later when you have several kits focused on different aspects of your career.

We'll talk about those subfolders for each section of your kit later in this chapter. For now you need to know that "immediacy" is a keyword. Whenever you have new information for your kit, drop it into the proper subfolder. You can format and edit as you go or just throw stuff in as it comes to you. Your mess quotient is not a consideration. What we're working on is the Prior-Planning-Prevents-Poor-Performance issue.

Making Contacts

Your contact list—the one you've been building in your computer—is not part of your media kit, but without it your kit is nearly useless. Contact lists are the petrol that powers your promotion. In fact, your contact list is not one list. It's many. The idea is to get your promotional materials to those most likely to be interested in the information you are disseminating.

There are three ways to build your list. Buy a list, assemble a list from online and library resources, and build your own list as you personally come in contact with folks—everyone from readers to editors to new media outlets. Of course, you can always combine these methods, but the list you build yourself will reap the most rewards—by far.

We'll work on your media list first. A good portion of it should be focused on media you know well. The better you know a medium, the better you'll understand how to pitch ideas to them.

So, you are on the lookout for media when you're out and about. You run across a newspaper, a magazine, or even a throwaway (remember what we said about finding important information where we least expect it?). "Aha!" you say. "This community weekly may be interested in my story because it's just for women... or seniors... or natural food." A roster that lists contact information is usually on page two. Enter applicable data to your list as soon as you can.

You separate your lists for different purposes by assigning codes to your entries. My codes include NAT for national, LOC for local, LIB for libraries, BKST for bookstores, CAT for catalogs, and several other codes that work for the kinds of books I write including WRT for media with an audience of writers. I also make notes that will help me address an editor in a more personal way. The note might give me the name of a humor column or section of the newspaper that would be an especially suitable target for the topic of my book.

A properly coded entry lets you use your filter function and email-merge function to target your kit, invitation, or media release to editors who might have an interest in the information you are sending out or to readers interested in the different genres you write in. (Stay tuned. How to write a media release—the new term for the oh-so-dated "press release"—is coming up!)

> **Hint:** New authors may have trouble accepting the idea that information they disseminate won't always be about their books. That's part of the tuning-in process we discussed in Chapter Ten.

When editors get information that fits their needs, you build credibility. When you send what appears to them to be unrelated to their audience, you lose it. Editors open mail they are certain will benefit them.

The tuning-in process works when you're watching TV, listening to radio, or whatever. Make notes. Google that medium as soon as you can, and keep building that database.

With 350 million magazines published in the U. S. each year, a few should be interested in what you write. Find newspapers—dailies and weeklies and TV and radio stations—at www.newslink.org/news.html and usnpl.com.

My favorite resources are *Bacon's Directories* and Cision. They are too expensive for most authors or even small publishing companies to buy, but your library is sure to have access to these powerhouses for information on all kinds of media. When I promote at out-of-town venues, I use them to find resources for regional publicity for the event.

Let's talk about your personal or general contact list, (think "reader" when you see these terms). Your contact-list thinking cap should be on at all times. Your goal is not to lose anyone. When I forget to make an entry, I'm sure to regret it later.

You want the names, emails, and addresses of anyone you meet who might be interested in your book or your expertise. Don't overlook your holiday card list, lists from club rosters, social groups, and your mother's bridge club list. You'll use them for your book launch and forever after.

12 The Media Release

> A compelling media release is like a good quarterback; even if he can make a perfect pass, he needs his team to be consistently effective. ~ CHJ

Now you have a media list, you need a media release. A media release is often effective all by itself, but when you want to supply the kind of support that makes it hard for gatekeepers to ignore your story, your release needs backup. The release becomes part—albeit one of the most important parts—of your media kit.

To clarify, press releases *are* media releases. We wouldn't want to offend those TV producers, radio hosts, or online folks by using a term that neglects their existence, now would we!

Media releases come in all shapes, sizes, and formats but you still need to be familiar with what is accepted or expected by the gatekeepers. You can drive yourself crazy finding and imitating different media release formats, but the step-by-step instructions I give you in this chapter are basic, generally accepted, and will save you time and keep an Excedrin headache at bay.

Building Your Media Release

A media release can be easy if you do it one step at a time. Writing a media release is less like manipulating a Rubik's Cube and more like putting together a puzzle—the kind of puzzle with big, easy pieces that you could do when you were three.

If your release is assembled as a template before you need it or before a publicist's fee-clock starts ticking, you'll save a lot of money and time. Leave blanks where you don't have the information you need. Save it as MEDIA RELEASE TEMPLATE in your computer.

When we put a puzzle together, we spread out the parts on a tabletop. I'm providing the parts for assembling your release below. Before you read it, find the sample release in the Appendix of this book. Like the cover of a puzzle's box, an example serves as a visual aid for the work you're doing. Go ahead. Read it now.

Here are ten puzzle parts to fit together for a basic news-style release that won't appear unprofessional because you don't know the rules or because you're trying too hard.

Puzzle Piece One: The header consists of five lines below your stationery's letterhead.

- Use a distinctive Media Release header like this:
  M E D I A R E L E A S E.
  Use caps, large type, boldface, 18 point Arial typeface with a space between each letter and three spaces between the words. Justify it on the left of your page.

- Double space. Enter **CONTACT:** in 12 point, Arial caps, left justified. Your info or your publicist's goes here. Include a name, phone, and email address, each on its own line. Revert to upper and lower case for details. Include this information even if it is in your letterhead.

  Warning: Authors often hear that they should rig their do-it-yourself media kits and releases to appear as if they are being sent from a professional publicist's office by using a fake name. I hope you won't be tempted to do that. Of course, you'll want your publicity material to look professional, but any pretense beyond that will only make you look foolish when you're found out once an editor begins to work with you. See Chapter Four on ethics.

Puzzle Piece Two: Release information goes one space beneath the contact information. Type in **For Immediate Release** in 12 point bold Times New Roman, left justified. Change this to a specific date only if there is a very good reason for doing so. Both available space on any given day and timeliness is an issue for editors. Don't limit them with a specific date unless you must. In that case, this line would read: **For Release After Month/Day/Year.**

Puzzle Piece Three: Your headline is centered in sixteen point **Arial** bold. Your headline should seize an editor or producer's attention so she doesn't scrunch the release into a ball and toss it. Feature the most newsworthy (original, unique, or charity-driven) element of your release for your headline. Study newspaper headlines. Use active, strong verbs. Omit as many little words like "a," "the," "and," "but," and other articles and conjunctions as possible.

Puzzle Piece Four: Your dateline can be omitted if it seems irrelevant, but most print media appreciate it. It is simply the place—*not* the date—of the city from which the news originates. Usually that is where your office is located. These days some are using World Wide Web as a dateline.

Puzzle Piece Five: The lead is simple and brief. It is the first sentence in the body of your release. State who, how, where, when, and what. You will learn how to make this line more appealing to editors later, but until that can be mastered, a straightforward, old-fashioned journalist's lead is better than one that screams inexperience. Check to be sure that the "when" includes the date, not just the day of the week. Here's an example:

> "*Shades of Iris,* a novel by Marlena Reingold, was released by Schuster Arrow Press on August 1."

A year is not necessary. By definition, media releases are recent news.

Puzzle Piece Six: The body of the release follows, single spaced.

- Leave a space between paragraphs.
- Do not indent paragraphs.
- Mention the single most newsworthy aspect of your event in the paragraph after the lead.
- The next paragraph lists the author's most important credentials, including the author's hometown if the release is being sent to the local press or is otherwise relevant.

Puzzle Piece Seven: Your logline or pitch for your book comes next. You may have already written your first pitch. It's that mini synopsis of your book meant to snare an editor's attention that was explained earlier in Chapter Ten. Something like, "Just as Sky Eccles is about to make the biggest mistake of her life, she returns to her family's farm and the reverse example set by her feisty red-haired grandmother."

Puzzle Piece Eight: A paragraph about you comes next. It may be the mini biography we talked about in Chapter Ten. "Reingold has been writing ad copy and promotional pieces since she started her own party-planning business in 1988."

Don't worry if you don't have much writing-oriented information to include here. Use professional information that relates to your book or leave it blank. By the time you've finished reading this book, you'll be an expert on how to build your credentials.

- Do not include your hobbies unless they have something to do with the subject of the book.
- Reuse this paragraph in most releases unless it specifically calls for new information. Time is valuable. Recycling content saves time.
- As your credentials build, update this paragraph for subsequent releases. Eliminate older, less impressive ones or those that don't support the information you are presenting in this specific release. Slot in the new ones you've accrued.

Puzzle Piece Nine: Your close is easy.

- Type in a line where gatekeepers can find more information: "*This Is the Place* is available in bookstores or online at bit.ly/ThisIsthePlace." Do not use active links in media releases you mail. They clutter and must be typed in a URL window anyway.

- Limit active links in releases you send by email. Too many may make media release disseminators increase their fees and cause email platform to bounce or send them to spam.

- On another line type, "Learn more at: www.xxx.com." Use your website address, the site you use as a sales tool for both readers and the press.

- Leave a space and center three pound signs. "###" signify the end of the release.

Puzzle Piece Ten: Mention your media kit, photos, and other support material.

- This is not part of the body of your release, so center it in eight-point bold, Times New Roman. Type "A media kit and photos are available on request." on a line of its own right under ###. Adapt this line to the situation. You may only need "Support materials available on request."

Puzzle Piece Eleven: Save what you have done. This release is a template. Each time you send a new release you review it, tweak it and save it to categorized folders with titles like Book Signings, Teaching, Library Appearances. You will also have releases on news related to current news, seasons, awards, charities that are more likely to pique the interest of gatekeepers than "just another book signing." Ho, hum. That doesn't mean you should prejudge what editors might use. They may need something to fill a hole. Something you say may fit with another story they are doing. You want frequency to position yourself as an active author or expert. And these media release copies become a record of your promotions. Some day you may want to tell an agent, "I have presented at more than a dozen writers conferences worldwide." You get the count from these releases!

How to Write Your Release

Writing releases is part editing but it also uses the creative part of your brain. Yes, it does! And it requires you to use your analytical skills, too!

Let's tackle the nitty gritty stuff first. Here are techniques to make your media release professional:

- Your release should be one page or less. (Don't cheat by using a smaller typeface.)

- Give the media what they need to complete their jobs. If you are sending out a release to a host who uses several guests on a panel, include other resources or other authors who could give opposing views or flesh out the topic you are proposing. Include their contact information. To decide what resources editors might need, put yourself in their shoes.

- Verify the accuracy of the contact information you provide. Include as much information as you can and still maintain security. Incorrect information obviously renders a release useless.

- Introduce your release with the most powerful headline you can come up with such as "Sex Disappears from America's Bedrooms." Use large, bold typeface.

- The subject line of your email should not be vague or misleading. Remember the ad, "It isn't nice to fool Mother Nature?" In their own realm, editors are as powerful as Mother Nature. You don't want to tick them off. Your subject line reads, "Media Release," followed by a colon and punchy headline. Don't use anything intentionally vague or anything that might be interpreted as spam, like "Hello," "From a friend," or "Important information."

  Example: The late Walter Brasch, a journalism professor and author of several books on politics, sent a release with this subject line: **NEWS: Brasch Allowed Out in Public Again.** Believe me, as editor of the *SharingwithWriters* newsletter I opened that email to see what he was up to.

  Hint: I sent out a release on a book fair booth I was coordinating. My response rate doubled compared to many similar releases because I lead the release with a personal note suggesting that editors feel free to edit, cut, or otherwise utilize the release any way they wanted (many online newsletter editors don't have journalism backgrounds and seem to think they must use it exactly as it is written!) I also told them I had articles on how to navigate book fairs available for their use at no cost if they would prefer.

- Edit. Remove all the high-falutin' adjectives. In media releases. "Awesome" and "magnificent" are four-letter words. Your book is not "superb" until it has won the Pulitzer (Pulitzer.org), and even then, you show how "superb" it is with facts or quotes from credible sources.

- If it's appropriate, bullet your information. Bullets leave lots of white space and that lets your recipients easily glean what they need.

- If you can, include a link for a YouTube video or trailer featuring you or your book. (See Chapter Nineteen on New and Old Radio and TV or check this book's Index under "videos.")

- Punch up the copy with active verbs. Use image-laden, specific nouns when you can. Rather than "cookies," use "marzipan." Rather than "bike," use "Schwinn."

    Example: "Local Woman Writes Book," is humdrum. How about "Mystery Writer Stages Murder on Will Rogers Beach."

- No opinions allowed unless you have a blurb (endorsement) from an expert who might convince an editor of your stature. If you do, slice it into the release format.

    Example: "Dale Barton, President of Armand, & Co., says, 'This is the year's definitive book on world demographics.'"

If someone is available to proofread your release for typos, use that second pair of eyes. Microsoft Word's spell and grammar checker is helpful, not perfect. Everyone must edit themselves—at least on occasion. Usually things like query letters, and media releases. For help with that and lots more, read my multi award-winning *The Frugal Editor*, second in this *HowToDoItFrugally Series* of books for writers (bit.ly/FrugalEditor).

For dozens of sample media releases covering everything from book launches to winning contests, go to the release page in my Media Room (bit.ly/RecentReleases).

Dolling Up Your Release

Tuning up your release is like writing in general; you need to know the basics so you'll know when to break the rules and when you've gone too far. Most releases don't lend themselves to mascara and lipstick.

There is nothing wrong with keeping a media release simple, but if the subject calls for a more enticing lead than the usual how, where, when, and why lead used by journalists, here are a couple of approaches that might work. If your generic release reads:

> "Palm Springs—Peter Morton, CEO of Tyr Publishing, Los Angeles, signed a contract for *Christmas Cookies Are for Giving* (bit.ly/Cookies4Xmas) with longtime Palm Springs resident, Kristin J. Johnson. This book, a combination of cookbook and book of inspiration, will be released in August of this year."

The Frugal Book Promoter

Christmas Cookies is a combination cookbook and book of inspiration and "inspiration" part is the most interesting part of this lead. That's what makes this news—not that it's a book that's just been released. So, this might be more likely to interest an editor:

> "Palm Springs—A combination of inspirational essays and recipes that will have you licking the mixing bowl during the holidays, Kristin J. Johnson's *Christmas Cookies Are for Giving*, (bit.ly/Cookies4Xmas) is in release. Tyr Publishing CEO Peter Morton says, "It will be in bookstores in plenty of time for people to add it to their gift lists and available online for last-minute shoppers."

You could skip poor old Peter the Publisher altogether unless he is a Palm Springs local. Or you could work him into a later paragraph, but a quotation like this makes the release current and lends authenticity to the pitch.

To tackle something more daring and probably more effective, write a lead that points out the *benefits* of your book or warns of the *dangers* inherent in ignoring it. We discussed benefits and consequences in Chapter Ten under "Your Pitches." Here's an example of a lead that uses a little scare along with a bit of benefit.

> Carolyn Howard-Johnson, author of the multi award-winning *HowToDoItFrugally Series* of books, spent the first four years of her career stepping into dangerous publicity potholes. She shares her hard-won expertise with the release of *The Frugal Book Promoter* to help other authors avoid her booboos.

When a lead like this is used, some of the essential details need to be moved down to the next paragraph. This may misalign that puzzle you are building but you're a writer. You will figure it out.

A variation that sets your release apart from thousands of others is a good idea if it doesn't look as if you are trying too hard. You might use a memorable quote from your book, an endorsement from a celebrity, or a fact that shows why your book is important. Indent it, and place it just above your lead. I chose this one for the release from my book of creative nonfiction because it reflects the book's voice and gives the reader an immediate idea of its setting:

> *My city is like a saltwater pearl, gently, gently cradled by the Wasatch Mountains. The crescent of the foothills tenderly curves around the city like the palm of a mother's hand...*

Notice that I didn't use quotation marks (though I could have). Italicized font is a style choice. Rules are not laws. They are made to be broken—or not.

A subhead (sometimes called a deck) under the headline is another approach that is rarely don but rooted in traditional journalism. It appears indented in a slightly smaller size font than the headline of the release. It needs nothing more to separate it from the rest of the release. It may focus on conflict or a benefit, and it can be quite a bit longer than a headline. This is an example of a short one:

> Academics are looking to erotic politics in a search for trends.

The word "erotic" will hook your gatekeepers, but editors are also intrigued by "trends." For more words that influence others read *Words that Work* by Frank Luntz (bit.ly/FrankLuntz).

Distribution of Your Release

Distribution may be done several ways. It may accompany your media kit, either inside the folder or attached with a paperclip to the outside. You may mail, fax, or email your release or use a combination of two or more methods. You may use a free or pay-for press release platform.

- If you don't use your release as part of your media kit, send it first by email rather than snail mail. Editors prefer email because they can save time by copying and pasting. They must scan or retype something that comes by post. Have I told you before how busy editors are? You can follow up with another release—one that is slightly different—by snail mail or fax.

- To give snail mail envelopes a more professional look, send them through the feeder on your printer rather than handwriting them.

- If you fax your release, direct it to the proper editor with a separate cover sheet. This will usually be the feature or managing editor. For radio and TV, it will be the producer (or sometimes the host) of each show.

- Use the current editor's name and spell it correctly.

- If you have a photo that will convince an editor your story is visual, send it by USPS, FedEx, or UPS along with the release and a query letter. Attach the photo with a paperclip to the query letter (more on how query letters differ from releases is coming!) You may offer to send the image at the bottom of your emailed release, but it will not be as effective.

    Hint: I know. I know. But this bears repeating: Don't attach your release, photo, or anything else to your emails. Many media outlets don't let email with attachments through their servers and many editors won't open them if they do make it through.

The Frugal Book Promoter

Avoid letting your release die a slow death on a gatekeeper's desktop. Remember that relationship thing. This is your chance to build on it. Follow-up is as important to clinching a publicity deal as a homerun at the bottom of the ninth inning is to the World Series. After a reasonable wait, phone your contact. Ask her if she received your release. Be prepared to pitch a new angle on the story if the editor says your first idea isn't quite right. It wouldn't hurt to guarantee exclusivity on any new idea you present to him or her, either

Announcements vs. Releases

Media announcements are shorter than media releases and sometimes sweeter, especially to the eyes of someone who is in charge of a calendar or the mini features in the frontmatter of their magazine. They are especially useful as followups, as introductions to a planned media blitz of well-spaced releases (each touting a different angle), or to notify editors of an upcoming event. A different version of your release might be faxed or emailed a few days after the first one.

Media announcements read like barebones invitations. They include:

- The term "Media Announcement" as a header.
- Contact information.
- A captivating headline.
- A pithy lead or pitch.
- Follow up with the place, time, date, and a resource for gleaning more information.

Media announcements are quickies. Don't put much more than what's on this list into yours.

Up next, one of the most important ways to use your release. It's what gives your media kit a reason for being.

13 The Rest of Your Media Kit

> Media kits are the body and soul of your writing career. They are record keepers, confidence boosters, and organization wizards. ~ CHJ

We have discussed how handy media kits are to your marketing process. As your writing career grows, you will save eons of time if you plop new achievements and ideas into the appropriate subfolders as they occur. Your additions needn't be polished. Think of them as first-draft folders. You'll reorganize, edit, and polish them when you need your media kit or any of its parts.

In this chapter, I give you a list of folders that substitute as the sections you may use in your kit. The list is not engraved on sterling. With each kit you send, you may eliminate some segments or subfolders and add others.

If you are familiar with media kits, you may notice that I suggest more sections (or subfolders) than you might see in kits for other industries. Because I have been on the receiving end of media kits as a staff writer for a newspaper, I know how important it is for you to put what the editor *needs* in the kit and make it easy—v-e-r-r-r-y easy!—for editors to find the details they need to flesh out their story. Without making a phone call. Without online research. And without shuffling through too many papers. When a contents page is included in your kit, it is more likely it will do what it is intended to do. That is, get you free exposure. Here are subfolders you need for your kit:

- Contents page, sometimes known—redundantly—as "Table of Contents"
- About-the-Author page (Your bio and/or credit line).
- An Awards page
- A Publications page or Published Works Almanac.
- List of Appearances
- Praise-for-the-Author's-Work (or the Author's Book) page (Endorsements/Blurbs/Testimonials)

- Sample Review (with permission to reprint)
- Sample Interview (with permission to reprint).
- First-Person Essay (with permission to reprint)
- List of Your Available Seminars
- List of Fellow Experts for Panels.
- Tip Sheet highlighting your expertise
- Other media-kit items.

You pick and choose from among these subfolders depending on how your kit is being used. If you are sending it to a feature editor with a query about a story, you will include your tip sheet. If you are sending it with a pitch to a radio host, you might include a fun list of soundbites instead.

Next, let's learn what each of these subfolders (or segments of your media kit) contain and what they do for the gatekeeper who receives your kit.

Your Contents Page

A *contents* page is rarely seen in media kits. Having one, however, makes it easier for gatekeepers who receive your kit to find what they need. And you already know how important that is!

Go to your word processor's manual and learn how to format titles and chapters. Knowing how to let Word do it for you is a skill you will use many times over the life of your writing career. Of course, if that sounds like too much work, you can do it manually.

Divide your Contents (call it "Contents" if you don't want your gatekeeper to roll her eyes!) into two parts. One part shows the gatekeeper what she will find in the left pocket of your media kit folder. The other part lists what she will find in the right. You decide the order depending on what is most important for the title of your book or the pitch you are making. You'll ditch the right/left thing for digital kits. For them you might divide your kit into related segments with titles something like "The Essentials" and "Permission-to-Print: Make Your Job Easier." The latter would include copy-and-paste items like a review or interview that has carefully indicated that permission from whoever owns the copyright. I have starred the items that might qualify for such permission.

Your About-The-Author Page

About-the-Author is a third-person credit about you. Call it a biography if you prefer, but it is focused on information that pertains to your writing life. It contains details similar to what publishers use on the flyleaf of your book's dustcover or on the back cover of your book. However, it includes more information than you usually see there. It's a place where editors go to glean both personal and professional information about you and to get a feel for your voice or ideas for a story angle.

Your About-the-Author page should be written by you rather than by your publicist or publisher. If you must give them the information to write it for you, the work is being done twice. You pay for it in time when you write it. You pay them in real money when they take that information and rewrite it. Further, you know yourself better than they do. You have more passion about your life and how it relates to your book than anyone else. This is a place where you can let your voice, even some humor, come through.

Until your relevant credentials grow, you may prefer to title this page "Mini Biography." Later you can add a longer Author page but keep your Mini Biography as part of your kit. An editor may find it convenient to have a choice. The idea is to provide editors with the information they need and in the format that will be most helpful to them. Here are some tips:

- If you don't have much information yet, widen the margins.

- Avoid clichés. One of the most common errors new writers make is saying that they "always" wanted to write. I made this mistake myself and cringe every time I see printed matter that used this old version of my Author page.

- Carefully select what you tell about yourself. Readers of a novel set on Wall Street would find it relevant if the author is a financial advisor. If the author's book has no relationship to the world of money, that author should highlight other achievements.

- Don't be afraid to offer several choices, from a bio like the ones on the back dustcover of hardback novels to the two-line credits that editors of *The New York Times* put at the end of their op-ed pieces.

- I have a bio for my poetry and one for my speaking credentials that I substitute for a more general one when the occasion requires that.

- Don't forget a suggestion that editors have permission to copy-and-paste any version of bio in your kit. The editor may choose to use something different, but it's worthwhile to point your branding in the direction you want it to go. (See Chapter Ten for more information on writing biographies and credit lines.)

Your Awards and Publications

Awards and *Publications* are two of the most important pages in your kit. On slow news days, editors see words like "prize" and "award" as unset jewels. They will not care if they are semiprecious stones or the finest cut diamonds because they know either will add luster to a story. Agents and editors of journals love it when you have an impressive record of publishing records.

Having said that, lacking stellar lists on either page is not a death knell. Much will depend on how you present your other passions and credentials.

At first—until you have a long list of awards or places your work has been published—you may include both publications and awards on the same page. In some ways, a published article is an award. It's an affirmation of the quality of your work. When your lists become longer, use two pages or prune the less influential entries.

Organize your lists of awards and publications the way you would organize them for a résumé. Place the "Awards" first on the page, "Publications" next. List your most recent achievements first because, as your career progresses, the more current ones tend to be more pertinent and prominent. Occasionally you'll have an important award or publishing credit that should be featured. Put it first or make it stand out with special formatting. Don't hesitate to place only one such an honor on a page if that is all you have. Carefully word your entries make the best appearance possible and for heaven's sake, don't apologize for it! Keep reading for help with ideas for finding brag-worthy items in your background that you might overlook.

Your List of Appearances

The Appearances list is designed to impress gatekeepers. Oscar Wilde's satirical nature showed when he said, "It is only shallow people who do not judge by appearances. The true mystery of the world is the visible, not the invisible." His observation is funny because it reflects the way so many of us see things.

We *are* judged by the kits we present to the media. Our Appearances page is probably right up there in importance with Awards and Publications because radio and TV producers and other gatekeepers look for authors with enough *presence* to make them proud. After all, when they invite you as a guest, their reputation is at stake. Like it or not, you include this page in your kit.

Because this page of appearances is so important, try to find something in your background that convinces folks that you are capable of handling exposure, that you will be comfortable before a camera or mic. Here are some possibilities:

- Did you study drama in college? High school? Been in a play?
- Have you taken a Dale Carnegie course? Or joined Toastmasters? Done any modeling?
- Have you been on a debate team?
- Have you led seminars or been a panelist as part of your business or publishing experience?
- Have you been an instructor in the education or business worlds?
- Do you sing? Been a member of a choir that performed?
- Have you read an excerpt from your book at a signing?

All-star credentials are not essential. Nor is quantity. As you can see, this page may not be a list at first, but rather a little pitch that gives gatekeepers a sense that you can present yourself well. Something like, "References on request," will do nicely as a start. It's a trick used by beginning actors on their résumés.

If you have nothing for this Appearance page, make a subfolder for it anyway. The universe has a very nice way of filling empty spaces and meeting positive demands. In the meantime, take a speech class. Now you're an author, you'll find a thousand reasons to be grateful you did. Even book signings benefit from learning to be more comfortable in the spotlight.

Your Praise and Endorsement Page

Praise and Endorsement includes what our industry usually calls blurbs. My favorite way to accumulate these is to ask if I can use nice comments I get from readers and other associates in my email. Learn other ways to get them and other uses for them by looking up "blurbs" in the Index of this book.

This blurb-collecting process is fun. Each great blurb is like a positive affirmation that helps your confidence grow. Put your blurbs in this folder as they come to you. You'll eventually separate them into categories for different books or the different kinds of marketing you're doing.

Your Book Review Page

Your *Book Review* page is used by a gatekeeper as an indicator of the quality of your work. Occasionally, an editor may want to reprint a review just as they find it in your kit.

As soon as you have a positive review, add it to a Review subfolder in your media kit file. Here is how to do that:

- Ask permission from the reviewer to add it to your media kit.

- Get permission from to reviewer to reprint it or allow others to do so and mention that in the header of the media kit review page. Include a request that editors print the review in full using the reviewer's byline and tag or credit line.

  Hint: Once permission is granted, use the review on your website and submit it to my TheNewBookReview.blogspot.com and other review blogs and sites. Submission guidelines are in the left column of my blog.

- State where the review originally appeared.
- Type in the reviewer's byline.
- When you have many reviews, select the one written by the most prestigious reviewer or appeared in the most prestigious publication. High praise is good, but credibility is better.
- If the original review does not include a headline, provide one that is true to the reviewer's intent.

If you have a review that isn't as good as you'd like, resist the temptation to extract only a positive excerpt from the review itself (though it is kosher to excerpt it to be used as a blurb!) Media people know a review that is critical of one aspect of your book is more credible than one that praises a book excessively. Editors suspect that a pie-in-the-sky review was probably written by your mother. Please take a minute to reread Chapter Four on publishing industry ethics.

If you have a short review and a longer one that includes a synopsis of your book, use them both. An editor may find one suits her style or space requirements better than the other. Label them "Sample Short Review" and "Sample Longer Review" on separate pages in your kit.

Hint #1: If you don't yet have a review, substitute a mini synopsis you write yourself. Make it a tease that entices even a jaded reviewer or editor to want to know more. Don't attribute it to anyone. Learn more about writing reviews and getting and using reviews in my *How to Get Great Book Reviews Frugally and Ethically* (bit.ly/GreatBkReviews).

Hint #2: If you want to extract little phrases that rave about your book from a review, they go on your Praise page where gleaning the best of the best from reviews and elsewhere is acceptable. And you don't need permission to use excerpts under 25 words.

Your Sample Interview Page

You also need the text of an interview, imagined or real, that a reporter, blogger, or radio host might use to glean questions to use when she interviews you. You have seen interview formats in *People* and *Time* magazines. They look like transcripts of—usually very short—questions and answers.

Some reporters use the Sample Interview that you supply verbatim. Others adapt the questions to their needs, and others may not use them at all. Bloggers and radio and TV hosts often ask for talking points. To save time, give them select questions from your Sample Interview. You'll be familiar with the questions and therefore better prepared with your answers.

The Sample Interview in your media kit is your chance to combat the inferior quality of interviews—both the questions and answers—that James Thurber described when he said, "My opposition [to interviews] lies in the fact that offhand answers have little value or grace of expression, and that such oral give and take helps to perpetuate the decline of the English language."

A little name-dropping in a media kit is essential, not a social *faux pas*. When the name of the journal or the interviewer will lend an air of prestige to your kit, that's the one you select.

Having said that, if the interviews available to you do not focus on content you consider essential, write your own. That gives you as much control over the interview process as possible. Of course, your answers (also written by you) will be witty, entertaining, and... I did mention short, didn't I?

If you can't get permission from a host to reprint an interview, there are no media-kit cops who will object if you list the names and links of their blogs or journals at the bottom of your Sample Interview page or even links to the original review.

You could also mention influential reviews as one of the answers in your self-written interview or include them with links on your Appearances page. A media kit should follow guidelines closely, but the content is more flexible than the inscription on your great grandfather's headstone.

Hint: You might substitute a Frequently Asked Questions (FAQ) page for a sample interview, perhaps the same one you will eventually use for your website.

Your First-Person Essay

This requirement is often ignored by authors. What a missed opportunity! These essays bring people (in this case, gatekeepers) into your circle—up close and intimate. In *On Writing Well* (bit.ly/OnWritWell), William Zinsser said, "I almost always urge people to write in the first person.... Writing is an act of ego and you might as well admit it."

Zinsser might be alluding to the fact that it is disingenuousness to remove the author from the telling of her own story by using third person. After all, the author is the ultimate expert on herself and the pronoun "I" is not a dirty word.

Hint: A first-person essay is a narrative. The one you use in your media kit is a little story with you and your writing as central characters. It is quite different from the About the Author piece (or biography) you wrote for your media kit's About-the-Author page. Editors use it differently, too.

Because you're a writer you are probably aware of how frequently the press uses first-person essays. Some newspapers label a column "First-Person Essay." Others vary the titles. The *Los Angeles Times* used "First Column" before it was sold. You usually find first-person essays in the left column of the front page and in the same location on the front pages of their other sections. *Guideposts* (guideposts.org) is a widely read magazine that has been around a long time and often uses first-person essays. They are often used in anthologies and collections of essays, too.

When authors write about themselves, their style sometimes becomes so stilted it reads like a college text. A first-person essay should be lively and full of anecdotes and dialogue, even if you write nonfiction.

Eventually you may want to have several different essays or versions of your essay stowed away in your computer because different publications target different audiences. One of my essays talks about my bout with cancer and how my search for health brought me back to writing after a long hiatus. Another is about my struggle with repression of women in an earlier decade and how that affected my early writing career. One tells of my love of yoga, and—you guessed it—how it helps my writing. Another, how travel informs my writing. One relates to how writing has affected my life as a senior. I switch out the essay I include in my media kit depending on where I am sending it. It doesn't take me long to rewrite one of these (dare I say "canned") essays when a new opportunity presents itself. For me, it's a bigger trick to remember to save each version under a different name.

Here are some pointers for the first-person section in your media kit:

- Label this page "First-Person Story."
- It should run from 700 to 1000 words. Number these pages separately from the rest of the kit and staple them together when you are submitting a hardcopy of your kit.
- Use an attention-getting title.
- Include a free-use permission statement.
- Include your byline and tagline. See Chapter Ten under "credits."

- Try to include the title of your book in the body of the piece, but only if it is an integral part of the story, not an obvious add-on.
- As a favor to your editor (and yourself), include your own tagline or credit.

A well-written first-person essay might be reprinted by an editor exactly as it is presented. Sometimes you will be asked for more information or for permission to rewrite it under another byline (the answer is always "Yes!"). Other times this essay may trigger interest in featuring you in a different story.

Caveat: If you hire a publicist, she may not use first-person essays in her kits. It may be up to you to convince her to use yours. You, after all, are the client. She should accommodate your suggestion.

Your Available Seminars List

Having a list of available seminars is an essential part of your kit, especially when you send your kit to bookstore event directors, to program directors of tradeshows or conferences, to schools and universities where you may want to teach, to library program directors, and even to TV and radio producers who will get an idea of the variety of topics you can address if you should become a guest.

Excellent speakers tend to be successful in the business world. That is especially true for authors. If fear keeps you from sharing your expertise, take a baby step toward overcoming it for the sake of your personal growth and the success of your publicity campaign, not to mention the what we call back-of-the-room sales of your books when you are lecturing or speaking. Author Ester Benjamin Shifrin is an example of how well this can work; she sells most of her books in rooms where she speaks to groups about her book, *Hiding in a Cave of Trunks.*

Settling on your seminar topics is similar to searching for angles that will interest editors. Examine every aspect of your book. Rediscover the passion that inspired you to write it. Come up with at least two topics that appeal to audiences with diverse tastes. These might include a writing workshop, a moderated panel on publishing, or a seminar on the premise of your book. Keep adding ideas to this subfolder as they occur to you.

You needn't write the synopses of the presentations that go with each of your ideas, but do consider whether you have (or can research) enough material to make the seminars or workshops you offer successful. Write a catchy title and an intriguing pitch for each topic. Use the skills you learned in Chapter Ten for writing loglines, pitches, and beguiling synopses of your book. Study university extension catalogs for ideas on writing seminar descriptions and then spice yours up a bit.

Hint: The Seminars page in your media kit indicates that you have presentation skills many gatekeepers need even if you choose not to pursue speaking as an essential part of your campaign.

Your Fellow Experts List

An *Experts List* is a companion to your Seminar page. When you include a list of experts who complement your expertise—ones who are charismatic and know how to work as a team—you mark yourself as a professional and make it oh, so easy for an editor or producer to style a story or segment in which you are an integral part. That one feature may give you an edge.

Here are some quick tips for your expert list:

- Get permission from your fellow experts to list them in your kit.
- Your Expert list should be on a page by itself, very brief, just the facts, ma'am.
- Include at least one expert who holds an opinion different from yours. Include another whose expertise adds a different dimension to the topic.
- Include contact information and one-sentence descriptions of what makes them experts and what they can add to the conversation.

Other Media Kit Items

These items might not be pages in your media kit *per se*. It is a list of ideas or reminders of stuff you need. Each entry is like a "do-or-don't-do" string around your finger.

You put items you *need* reminders for in this subfolder:

- Your picture. (See Chapter Ten under "Your Photo.") You need a few hard copies and a digital file.
- Your business card.
- Your galley or Advanced Reader Copy, both a hardcopy and an e-copy. (See Chapter Fifteen on how to use ARCs to get reviews.)
- A color image of your bookcover.
- Get a logo and website banner designed. Canva is free and good for do-it-yourselfers (canva.com/create/banners).

You randomly toss other items into this folder like bookmarks and ideas for your promotional gifts (if you insist on buying them). But keep reading before you spend any money on these doodads.

As you complete each task, delete the reminder from this subfolder. In this subfolder you don't hoard entries as a record and resource as you do in others.

I once put an idea for a tip sheet in this folder. It helped me design a line of questioning for a late-night radio host so it didn't go completely to waste, but I never got around to writing all ten tips. The note remains there to silently nag me. It is my prerogative to ignore it, just as it will be yours.

Souvenir and promotional gifts for media kits are not what they are cracked up to be. With the exception of quality thank-you gifts, authors will do fine without gizmos, especially the kind that all too soon get tossed into gatekeepers' clutter drawers.

I've rarely seen giveaways for media kits used effectively. Nicer ones may be used to attract editors to take a kit from the pressroom at a tradeshow. To work that way, the gift must be suited to the theme of your book and have a high perceived value!

I viewed my first promotional item more as a thank-you gift than as advertising. I wanted something that suited the material in my book, but I hadn't yet learned that most of the stuff authors were spending money on was not effective. I bought miniature porcelain thimbles with "Utah" printed on them because my book is set in that state. My mother made little felt slipcases for them and my husband tied tiny gift tags with a quote from my novel to each pouch with thin grosgrain ribbon. Mom refused to make more than the original 100 or so pleading poor eyesight. My next promotion gifts were miniature, hand-crocheted doilies made in China, presumably by women with no such excuses. We used similar tie-on tags. These worked better than thimbles because they more easily lay flat in books, envelopes, or thank-you cards. But think of the expense. Think of the time. Think of the guilt I felt about those poor Chinese women once I had time to think about it!

I made these choices because each had something to do with the sewing imagery I used in both *This Is the Place* and *Harkening*. I have heard of authors who make artistic blank journals and notebooks by hand for prizes and contests and tuck them into gift baskets.

If you must use items like this, your serenity quotient will go up if you forget about measuring their effectiveness in terms of book sales and think of them as means to promote goodwill. Here are guidelines to help you choose promotional items when you think you absolutely must have them:

- Shun the politically incorrect unless your book is a steaming gossip sheet. Avoid smoking accoutrements unless the title of your book is *Up in Smoke*.

- Hand or homemade items are appropriate only if those qualities are integral to the image you want to project. Unless you are a graphics and computer production whiz, handmade bookmarks—unlike some homemade gifts— might as well be printed with "Don't buy my book. I'm an amateur."

- Most gatekeepers appreciate food, but your edible should tie into the theme of your book unless the food is a thank-you after the fact.

- Buy in bulk to keep costs down but don't be overly optimistic. Your needs will change.

- Flat is best. Lightweight is a plus. Ecology-friendly, these days, is a plus-plus.

- Consider cost and distribution. You can easily give away thousands of promotional gifts and if you restrict distribution because of the expense, you defeat your purpose.

Bookmarks are often used instead of business cards. They are given away at book signings, tucked into books sent to reviewers, and even left in public bathrooms or at coffeehouses. I have never used them; my budget got in the way and they didn't make the cut. However, they are often keepers (some readers collect them!) and when they are printed with a great endorsement, bookcover art, and complete information for buying your book, they are effective because:

- They mail flat.

- They target the audience you want to reach.

- Readers don't discard them as readily as some promotional material.

- They may be produced relatively inexpensively. Printer duplicate an image on postcard-size, heavy-weight paper and cut the card lengthwise.

- They are two-sided so they can feature effective marketing techniques like endorsements and links to offers of freebies that drive traffic to your website.

Note: Bookmarks cannot substitute for business cards because they can't fit into media-kit folders' slots and they don't fit into people's wallets.

Logo- or bookcover-printed items like mugs, shirts, bags, and even baby clothes from local printers or websites like CafePress.com or Zazzle.com may be used for a variety of events:

- T-shirts work well at book fairs if they are designed to let fair visitors pair you and your book cover with the shirts. Use a headshot, your cover image, and booth number on your shirts. Humor helps. A shirt that said, "I was a lousy mother!" had people stopping the author in the aisles of BookExpo America.

- Carry necessities to book signings with a logo tote bag. Authors often sell books right out of the bag they carry when they run errands.
- Items that might get used on someone's desk like mugs or coasters remind editors, reviewers, and producers of you after the fact. MSNBC anchors use them instead of water bottles.
- Use them for prizes and drawings.

Online businesses that specialize in printing and shipping these items sometimes promise authors they can sell logo items to their readers for a profit. Readers can go online to order a mug or shirt for themselves or the author may stock a few to sell at book events. You know, like the concert promoters for Madonna do? Don't you believe it. Your mother probably won't buy one. How many coffee mugs that celebrate your favorite authors do *you* own? Rock stars, we're not.

Buy souvenir items wholesale. When you see something in a store that shouts, "Zinngg! This fits your book better than latex gloves," buy one as a sample (it seems only fair to the retailer!). Ask for the original box and, when you get home, check for the manufacturer's name. The tag or box may include a website address or phone number so you can contact the manufacturer or their distributor to sell directly to you.

If you have no luck buying the item of your dreams from the manufacturer, ask your retail owner or manager for a quantity discount. Expect greater cooperation and a bigger discount for very large orders.

Find gift and souvenir items at tradeshows and to-the-trade-only markets. Las Vegas has an excellent one for surplus merchandise bargains. Your city's convention center may host several tradeshows.

Assembling Your Media Kit

Of course, putting it all together is the last step before you send your kit off to gatekeepers. It is a little like designing floral art. Floral designers place the healthiest, most impressive flowers up front for effect.

You've seen that you might assemble your kit differently from one mailing occasion to the next. You've seen that you may end up with several kits, each with a distinct focus. The basics may or may not remain the same regardless of what you do.

You've learned that your kit must make it easy for editors to do their jobs. And it is only reasonable that we also make ourselves look as good as we can. It's a lot to keep in mind, so you do it one step at a time and make decisions as you go.

To save stress and time, shop stationers, office supply businesses, and online suppliers in advance. Your ideas and needs will change as you encounter new possibilities (and prices!) and you'll want to have samples of the stationery supplies you might use in your kit on hand to help you visualize your overall presentation. They might include:

- Two-pocket folders, the kind with tiny diagonal slits in the fold-up pocket portion to accommodate business cards.

  Hint: It's seldom necessary to buy four-color, professionally designed, slick, heavy-weight folders. Order printed professional-looking labels that sport your book's cover art, instead.

- A variety of possible paper choices.
- A printout of your assembled and formatted kit.
- Samples or mockups of your business cards and professional photo.
- A few media kits borrowed from other industries. I often pass kits from other industries around the room when I talk about marketing at writers' conferences. Use a couple of mine as examples. Go to howtodoitfrugally.com/media_room.htm and download the kit I offer as PDFs.

Play with these materials and the pages in your kit. Pretend they're playing cards. Shuffle them to their best advantage depending upon the branch of the media you are sending your kit to and the aspect of your writing career you want to emphasize. Which pages should come first? Which go in the left pocket? The right? Once decided you can format your Contents page.

Usually you assemble your material so the media release comes first in the left-hand pocket. Place your headshot (see Chapter Ten), your promotion gift (if any), a copy of your bookcover, and your book—if you are including one—on the left. Pages that are not in the realm of the usual media kit fare goes on the left, too.

On the right, put your About-the-Author page on top, your Awards page and then... well, you decide this order by determining which pages will most effectively convince an editor of your newsworthiness.

As a courtesy, attach a query or cover letter to the outside of the kit with a paperclip—maybe one that contributes to the design either by shape or color.

Your letter should be a brief and not necessarily formal introduction that piques an editor's interest.

The headers or footers of each page in your kit include simple contact information like those you find on thesis papers or in the top margins of books. Use a gray-tone font to keep them from competing with the rest

The Frugal Book Promoter 93

of the page. Don't use page numbers because you will rearrange the page order as the need arises.

Here are some quick don'ts:

- Don't print and assemble too many kits. It's sad to see a gross of folders and pre-printed interiors you can't use sitting in your garage.

- Don't use a designed letterhead on each page. It clutters and increases the time it takes your computer to print your kit.

- Don't use four-color printing on your folder or in the interior of your kit. Color adds to the cost of print jobs. Try a design using one-color ink on contrasting paper. Make your statement with quality paper instead.

- Don't attach your digital kit to emails unless an editor requests it. Instead, explain that it is available on request in your media release.

- As your kit grows, don't squash everything you've done into it. Pick the recent, most prestigious, or most relevant entries.

- Don't trick up your kit with gifts. Since the payola scandal of the 60s, editors often refuse gifts, anyway. Instead, send a modest thank-you gift a few days after the reporter or producer's work has been printed or aired.

- **Caveat:** Don't miss tradeshow opportunities. A kit displayed in an expo or tradeshow pressroom competes with dozens of others. Sometimes you're a signed copy of your book is the gift most likely to coax editors to pick up your kit and tote it around. Your kit attracts attention by sheer force of its design or because it includes a freebie. Some authors worry that an editor who can't possibly use the information in their kit will take a kit just to get a copy of their book, but editors are VIPs in the publishing industry—they may pass their knowledge interest on to others. They're also readers. And readers recommend books.

- Don't be too uptight about trying something different. As an example, there is not a right or wrong kind of presentation folder as long as it fits your brand. Some brands may call for something with a handmade look. I cut corners with my *HowToDoItFrugally* kits because "frugal" is the brand. A kit for a children's book made with Kraft paper and colored with Crayons and reverse-image letters may be more effective than an expensive printer-produced kit.

When you network at a cocktail party, you make eye contact, extend your hand, make a little small talk (my son calls it schmoozing) before you get down to serious business. The query and cover letters we discussed—the ones that get clipped to your media kit—are a lot like that process, even though they may be a little less... mmmm, schmoozy.

Next, we'll talk about your query or cover letters. They aren't enclosed within the kit but that doesn't mean they aren't an essential part of your presentation. The recipient needs to know *why* you are sending a kit and what you would like them to do for you. Don't forget to mention any prior contact you have had with the recipient of the kit. Queries and cover letters are the introductions that do all that for you.

14 Your Query and Cover Letters

> Query letters are the ultimate assertiveness-training tool at far less cost than a therapist with a half dozen initials behind her name. ~ CHJ

You just about have this publicity thing ready to roll. Your contact list is growing by the day. You've prepared your media release and kit using time-honored basics of branding and pitching. You're almost done except for the important cover or query letter.

Gatekeepers—folks like agents, editors, publishers, and bloggers—might first learn about you when they open a letter or email with your query or cover letter in it. Sometimes you send it to them with only an offer to provide the kit you've prepared. You also use them without a kit when you submit your manuscript. That means they carry a very heavy load in a single page!

You can see that we've saved this most important part of your presentation until last. Many of the skills you used developing your kit and release will help you write a great query or cover letter. Those skills make it easier than you ever thought possible.

There is little difference between a cover letter and a query letter. A *query* letter asks or tells the person it addresses what the author of the letter needs. A *cover* is an introduction to what is being presented. It may not ask for something specific, though you may benefit if it, too, specifies your needs.

You might be surprised at how many gatekeepers out there wear more than one hat. Without information about what you expect, they won't know what to do with your letter and it may get deleted or deep-sixed.

So, what *do* you want? A spot on a radio show? A featured article in a newsletter? To present at a conference or tradeshow? To be published? Do you want representation? The list goes on and on.

Of course you want to ask diplomatically. Making gatekeepers' jobs easier is considerate. It is tactful (and smart) to make them aware that you know who they are and what they do by naming their business, their TV show, or someone they represent. Or by letting them know where you met them or who recommended them. In fact, that information is a very good opener for a query or cover letter.

Your query or cover needs:
- An opener. Politely introduce yourself or start with a quotation from your book or an amazing fact that illustrates how important what you have to offer is and then introduce yourself.
- Next comes a bit about the idea you have for them (your pitch). That may require you to include a logline (a very short synopsis). Look up "loglines" and "pitches" in this book's Index. It generally does *not* include a lengthy synopsis!
- Your letter should be one page or less, but occasionally when you're pitching a story idea to an editor, it may be longer because it doesn't have an accompanying document. However, the format stays about the same.
- Then comes a short paragraph on your credentials.
- A simple thank-you and close follows. This may include the query or an indication of what you need from them, though you may want to work it into your letter earlier. It goes something like this: "I hope you will consider representing my (your title here). Please let me know if you need more information. Sincerely, (your name here)."

Here are a few don'ts for your query or cover letter:
- Don't make your letter into the driest business letter this side of the Sahara. It helps if your contact has a sense of your voice. Avoid words that are too formal or longer than three syllables.
- Avoid adjectives. Your contact—not you—should decide if your story idea is "amazing."
- Don't use the term "fictional novel." A novel by definition is fiction.
- Avoid saying "I think" or "I believe." The letter is written by you. Those words weaken your position.
- Avoid exclamation points.
- Don't say your book is "entitled." That's the wrong word. It is "titled."
- Don't include a chapter of your manuscript that relies on italics to indicate internal thought.

Hint: When you email a query, use the word "query" in the subject line. Follow it with a teaser or headline: "Query: Local Story to Build on Yesterday's *News-Press* Headline."

There are sample query letters in the Appendices of this book and a couple more in *The Frugal Editor* (bit.ly/FrugalEditor) where you'll also find more on editing query letters and pet query-letter peeves straight from some of our industry's most powerful literary agents who shared their thoughts with me. You'll need pristine query letters to get great reviews, too. It's one of my favorite ways to market a book. Regardless of who published it, you can assure your book's longevity with reviews! And they're up next.

15 Your Reviews

> ... newspapers and magazines are trimming back their review coverage
> ~ Christopher Dreyer for *Salon*

Many authors think it's worth it to learn all this marketing business—especially the writing of query letters—just to get reviews even though they're scared spitless of what those reviews might say. Byron once asked his publisher to "send me no more reviews of any kind." He thought Keats had been killed by one bad review (which, we know in retrospect, was not true).

Some writers—particularly those who have made it to bestseller lists—believe that reviews were responsible for their success; many others have been successful without them or in spite of them.

What can't be argued is that librarians and bookstore buyers peruse *Library Journal* and other major review journals, book review sections, as well as media material the major publishers send to them. Most authors would like to see their books in libraries and on bookstore shelves and good reviews are the fast lanes to those shelves—sometimes the only lanes.

You, as a promotion-minded author, would like to have reviews. They are my favorite form of promotion for a host of reasons not least of which is how many ways they can be used for your entire book marketing campaign. See *How to Get Great Book Reviews Frugally and Ethically* (bit.ly/GreatBkReviews) for everything you need to get them and use them effectively! Still, it may please you to know that authors are no longer at the mercy of reviews.

The publishing world has changed, in good part because of the web. Reviews are but one form of free ink. An author who has difficulty getting reviews can use other means of promotion including interviews, feature articles, book clubs, catalog sales, and social networking. I've seen authors addictively chase unproductive reviews when they could have used the same time to promote in other ways.

Do not judge book reviews by how well they produce sales. I have a traditionally published friend whose book was reviewed by *Newsweek* and her book still did not earn royalties over her advance.

Finding reviewers isn't easy and your publisher may not help much. No offense, publishers. I know many of you do a terrific job. Let's face it, you can use help, and you don't need to deal with disappointed (irate?) authors. And, authors! We are ultimately responsible for our own careers. Sometimes when we wait to take responsibility, it is too late.

One of my writing critique partners was published by a fine small press. When she learned her publisher had not sent advance review copies of her literary novel to the most prestigious review journals before their strict sixteen-week deadline, she was naturally upset. They explained it was a snafu. She and I used some of the alternative review-getting methods in this chapter. But mostly (because she had me to nag her), she moved on to other marketing strategies to make up for the neglect.

Most large publishers send advance review copies. Still, these days they are relying more on bloggers and review websites because they understand that grassroots publicity—reviews or otherwise—produces a very green crop.

Because thousands of galleys sent to the important review publications lie fallow in slush piles, the chances of having your book reviewed by a major journal, let alone getting a glowing review, is remote.

Beware of publishers—even traditional publishers—who don't respect tradition. My first publisher supplied review copies upon written request *from individual reviewers*. They did not honor requests that were generated from their authors' initiative. This method is cumbersome, unprofessional, and discourages authors from trying to get reviews on their own. Further, publishers should *offer* review copies to a list of reviewers—even those grassroots bloggers—who have been responsive to their authors in the past.

Ask potential publishers about their marketing process before you sign with them, but—even if you feel assured after having that conversation—it's best to assume you are on your own. We'll discuss how to do that next, beginning with how to get reviews from the biggest and best.

Big-Journal Reviews May Still Be Available To You.

Books that have been ignored by *The New York Times* have become bestsellers; others that received rave reviews never made it to that same publication's bestseller list. It is all a game. We can choose not to play, but if we don't play, we'll never know if we could have won, much less experience, the thrill of winning.

To win, you need to know the rules—especially the be-on-time rule—and you need to be very, very lucky.

- When you sign your contract with a publisher, be sure that they send advance review copies to major journals before their twelve-to-sixteen-week deadline.

The Frugal Book Promoter

- Big influencers in the publishing world pay more attention to a query or a review copy that comes directly from a publisher than one from an author or an independent publicist.
- If you are unable to get your publisher to accommodate review journals' needs, you can:
  - Buy extra review copies from your publisher to send to the reviewers. Ask for the list of review journals they submit to and expand on it by sending copies to others you think might be interested. Find my lists at howtodoitfrugally.com/reviewers.htm.
  - If your publisher will not have your book ready for release before that sixteen-week cutoff date, self-publish your own advance review or readers' copies (also called ARCs) and distribute them yourself. You learn how to do that in the next section of this chapter. Most publishers own the rights to your book so you must ask their permission to do this. How they supply review copies and what they charge you for them is something else you should discuss with them before signing a contract.

    Caveat: Distribute your own ARCs only if you are willing to risk the expense for limited results, and to take the pains to do it according to the firm and fast industry rules discussed in this chapter.

Making your own ARC or galley takes tons of planning, but you can do it.

Few use the term "galley" since print-on-demand has made publishing so quick and easy, but it is important you know this word for old-fashioned bound manuscripts because you will occasionally see it used to describe digitally printed review copies. Many use the term ARC—though no one seems to agree on whether the acronym stands for "Advance Review Copy" or "Advance Reader Copy." The word "ARC" seems to keep everyone in the industry using the same vocabulary to communicate.

If you are self-published, start the galley/ARC process by fudging with the release date of your book. If not, ask your publisher to list the official release date about twenty weeks to six months from the day your book is set to first roll off the press.

Delayed release dates are an industry standard. A book's delayed date *is* the release date. It is the one you or your publisher *say* it is and the one you use in your media releases. It isn't a fake date, so don't feel guilty. I know you won't want to wait, but that lead time will do the same thing for indie authors and publishers it does for big publishers. It gives you time to get a professional publicity campaign going including the intricate review process.

You arrange to buy books from your publisher or produce your own ARCs keeping copyright laws in mind. If you produce your own, you must reformat your manuscript in your own computer. It's obviously easier if your publisher provides ARCs to you at a favorable price. They will benefit from your efforts.

If you make your own ARCs, print them using a printer of your choice or a subsidy press (a publisher who charges you for their services). Plain vanilla (generic) covers are just fine for ARCs if they are clearly marked "Unedited Review Copy." You can also stamp or label a few of your regular run books with a violation notice, "For Review Purposes Only." Sometimes reviewers expressly ask that their review copies not be "defaced." In that case put your violation notice on a sell sheet. Keep reading for more details on sell sheets.

I like to use Amazon.com's KDP to print ARCs. They are especially cost efficient if you pay only for services that you can afford or that save you learning-curve time that you don't want to give over to the ARC process. You can upload your review copy free and pay two to five dollars per black and white copy (depending on the size of your book) not including shipping, and you may order any quantity you need, even just one. Many self-publishing platforms' profit margins are built into that price structure, so you are not cheating them by not utilizing all their services like formatting, interior design, etc. You may *need* to use them or *want* to use them if frugality is not an issue for you.

Many authors use Lulu or Ingram's Lightning Source (LSI) to print. Each has its own benefits and drawbacks. I know some who have used local printers, but they usually require a minimum print run which is usually too large for a run of ARCs or full runs for self-publishing or first books, for that matter.

Your review copies benefit from having your book's essential information printed on the first page, inside the front cover, on a label placed inside the front cover or as an insert, often called a sell sheet. Include:

- Official release date—the one you and your publisher have decided on
- Title
- Author
- Illustrator when applicable
- Name of your cover designer if you wish
- ISBN 13 and ASIN when applicable
- Number of pages.

- Retail price (the price a customer in a bookstore pays for your book) in both the US and Canada
- Trim size (the size of the finished, final copy of your book)
- Define as hardcover, mass market paperback, trade paperback, or other specification
- Number of illustrations and/or photographs
- Publisher's name and contact information—that could be you, the name of your own publishing company if you are self-publishing your book, or the name of your publisher
- Distributor's name and contact information
- Agent's name and contact information
- Publicist's name and contact information
- A "Review Copy Only" violation notice if you haven't otherwise used one

Caveat: Did I mention the twelve-to-sixteen week pre-release requirement of most top review journals? If it's too late for that, there are many other good ones like *Midwest Book Review* that welcome review queries after the release date. Find a list of some of those in my *How to Get Great Book Reviews Frugally and Ethically* (bit.ly/GreatBkReviews) along with everything else you need to make your review campaign your favorite, most successful promotion.

You're now ready to send your ARCs out with your releases or media kits according to each review journal's guidelines.

The big journals that require a fourteen-to-sixteen-week lead are:

- *Booklist, American Library Assoc.,* ala.org/booklist.
- *Entertainment Weekly Magazine,* EW.com.
- *Kirkus Reviews,* kirkusreviews.com.
- *Library Journal,* libraryjournal.com.
- *The New York Times Book Review,* nytimes.com.
- *Los Angeles Times Book Review,* latimes.com.
- *Chicago Tribune Books,* chicagotribune.com.
- *American Book Review,* americanbookreview.org/.
- *Small Press Review,* dustbooks.com. Poetry and fiction only
- *Publishers Weekly,* publishersweekly.com.

- Amazon.com, Editorial, 520 Pike St., Suite 1800, Seattle, WA 98101.
- *Ruminator Review*, www.ruminator.com.
- Book Page, bookpage.com. Submissions needn't be new titles.

Media associated with the topic of your book Use Cision.com, formerly *Bacon's Directories*. Check with your librarian for access.

- The book or arts and entertainment section of your metropolitan newspaper. Find a list of major newspapers and other review help at howtodoitfrugally.com/reviewers.htm#newspapers.

Caveat: Many of the same journals who appear to disregard or say they do not consider self- or POD-published books for review occasionally *do* review books published independently. Those privileged authors feel it was worth sending an ARC so professionally wrought the gatekeepers couldn't ascertain that it did not come from the most respected publisher or publicist and worth it to have built a sturdy platform while they were writing their book (and before!).

The following review journals are amenable to reviewing alternative forms of publishing though no reviewer, review journal, or site guarantees review for all submissions:

- *Independent Publisher*, independentpublisher.com.
- *Midwest Book Review*, midwestbookreview.com
- *Foreword Magazine*, forewordmagazine.com
- Lots of online review sites like MyShelf.com, CompulsiveReader.com, BookPleasures.com
- Book clubs for general readers and clubs for niche markets (think Oprah's book club associated with Holland America Cruise Line.). Find ideas at literarymarketplace.com.

Caveat: When you submit galleys or self-published ARCs, some journals ask you to send a final copy of your book when it is finished as proof that it was released.

Warning: Do not pay for a review. It it not considered ethical by journalism standards and your expensive review will *not* impress gatekeepers like librarians and editors. Trust me. They *do* know the difference. For more information on this topic, read my *How to Get Great Book Reviews Frugally and Ethically* (bit.ly/GreatBkReview).

The lists I've given you are compiled for the frugal author. They can be expanded a thousand-fold if your budget allows. Work with your publisher. Do not duplicate her efforts.

Check for changes in a journal's contact information and submission guidelines.

> **Hint:** Send a book or ARC with your query only when submission guidelines ask for it. For all others, wait to send your ARC until the reviewer indicates an interest in your book based on the query letter you send to them.

Alternatives To Major Review Journals

Alternatives are available if you miss the deadline for the biggies. We have to love them because they give authors and small publishers more control over the success of their books.

Here are the advantages of using review alternatives:

- Some review blogs, websites, and journals specialize in specific genres. That allows you to target your readers.

- You can build relationships with editors or reviewers of small and alternative journals more easily. That can lead to more publicity—like an interview or publication of an excerpt—for your book. And for your next. (Check the Index of this book for more on building your contact lists! You'll want one specifically for reviewers.)

- Many of these alternatives do not have deadlines or limit reviews to a recent copyright year.

- Many accept reader reviews and many readers are elated to be asked to share their opinions with others. It may be a first for them.

- Reader reviews usually include links to your website, to your blog, and to your online sales page. Click-and-buy is an easier sale than delayed purchases produced by print journals.

- Blog and online reviews are gaining prestige.

- Blog tour services will contact online reviewers for you. They are often inexpensive. They get reviews for you, and their contacts become your contacts. Keep reading for a short list of some of my favorites.

> **Hint:** my *New Book Review* blog (TheNewBookReview.blogspot.com) was specifically set up to help writers get more exposure for their books. Lacking a review, authors may submit a syn-

opsis. Please use the submission guidelines in the left column of the blog.

Sending an electronic copy of your book attached to an email query seems like a time saver, but don't. Many reviewers won't open email with attachments so your query may not get read. Offer to send an electronic copy in another email or through your eBook publisher or a hardcopy by post. And *don't* try to convince reviewers to accept the e-copy over the paperback. It's insensitive; if they accept your book, they should be able to read it in the form they prefer.

When reviewers prefer to review from digital copies, they may specifically ask for an "e-galley" or "eBook" which may be a bit confusing. Don't panic if you haven't yet published an e-version of your book; these reviewers will probably accept a PDF copy.

Alternatives to the Alternatives

Even more alternatives are avenues for exposure long after your book's release. Here are some ideas for finding them and using them:

- Don't overlook staff members at bookstores located in areas where you live or were raised. Many review for the bookstore's newsletter. Sometimes they post brief reviews on the shelf where the book is displayed.

- Ask a writer friend from your critique group to write a review. Send that review to art and entertainment and book editors with a query for a review and permission to print your friend's review if they prefer to.

- In general I don't recommend paying for reviews, even from respected review journals.

- I also don't recommend paid advertising of any kind with very few exceptions. If seeing your book advertised is a dream, you probably should try the traditional publishing route. Keep reading this chapter for more on this topic.

- Subscribe to newsletters to look for review resources. Sometimes the editor will be willing to print one of your existing reviews with permission from the reviewer.

- Go in the back door. When a review journal doesn't accept your book for review, research their individual reviewers, and query them directly. Use search engines to find them or call the journal and ask for contact information. You may have more luck if you send a personal query directly to the reviewers who write for these sites right from the start.

- Read reviews in journals and online to find reviewers whose style you like and who review books similar to yours. Some may write for websites that obviously prefer a genre other than yours, so when you send them a query, mention the review you liked, where you found it, and why it made you think they might be interested in your book.

Hint: I'm thinking of publishing a couple of chapters of my next novel—sort of a combination ARC and chapbook—to send to a long list of booksellers with query letters suggesting we plan well ahead for a reading or workshop. I'll make it clear in the query that I would be pleased to send the finished book to them upon request once it is available.

- Submit a short, ready-to-go review request to me to put into the Opportunities section of my *SharingwithWriters* newsletter. Dan Poynter once offered this service. I want to honor him, not fill his very big shoes. Put "SWW Opp" in the subject line of an email to HoJoNews@aol.com. The only cost is your book. Offer paper copies for best results.

Now You Have A Review, What?

Depending on the reviewer, your review may get published where it will rarely be seen or where it will be seen thousands of times. You have some control over that:

- If your reviewer doesn't normally write reviews, ask her to send her review to her friends and to magazines that publish reviews that are not written by their own staff writers. If she is an author or a professional in the field your book addresses, she will benefit from the exposure.

- Ask your reviewer—even one who writes for a review journal—to post her review on Amazon.com, BN.com, and other online booksellers that have reader-review features. This is OK if she still holds the copyright for the review.

- Ask permission from the reviewer to reprint the review and then post it on your blog, on your website, and in your newsletter. Use quotations from the reviews to give credibility to selected media releases and queries.

- Once you have permission to use reviews, send copies of the best ones to bookstore buyers. For a starter list of bookstores, go to midwestbookreview.com/links/bookstor.htm

- Send quotations (blurbs) from the reviews you get to librarians. Include order information. For a list of libraries try Midwest Book Review, midwestbookreview.com/links/library.htm.

- Use snippets from positive reviews as blurbs in everything from your stationery to your blog. (Check "blurbs" in the Index in this book for other ideas for their use.)

- Post blurbs from reviews you get on your Amazon sales page. Read Chapter Twenty-One to learn how to use the benefits they offer.

- Include the *crème de la crème* of your reviews on the Praise page of your media kit.

Facing Reviewer Prejudice Head On Is Essential.

Many authors have trouble finding reviewers because some judge books by their covers and even more judge books by the name of the publisher or the kind of presses they are published on. This book bigotry is changing, but slowly. If your book is self- or subsidy-published, traditionally published but printed with a print-on-demand (POD) press, or printed by a very small, unknown press, you may learn firsthand about how debilitating it is to be judged unfairly. You can fight this kind of prejudice:

When you subsidy-publish or use publishers that have names that are known industry-wide as subsidy publishers, negotiate with the publisher for your own imprint. Big publishers often publish books under several names. Doubleday, as an example, is an imprint of Random House.

Produce a great product. That means you need to learn a lot about every aspect of publishing and, when you need help, own up. Hire it out. That includes editing, indexing, formatting, interior design, and book-cover design.

When you feel yourself at a disadvantage, know that all authors—traditionally published and self-published—sometimes feel that way, too.

When you write articles debunking book bigotry, use my hashtag #bookbigotry. We're all in this together.

Don't get discouraged. Keep at it. We now have control over our own careers.

Review Scams Abound

There are a few pay-for review services that may be worth the money—like those that package the review you pay for with other services. But authors who are new to the industry are easy targets for those who want to make money from them. Even respectable Kirkus has a paid-for review service. Their reviews are probably as reputable as paid-for reviews can be, but booksellers, librarians, and some readers know paid-for reviews when they see them and they generally are not influenced by them.

Think about it. It is difficult for a reviewer employed by the author or publisher of that book not to be influenced by that relationship. Readers and gatekeepers don't consider them credible. That is why paid-for reviews fly in the face of accepted journalism ethics.

In general, I advise against paying for reviews. There are a zillion other free ways to get attention for little old author-you or your book. Why pay for something few give any credence to anyway? Besides, authors can Tweet a request for a book review and probably get one from a reader or blogger. It's that easy. If you send a book and get no review, look at it this way: It may be better than getting an unfavorable review.

For the best ways to get reviews and make the most of the ones you get including how they can help power your book into gift catalogs and how to legally excerpt and use great blurbs from them, read my *How to Get Great Book Reviews Frugally and Ethically* (bit.ly/GreatBkReviews).

Making a Great First Impression with Books or ARCs

Sending books or ARCs is a little like sending your first child off to kindergarten. You want to help her make a great first impression. To extend that simile, some parents are so anxiety ridden they overdo it. Clean stockings and panties and a nourishing lunch may serve her better than fussing over buttons and bows. The ARCs you send to gatekeepers must have the essentials, not a lot of frills:

- Reread the media release and query and cover letter sections of this book so you can spruce yours up before you send your kit off.

- Use computer-generated labels instead of handwriting the envelope's address.

- Send your kit and book Priority Mail. It looks great, isn't much more expensive than first class, and USPS supplies envelope and labels at no extra cost.

- If a reviewer asks for a copy of your book, write "Requested Material" on the envelope. Please don't pretend it's been requested if it hasn't. You won't fool anyone.

- When the envelope is opened, the reviewer should find a brief cover or query letter front, center, and face up.

- Follow submission guidelines. Certainly, don't send a copy of your book by post unless they specify that as a preference. It's not very frugal!

- When you contact gatekeepers by email, your subject line must be professional. Your recipients need to know exactly what they will find when they open the email. If they don't, they may not open it at all. It starts with "Query," and then a headline-like "Bill Gates Recommends Local Author's New Novel."

- Update and spruce up your media kit so you can send it along with the book copies you are asked to submit by mail. Remember our adage about making it as easy as possible for editors to do their work? The same goes for reviewers. Your media kit will have lots in it she can use.

If you're reading this book all the way through rather than using it as a handy reference when you encounter something new, you are aware my *HowToDoItFrugally Series* of books is one big share, one big wish for your success! So, forward! On to the next chapter, "Promote by Doing What You Love." What do you love? Writing!

Section IV – Promote Your Book by Doing What You Love

> If my doctor told me I had only six minutes to live, I wouldn't brood. I'd type a little faster.
>
> ~ Isaac Asimov

This section of *The Frugal Book Promoter* is good medicine. It's good for those who think they don't like to promote but do love writing. Because a good portion of book promotion *is* writing it will help you get started and you'll learn to love some things you didn't think you could.

This section is also a tonic for those who get a thrill from marketing. What a delight to find that you get to combine two things you love to do.

Many of the promotion ideas in this section can be used online or in more traditional venues. There are marketing remedies for those who hate anything that smacks of tech and a few ideas for those who adore what tech can do. In either case, put your lab coat on and devise a plan that fits your career goals. Mix ideas from elsewhere in this book to build a marketing campaign tailored to your personality and book's title.

16 Loving Writing and Recycling

> The writing-and-recycling combination is the Prius of promotion. If marketing a book were measured in miles, you'd go farther on less fuel with your writing than about anything else. ~ CHJ

This chapter on using your writing skills to promote is perfect for those who love writing, but it's also great for those who are shy. Put these ideas in your mortar and mash them with your pestle until you have the perfect marketing mix for your personality and your title.

Recycle Creative Work

When I began to think about promoting my book, I had scraps of my writing secreted away in the nooks and crannies of my computer. They were like emerald-cut diamonds in the dark recesses of a safe. What good were they hidden away like that? Some had been submitted and rejected and some had never been submitted at all. Some were unfinished. That made them equal because regardless of the reason they were hidden, no one had read them! There were even a few that had been printed—some on obscure websites that had purchased first-time rights only and these cried out to be read again.

Then I noticed new literary journals sprouting up everywhere on the web. Many were edited by people who care about literature even though they did not pay their authors a cent for their creative work. They seemed likely resources because they didn't already have a battery of favored contributors. I began a rescue mission. I retrieved a few stories and poems from my files and submitted them.

Some pieces I resold. Some I gave away. You can do this, too. Collect and edit your old writing. Rewrite sections of your book as excerpts or short stories. As you learn new things or do new things, write about them. Put on your big-idea sombrero and think of articles, stories, or poems that relate to your book or will appeal to your readers. Then find a publisher to showcase them. Or do it the other way around. Find publishers who appeal to the reader you want to reach and tailor what you write for them. You add a plank to your platform each time your work appears in print. You also expose your writing style and name to readers and have new content to recycle elsewhere.

Caveat: When previously published material is used, the first publisher may be credited along with the author but *must* be if the publisher paid for first rights. If the name of the original publisher will burnish your piece with additional credibility, it benefits both author and publisher to include it.

Submitting material for no pay may be an idea that makes you cringe. However, it is a time-honored tradition among poets and literary writers. People have bartered for eons and considered it fair and just. When the article you give away appears with a tagline and a link to your website, it will:

- Add to your name recognition (your branding).
- Help build your platform.
- Boost your search-engine ranking.
- Increase traffic to your site or blog.

Hint: Print journals often have websites so when they publish work that includes a link to your website, blog, or Buy page in the tagline, you get a bigger footprint on search engines, a better trafficked blog or website, and exposure for your other work long after the print journal has gone extinct.

A list of print and electronic journals that have published my work, many just thirty days or so after I began my recycling campaign, is on my website. It will encourage you to try this platform-building campaign and serve as a resource for approachable journals, see bit.ly/CarolynsPublishedLiteraryWorks.

If you haven't yet published a book, this published-works list reassures you that your voice is worth listening to and illustrates that even a piece once rejected by the *Atlantic Review* (that, mind you, gets something like 30,000 submissions a year!) might bring readers pleasure and serve as a promotion tool. If any publication listed there suits the material you have closeted away, edit and submit! That one action may turn you from a literary couch potato into a PR genius.

Submit your article with a title, a byline, and a credit line exactly as you would like to see it in print. (Look up "taglines" in the Index of this book.) Don't expect your editors to do it for you. They may not use your suggestion, but it is *your* job to make it easy for them to do *their* jobs.

Many of these publishers reimbursed me with no more than a thank-you, a lovely link, byline, tagline, and, occasionally, copies of their journal. It was worthwhile because of new relationships were formed and old ones rekindled. We all must choose our goals. Choose to network, share, and expose your work.

Write Nonfiction Articles

You'll need some nonfiction articles associated with your title or genre. You can place them one at a time using traditional market directories to guide your submissions or by using article banks, online sites where publishers go to find professional content. Here is a list of some of those article banks: PowerHomeBiz.com, ClickforContent.com. Ezine-writer.com, Writers.net, ThePhantomWriters.com, eHow.com.

Caveat: Do not post or offer any article in trade that you may want to sell later. Many journals buy only first rights; if your piece has appeared on the web, it will not qualify under many publishers' guidelines.

These tips will help you get more promotional mileage out of your articles regardless of how you disseminate them:

- Include information about your book in the article itself if you can figure out how to make that information pertinent to the article. Editors who use free material expect a little self-promotion if it is relevant and isn't blatant.

- Submit a resource box or sidebar (the helpful informationals that are sometimes surrounded by a border) with your article. They often appear with articles on the web and in print. Some sites and journals pay more for articles that include a thoughtfully written sidebar.

- Invite editors to visit your website to get free content and sign up for your notices about available articles. Capture their information and categorize it in a list so you can better serve them in the future. Use the index in this book to refresh your memory on building cracker-jack lists! Lean about my free article policy at howtodoitfrugally.com/free_content.htm. Use the contact page to ask me for free articles on writing-related and book-marketing related topics for your own blog, anthology, or newsletter.

- Don't date your articles with limiting content. Use "recently" instead of a specific date. Use the copyright insignia (©) your name and title of the article.

- Avoid sending an article to an editor twice by tracking where you send each of them.

Write a Column or Blog

Columns and blogs may be more productive than you imagine. After you've written many, you can categorize and assemble them and get a new book out of it for your income stream. Read Nina Amir's *How to Blog a Book* (bit.ly/NinasHowTo).

A logical way to land a regular column of your own is to examine the articles you've written, identify a media trend, and parlay a select few with a specific theme into a proposal or query. One of my clients, Patricia Bunin, did this with very short anecdotes about her senior experiences. She believes her column sold primarily because they were short. These little essays became the samples that helped convince an editor of her expertise.

To make this model work you need a column name, a platform that shows an editor you can attract readers, and the courage to send a query letter!

When my husband and I closed our last retail shop, I took old, yellowed clips from columns I had written before we had shops into the *Pasadena Star-News*. Because they were so ancient, I was sure the features editor would politely show me the door, but I figured nothing ventured, nothing gained. The editor immediately assigned me a column called "Savvy Shopper" for that newspaper and its affiliates. Sometimes being brazen is an advantage. Sometimes we need to be in the right place at the right time. We can't be there if we don't put ourselves out there.

Don't assume the samples you have aren't good enough. I thought the way I addressed the readers as "you" in my old was dated. The editor thought it was "fresh." That your samples have been published gives you credibility, but you might present something new you have written. If you have written frequent op-ed pieces or letters-to-the editor they may be an entrée to your own column, too.

Once you have experience, an editor may be willing to take a chance on something with a different slant. They need responsible writers who write well and submit on time. Find suitable periodicals in *Bacon's Directory* or *Cision*, either online or in your library.

Once you're accepted as a columnist, sell only first rights so you can reprint and resell them. Repurpose material you've gathered in the past for a new column.

Blogs work very nearly the same way, but bloggers are at an advantage. They get to run things their own way. The disadvantages are that they don't have deadlines to motivate them and they need a little online savvy to run a blog. See Chapter Twenty-One for more on blogging.

Syndicate your articles or columns. Some columns with a specific thread like fashion or grammar lend themselves to syndication. Imagine how much better books sell for nationally known columnists like Dear Amy or Liz Smith (and how fondly we remember TV columnist Andy Rooney). That columnist could be you.

Once you have a track record, submit a proposal to small syndication services or large ones like the Associated Press (AP). Do a search on "syndicates" for ideas. You want to know what kinds of columns they already have, where yours might fit in, and the appropriate editors' names.

Self-syndicate your column or your blog posts. Approach small newspapers, newsletters, etc. with suggestions for your own syndicated series. You can also email columns or post them at intervals to your contact list. As your list grows, so grows your platform for selling to a syndicate. Or you can give your articles away, syndication style. The latter is an efficient way to recycle essays, columns, commentaries, and rants. I organized this process to meet my needs. I have no idea if anyone else does it similarly, but it disseminates writing at the grassroots level widely and quickly.

My approach is informal. I keep a separate list in my computer of all the editors I know who don't require exclusive material. I send articles I write on how authors can get free ink to one group of editors, my pieces on tolerance to another group, and so on. (See Chapter Eleven to learn how to categorize your media list.)

When you write an opinion piece, review, or rant, open your file for a particular group of editors and copy-and-paste their addresses into an email blind copy address window. You may later choose to use an email marketing list like the service from GoDaddy.com. The next steps are:

- Use the help feature on your email service to learn how to make each email address blind. Your query or submission will look more personal to those who receive it.

- Think of a clear and catchy subject line.

- Include a signature line with complete contact information.

- It is unorthodox, but because eventually all the editors on my list have come to know me, I introduce my article with a short note that is generic enough to work for any editor who receives it and then paste my article beneath it. I make these points in the introduction:

    o The article is free.

    o I would like the editor to use the piece in its entirety and include the byline and tagline as submitted. Clearly delineating your expectations is not demanding; it is professional.

    o I would like notification when the article appears (along with my contact's Twitter moniker and the permalink that always takes readers to that specific article) so I can promote it in my newsletter and blog and on Facebook and Twitter.

    Caveat: This is a caveat that bears repeating. Do not attach your article. Many virus-wary editors (and others) will not open an email or its attachment if one is included.

- Check for typos (which, I'm not happy to tell you, I sometimes miss, so I know firsthand it's a good idea to ask someone else to check, too).

- Sometimes, I offer an editor an exclusive, especially if I can parlay it into extra exposure by gently asking for more than a byline and tagline. I might ask for a display or classified ad on their website or suggest we guest blog for one another or work in some other cross-promotional way.

- Include website managers, bloggers, newsletter editors—even other authors—on your article placement list.

Grassroots marketing like this works. Of course, you can also target big-time editors.

Publish Your Own Newsletter

Use your newsletters to promote your book and keep readers involved until the next one is released. If your book hasn't yet been published, your readers will enjoy following the publishing process.

Newsletters needn't be fancy. Joe Klein told an anecdote in his *Time* magazine column about a simple flier Bryan Lentz chose to promote his run for congress. Lentz said his staff "...wanted something splashy." His simpler choice cost less. He says, "[My newsletter] looked real. People open and read 'em like a newspaper." Klein notes, "It was true, people [nearby] were reading the Bryan Lentz news."

That's the way it can be for your newsletter, too. I once asked my readers about my plain-text *SharingWithWriters* e-newsletters and they voted overwhelmingly for keeping them simple—and long—rather than short, colorful HTML.

Some authors skip a newsletter and contribute to others' letters instead. The trouble is, there are benefits to having your own newsletter that you can't get by playing someone else's game. Shel Horowitz reinstated the letter he once dropped for just that reason.

It may be easier for authors of some romance genres to fill their letters with material that will be of interest to their readers, but it can be done for any genre. Here are some tips on how to start:

- Keep your goals in mind. Entertainment? Staying in contact with readers? Garnering support? Book sales?

- Consider the time it takes to produce a letter.

- If you plan a snail mail edition, consider the cost *and* the increased effectiveness.

- Let your letter reflect your personality. Most letters start with a chatty piece from the author. C. Hope Clark includes a snapshot of herself doing something fun in her *Funds for Writers* newsletter (fundsforwriters.com/newsletter).

- Humor attracts and keeps readers.
- To increase readership, encourage readers to contribute articles and letters-to-the-editor.
- Include something to entertain your readers. Crossword puzzle of publishing terms, anyone?
- Ask your readers for suggestions on content they would like to see included.
- Post each newsletter on your website. Some of your regular subscribers will revisit your archived letters and the sites you link to in your newsletter, including your own.
- Use a signup window on your website and blog so visitors can subscribe to your letter.
- Recycle your feature articles and tips onto your blog and vice versa. Allow plenty of time between each appearance. Recycle again to others' letters and blogs.
- Include a calendar of your events.
- To encourage readers to scroll to the end of the letter, end each one with something amusing. I use pun-oriented jokes because they relate to the fun of words. Publicity Hound Joan Stewart uses doggy videos and jokes and solicits new ones from her readers.

Write Book Reviews

Why not write book reviews? You read anyway. Reading contributes to the quality of your own writing, and it doesn't take much more time to write a review for your website or blog or for online bookstores after you've finished reading a book. Here are other advantages:

- When they are allowed, bylines and taglines on your reviews expose your name to a most important audience—people who read books.
- Include your website link in your tagline to improve your position on search engines.
- Reviewing connects you to editors and other reviewers at review sites who can help you get your book reviewed when the time comes.
- If you write about writing or the publishing industry or review for a review site or a journal and your editor is willing to write you a letter of assignment, you may apply to tradeshows like Frankfurt Book Fair and BookExpo America

(BEA) for a press pass. Such a pass affords you many other benefits. Use your e-reader's find function to find other mentions of "tradeshows" and use this book's Index to learn more about them and how they can benefit your book

- I go into more detail on using and writing reviews—even becoming a professional reviewer—in *How to Get Great Book Reviews Frugally and Ethiicall* (bit.ly/GreatBkReviews).

Mary Gannon, deputy editor of *Poets & Writers,* says reviewers take "a lot of heat... for some free books, a few bucks, and a byline." However, it's usually only the most famous reviewers who are disparaged for their criticism and only the radical or caustic ones at that.

Hint: The how-tos for writing a review are not in the purview of this book. Learn more by reading Magdalena Ball's *The Art of Assessment* (bit.lyArtAssessment).

Whether you are compensated with cash or with exposure for your book, your reviews will be good writing samples and publishing credentials for the future.

- MyShelf.com looks for reviewers who offer them exclusives.
- CompulsiveReader.com.
- MidwestBookReview.com.
- Bookpleasures.com.
- Don't forget to pop your reviews up on online review sites like BN.com.
- To extend the review you do for any other site, submit it to my *The New Book Review.* You'll find submission guidelines in the left column at TheNewBookReview.blogspot.com
- Don't neglect readers' social networks like Goodreads.com. Find more information on using them without spending too much time at it in Chapter Twenty-Two on social networking.

Hint: I once developed a type of review site (or blog) that I consider to be original, if such a thing as "original" exists. In Reviews for Riters, I assessed famous writers' books as if they had been submitted to a critique group. I looked for writing techniques used superbly or not so well, ones that emerging authors could emulate—or not. Editors of sites that cater to the needs of writers were enthusiastic about them. You might build such a niche with your own idea.

Hint: Many writers and reviewers who submit reviews to my free *The New Book Review* (TheNewBookReview.blogspot.com), don't know how to use a permalink to extend the life of their review when they promote it. A permalink lets your reader to go directly to what you are promoting. It's courteous and better use of your promotion time. When I accept a review for *The New Book Review*, I send you a how-to article on using permalinks with ideas for using them to promote your review as a thank-you for participating. Submission guidelines are in the left column of the blog.

Write For Anthologies

Anthologies are collections of similar articles, poetry, or stories assembled by an editor or group of editors. It is a wonderful way for new writers to get recognized.

Watch for calls for submissions in newsletters and magazines and send something you've written that matches the publication's needs. Sometimes they pay you, sometimes not. No matter. Your name and your book will receive exposure with an added measure of credibility because you are published within its covers. Often you receive much more than you give.

Some authors complain that they don't get paid, don't get paid enough, or that they are expected to buy the anthology and to promote it. These grievances seem shortsighted to me. You would probably *want* to buy a couple of books your work appears in to give to special people in your life and to editors who may then give you (and the anthology) some publicity. Inclusion in an anthology is, after all, part of your platform, a kind of clip that points to your experience and success.

Further, if you're contributing to an anthology as part of your marketing campaign, it's to your advantage to promote. If all the contributors do so... well think of the promotion power behind that!

These doubting Thomases also overlook that many of the finest review journals and anthologies do not pay their authors, and that these publications are accepted entrées into the upper echelons of the literary world.

Work published in anthologies is recyclable, too, providing you did not sign over all your rights to the publisher. A writer who recycles her work may feel less resentful about not being paid or by other demands.

My first anthology was a cross-promotional effort. We all knew our collaborative eBook would only be as successful as the sum of the participants' promotional efforts. We were to give our eBook away rather than sell it. We shared our promotional coups using an e-group on Yahoogroups.com, became friends, joined one another in other projects, supported one another. Where is the exploitation in that? The process worked so well, I began to consider using anthologies published by traditional publishers, university presses, and others.

Anthologies sometimes pay their authors and almost always credit them with a tagline or other acknowledgement. Here are other advantages:

- Anthologies may offer awards. One of my stories appeared in an unpaid anthology but it also carried with it the Red Sky Press Award. Awards, especially those chosen by prestigious judges like Rose A. O. Kleidon, Professor Emeritus in English at the University of Akron, can be used to promote in dozens of different ways. See the Index of this book for more on "contests" and "awards."

- Anthology editors may plan group book signings to promote the collection. A bookstore signing planned by *A Cup of Comfort* editors helped prepare contributor JayCe Crawford for marketing her soon-to-be released book. Anthology editors should not object to your passing out your business cards or bookmarks at their events. After such events, you have an entrée to the bookstores' events coordinator.

- The release of an anthology, book signings for anthologies, or any other related events or awards are opportunities for an author to send out her own media releases; this is not just exposure, it's credible exposure.

- Some anthologies give a portion or all of their net profit to a charity.

- When you participate in an anthology, you may meet someone in the publishing world from whom you can learn new things or meet people who will introduce you to others with similar interests. Hooray for networking!

Authors should be cautious. But they shouldn't reject an opportunity of being read and maybe even discovered based on someone else's bad experience or paranoia.

Write Forewords and Introductions for Other Authors

When I was asked to write my first foreword for a book, I had no idea of the benefits of doing so, but it sounded fun. Eric Dinyer is an artist who had a concept for a gift book called *Effort and Surrender: The Art and Wisdom of Yoga* (bit.ly/YogaForeword). I was surprised when Andrews McMeel Publishing used my name on the cover—nearly as prominently as the author's. The book was sold in Walmarts across the nation. That's not shabby exposure! The gift book is gorgeous with a little window in the cover that showcases Eric's artwork. It was a perfect addition to my branding campaign. Since then I have been asked to write other introductions and forewords. I never find it necessary to refuse because authors usually don't ask authors who are not a match for them.

An author might pursue these kinds of assignments by letting it be known they are available when they network with other writers and artists or on their websites.

Write Tip Sheets

A *tip sheet* is the way to editors' hearts. It is a list of quick, readable entries that relate to a specific subject. Editors use all the tips in an article like "Ten Great Tips for Writing Scintillating Headlines" at once or just one of the individual tips to fill nooks and crannies in their layouts. They know their readers love them. The subject line "Tip Sheet" is a most welcome message in an editor's email box.

It is true that fiction writers must tweeze their material to make a PR technique like this work, but the results are worth the effort. Nonfiction writers will likely find tip sheets come popping off the pages of their books. Here are some ideas:

- List events in a timeline. This is ideal for the writers of history, regency, and other period romances or historical novels.

- *Time* magazine itemizes opposing statistics to suggest conclusions. Your list of stats would deal with an aspect of your book, say the rebuilding of urban areas, if your book is about revitalizing inner cities.

- The publicity firm I once worked for instituted The Ten Best Dressed List. This was a publicity coup that built more than one career. Do a "best" or "worst" list that relates to something in your book.

- Editors like "Top Seven" or "Top Ten" lists. These lists adapt themselves to how-to books.

- Lists of unusual little tidbits are good. I used one about Utah's idiosyncrasies to intrigue radio show hosts when *This Is the Place* was released. I put my list in a "Did you know" format. "Did you know that residents of Utah consume more catsup per capita than any other state in the union?"

- Because quotes have mass appeal, *Time* magazine uses them in a column called "Verbatim" each week. Recycle short quotations from your book. Tweeters love quotations and often extend their life by retweeting them.

- With a few adjustments, I could submit the list on writing tip sheets that you are reading right now to sites where authors congregate. I would need to add a title, byline, and a credit with a buy link that would help market this book.

> **Hint:** For tip sheet ideas go to Top7business.com. It features a new list of seven ways to solve a problem each day. Submit a tip list suitable for their online publication—one that is related to your book or your body of writing as a whole.

Write Op-Ed Essays

You are probably familiar with the op-ed sections of the newspapers you read, but maybe you didn't know they are called "Op-eds." Not all papers identify these sections the same way. They are usually found near the letters-to-the editors section or on the page opposite their daily political cartoon. Though both letters-to-the-editor and op-eds are opinion pieces, op-eds tend to be longer than letters-to-and usually carry both a byline and tagline identifying the author as an expert. (Look up "taglines" and related keywords in the Index to learn more about how to use them.) Authors of letters-to-the-editor are not compensated, but the authors of op-ed pieces often are. Read a few each day to see if there are ways your book (including your book of fiction) might relate to current events and how your opinion might add to the conversation. Having an op-ed piece in a daily newspaper can propel you to expert status overnight.

Once you are a published author, it will be easier for your work to be accepted for op-ed sections. Send a query letter to the editor in charge of the paper's editorial page. You will probably find a roster of editors right on the op-ed page or on a newspaper's website by searching on "editorials."

> **Hint:** Pitch your op-ed ideas to newspapers that covered a current event related to the topic of your book. Don't wait. To newspapers, the word "current" is crucial.

Write Promotional eBooks

Bookstores offer a huge selection of books: Hardcovers, trade paperbacks, mass market paperbacks, books bound with twirly wires, pop-up books, large-print books, tactile books, and more. But there may be as many different kinds of electronic books as paper ones.

eBooks also come in all sizes from whitepapers (a term often used in the business world) that should, by all rights be called e-papers, to full-blown books. Some electronic books are given away. Some are sold. Readers can personalize their fiction using links to choose their own endings. eBooks also come in several formats for multimedia readers.

So how do you use them to your advantage? Lots of ways. When your book is published electronically as well as a traditional have-and-hold book, you let your readers (who, after all, are your *customers*) get your book in whatever form *they* want. Your eBook lets them get it fast. Some books, like books on tech, require frequent updates. eBooks allow authors to do that easily, Authors can also reach niche markets without much upfront expense. But mostly—tada!—eBooks make great tools for promotion. Here are some ways to do that:

Write a whitepaper or eBook to give away. Don't think that because it's free it can be slapdash. The idea is to let the eBook you're giving away entice readers to buy your other book (or become your client or customer). It should feature contact information, your motto, even, even an excerpt from your newest book—with a cover image and buy links, of course!

To get wider exposure than you could on your own, coauthor an eBook. Share your contacts, your publishing expenses, your promotion ideas, your time, and your different skills.

Write an eBook to entice others to do something you'd like them to do, like sign up for your newsletter. Like buy another of your books. Like subscribe to your blog. Okay, let's admit it. They're little bribes. You can use others' eBooks as bribes, too. It's a great way to help one another in a way that benefits you both. Shelley Hitz offers several free eBooks to authors on a variety of subjects including a free eBook I contributed to.

- You can see from the last bullet, your promotional eBook can be a round-robin kind of effort with a little help from your friends

- Write a sequel to your book and publish it as an eBook to spur sales that have become stale. Or the other way around. James Patterson gave away an early novel to create a flurry of media attention around a new one.

- An eBook format can breathe oxygen into a book that is about to expire.

- If your book isn't already available as an eBook, publish it that way and promote its new availability as a travel-easy and frugal format. To do that you must own the rights. Otherwise, encourage your publisher to do it or to allow you to do it.

    Hint: Copy for some eBook devices must be specially formatted. Making a .pdf file of your Word file may not cut it. There is a Kindle eBook formatting tutorial in the Appendix of my *The Frugal Editor* (bit.ly/FrugalEditor).

My students often complain that authors make less money on eBooks than paperbacks. Yes... and no. Think of this as Economics 101. There you learn about the importance of volume. Think of it as Marketing 101 where you learn about word-of-mouth and exposure. The more people who read your book in any format (and love it), the more you sell. This is why I make all my how-to books in this *HowToDoItFrugally Series* (and my poetry books) available as eBooks:

They can be offered inexpensively to starving or budget-conscious readers.

- They can be published fast. Once written, I had the first edition of this book ready to use as a text for the UCLA Extension Writers' Program class I taught in less than thirty days after writing it.
- It is easy to update them.
- The number of pages is not an environmental issue; you can include whatever you think best fills the reader's (or your story's) needs.
- People who live in other parts of the world can access your book quickly and inexpensively.
- Authors can publish eBooks free. Of course, it takes time and time is money. Still, if it's free advertising... that's pretty good!

I'm sold on eBooks. I often make my eBooks available free or at a discount when people buy the paperback using Amazon's Matchbook program.

An Anatomy of My First Free eBook

Let me break down how did this and it may help you use one of these magical, frugal tools in your own publicity campaigns. It was an anthology, a gift book, how-to book, and an advertisement in one! It was one of best, most long-lasting promotions I've done. eBooks are the new math: eBook + E-gift = Promotion. Oops. Make the answer FREE promotion.

Kathleen Walls, an online friend, asked more than two dozen authors from several countries to contribute to an eBook to be given away. Our *Cooking by the Book* could be used as a gift of appreciation to the support teams it takes to edit and market a book and to the legions of readers who cook but had never read any of our other books.

Authors who had at least one kitchen scene in their books contributed to *Cooking*. Each author's segment begins with an excerpt from that scene. A related recipe—often regional—comes next, and then a short blurb about the author with links so the reader can learn more about the authors and their books.

Contributing authors publicized this cross-pollinator any way they chose as long as they gave it away. Here are some of the ways we used to distribute *Cooking by the Book*:

- Some offered a free eBook as part of a promotion and let people email them for a copy. This was the least techie approach and it allowed personal contact with readers. It also allowed us to collect and categorize our readers' emails to use in later promotions.

- Some set up an autoresponder like sendfree.com that sent our eBooks directly to our readers' email boxes when they sent requests to a sendfree address we provided.

- Some contributors sent readers to their websites where they found a link to download a .pdf file of our free eBook. eBooks distributed like this are more effective if they include an offer or call-to-action—perhaps a discount on a series of your books—within its pages.

- Some contributors let others distribute our eBook as a gift to their clients, subscribers, or website visitors—either with a purchase or as an outright gift. When you use this method, you get to set the guidelines for its distribution because you provide the free eBook.

- If we were doing this promotion today, our eBook would be available to readers using any kind of device by using the free Kindle app. We could also do periodic freebie Kindle promotions.

Note: Use your eBook backmatter for special offers with live links to promotions or your Amazon Buy page.

- You may find other ways to distribute your eBook or alter these processes to meet your needs.

Contributors to our *Cooking by the Book* benefited from their efforts and from contacts with other authors. We had some superior promoters among us:

- Most of us set up a promotional page for the cookbook on our websites.

- One promoted it in her newsletter.

- Mary Emma Allen writes novels, but she also featured the cookbook in the columns she writes for New Hampshire dailies *The Citizen* and *The Union Leader*.

- David Leonhardt, our Canadian, incorporated the cookbook into a Happiness Game Show speech he delivered over a dozen times.

- We all offered coupons for this freebie at book signings. Because eBooks cost nothing to produce, they can be given to everyone, not just those who purchase a book. Some of us printed bookmarks featuring this offer.

- I put an "e-gift" offer for *Cookbook* on the back of my business cards.
- If we were doing this promotion today, we'd all blog about it and use Twitter, Facebook, YouTube, and other social networks.
- We treated the promotional book like a real book. We got blurbs and reviews. Reviewer JayCe Crawford said, "For a foodie-*cum*-fiction-freak like me, this cookbook is a dream come true." That review popped up in places we didn't know existed.
- We used *Cooking by the Book* as e-gifts to thank editors, producers, and others online.
- Each year Mother's Day beckons us to repeat our publicity blitzes, because, if you haven't noticed, mothers tend to do *lots* of cooking.

Our most startling successes came from sources we had no connection to at all. The idea for using a promotional eBook like this was featured in Joan Stewart's The *Publicity Hound*, in *Writer's Weekly*, in the iUniverse newsletter and more.

Some media found it newsworthy because it worked so well for writers of fiction. When I queried radio stations with programming ideas related to this cookbook, I had the highest rate of response I'd ever had, and that was in competition with a pitch for *This Is the Place* just before the Salt Lake City 2002 Olympic Games and an intolerance angle on the same novel right after 9/11.

Hint: I love Amazon.com (KDP) and Bookbaby.com for publishing both eBooks and paperbacks, whether or not they are to be used as promotions. You can do everything yourself and do it free except for the copies you buy and the shipping. They even offer free templates for designing covers. Be careful not to get caught up in the pay-for tracks if you are after "free." Second best is letting someone coach you through the your first eBook and you'll be set to do it on your own forever more.

Special E-Book Offer: I offer a free eBook for subscribing to my free *SharingwithWriters* newsletter which—contrary to the rules—comes out only sporadically. Find the offer on most pages of my website, upper right corner: howtodoitfrugally.com.

Translate Works You Love

If you speak more than one language, you could translate poems, plays, or about anything else. You might choose something famous or something obscure. If someone else has translated the same work, that's okay. You will bring your unique sensibility to the project. Edna Mine Karinski is a children's author at heart, but she is translating Mitsue Katsue Karinski's *Harvest Moon* from Japanese as a personal tribute to her mother.

You can make your marketing experience as joyful as I hope you are making your writing experience using the ideas in this chapter. You should know that—fortunately or unfortunately—the marketing that reaps the best results both for your own growth and the sales of your book may require you to stretch a bit. Even to take risks. The best marketing tools are in the next chapter. Give them a chance. Please keep reading.

17 Learning to Love What You Thought You Couldn't

> Don't let something you can't do keep you from doing what you can do.
> ~ John Wooden, advising his UCLA basketball players on facing the unknown

I like to take Wooden's advice a little further. You *can* do what you think you can't do—and learn to like doing it. I hope more authors accept this challenge because some scary aspects of marketing could keep our books from reaching their potential—and even keep us from publishing.

For some, speaking evokes as much fear as spiders or snakes. We think contests and reviews only set us up for rejection. If you think you could never learn to love the things you avoid, try anyway. They may be the brightest stars in the panoply of book promotion.

Speaking is the Star of PR and Life

The ability to speak in public will bring credibility to your résumé, and publicists dream about working with a client who can speak or is at least willing to learn.

If this seems scary, let the birth of your book nudge you toward learning this skill. If after giving speech-making an honest effort you decide not to give formal speeches, all your other less intimidating appearances—from book signings to recording videos to leading critique groups—will benefit from your new speaking skills.

If you think of speaking as sharing, you may find it fits your personality as well as a pair of comfy slippers. There are techniques that make being in front of a crowd less stressful. As an example, at your book launch you can take your microphone to the edge of the stage, sit down, and talk as if you were speaking one-on-one with those who have come to wish you well. At a seminar, use a wireless mic or one with a long cord so you can go into the audience to answer questions—a casual and effective way to touch those who have come to hear you. Beginning actors minimize their fear of performing before others by focusing their attention on a lucky-penny talisman they keep in their hand instead of focusing on the crowd. If you've ever taught or conducted meetings successfully, think of speaking on topics related to your book as an extension of those skills.

Here are ways to make your speaking appearances more effective and comfortable:

- Give handouts crammed with valuable information to the audience. Print your pitch, the image of your bookcover, and your contact information on each sheet.

- Use an old-fashioned flipchart—a giant notebook that fits on an easel. Write as you talk as if you were taking notes in your senior English class. Or you can use this technique as a cheat sheet by outlining major points before you start speaking. Leave space between your outline topics so you can fill in details and secondary categories as you speak.

- Breathe deeply before you start speaking. Have a bottle of water on hand. If you've also provided munchies for the audience, the entire situation will feel more relaxed.

- It might motivate you if you think about this: Authors sometimes make more money speaking than they do from their books.

- Learn to use PowerPoint. I'm not fond of PP presentations because they tend to reduce eye contact with a speaker's audience, but this little miracle from Microsoft's Seattle campus works a little like having a cheat sheet at the ready.

- So, you're ready to give speaking the good old college try, right? Here are some possibilities to help you prepare for the adventure:
  - Go to Toastmasters' meetings. See toastmasters.org.
  - Take a speech class at your local college.
  - Read Pam Kelly's book. She teaches master classes in speaking to UCLA's instructors and I learned everything I know from her. Find her book at bit.ly/PowerfulSpeaking.
  - Subscribe to Tom Antion's newsletter (antion.com). He's the online speaking guru.

Now you're ready to unearth potential speaking engagements. Watch the calendar sections in weekly and daily newspapers for coming events and do a web search for entertainment agencies and organizations related to your expertise. Write a query letter to each lead, only this time you're asking for speaking engagements. You wait a couple of weeks, call to ask if they received your letter, and follow up with a verbal pitch.

Pitching on the phone is good practice for speaking in general. Here are some other sources for finding places to speak:

- Fraternities and sororities
- Night clubs and coffee houses
- Corporations
- Professional organizations
- Charities
- Political groups
- Reading clubs
- Libraries
- University Career Centers
- Schools, especially college classes that are associated with some aspect of your book

You can propel one speech into others. In your handouts, include a form that asks the audience to recommend another organization that might benefit from your presentation. It will be more effective if you:

- Request that they turn the form back to you at the end of the meeting.
- Design your form as a self-mailer with pre-paid postage so they can send it later if they prefer.
- Ask for specific information like the name of the organization, preferred program topic or topics, the name of the program director and her phone number, and email address.
- Offer a discount or other perk (like your promotional eBook!) for the referral.
- Offer your service at a reduced rate or at no charge to charity events.

You may choose to charge for speaking or not. Occasionally an organization offers only an honorarium. In any case, they should let you display and sell your book as a service for their audience, and you should not be shy about listing your book as a resource in your handouts. I always ask those in charge of programming to mention my presentation in their newsletter and media releases and include my website address and images.

Handling the Hecklers

Dealing with a heckler in public is one reason some authors don't care for speaking, but think of it this way. It's better for authors to learn to handle iffy situations at a small public venue than on national TV.

Here are two secret words. Determine. Defensive. You *determine* you will not be *defensive* in advance. We are now public persons and must resist the urge to react. Take a deep breath and decide that these folks are not hecklers. They may be tactless or ignorant and neither are reasons to be offended.

A fellow author who is subsidy-published emailed this question for the column in my newsletter called, Q&A *a la* Ann Landers:

> **Author:** During my question-and-answer period at a book signing, a man asked me rather rudely why someone with my credentials should choose to subsidy publish and mentioned that he had found typos in my book. In an earlier interview, I was questioned about Jack Kelley's fabricated stories in *USA Today*, as if I had something to do with them.
>
> **My Answer:** Try to give people like this a break; assume they just want information and turn the question away from you and to the publishing industry in general. What's considered good about each form of publishing and what isn't. How the publishing industry, just like others, is not perfect. You might be armed with an anecdote of your own so the heckler (if that is, indeed, what she is) is disarmed by your candor. Humor is helpful. On a similar occasion, I told my questioner how *The New York Times* reported that major publishers were inflating their first-run figures for books in order to create buzz in the media and that compared to this kind of an... er... indiscretion, a typo or two, hardly seems like a sin of great proportions. You might then turn the occasion into something positive by mentioning how your book or another published by your subsidy publisher was recently optioned for a movie or received an award.

After an upsetting moment, we might examine our reaction to see what we can learn about ourselves. Did we feel insulted because we lack confidence in our choices? Do we feel our skills are inadequate to address criticism? Is there something deeper at work here we might tackle in the interest of self-improvement?

During a book tour (yep, a real *tour*—meaning several stops in a short period of time to promote one specific book) in Georgia, I was confronted by a woman who asked if I knew the Mormon religion was a cult. In Utah where I was raised, I frequently encountered intolerance because I was *not* a Mormon. I handled the situation well enough (but not perfectly!), returning her question with a question about how she would define "cult." Nevertheless, the experience helped me see how deeply rooted the hurts I experienced as a child and teenager were, that I hadn't, in fact, "gotten over" them as I thought I had, and that I am offended as much by bigotry aimed at others as at myself. Self-examination helps authors handle encounters of the hard-to-take kind more effectively. It might also enhance your writing skills.

Awards Set Your Book Apart

I pity the poor reader these days. Reviews can't be relied on for unbiased opinions, so a reader may have trouble telling which book is most likely to set her heart a'beating. As she shops, she often turns to the blurbs or endorsements on the back of the book. She may read a few of a book's first pages. But a book that has won an award from an organization like Reader Views, Eric Hoffer Awards or, yes, from universities like Columbia's Pulitzer (pulitzer.org), will probably clinch a sale faster than many other sales techniques.

Authors who have won literary contests for their work get bragging rights they can put into their media kits, query letters, websites and on their social media pages. That makes it easier to sell a promotion idea (or a next book!) than it would be for someone who is new to writing. Gatekeepers—anyone from acquisition editors to feature editors at newspapers—can be influenced by a contest. Notice I did not say, "A contest *win*." My highly praised book of poetry, *Imperfect Echoes* (bit.ly/ImperfectEchoes), was named honorary mention by the trusted *Writer's Digest*, and you can be sure I shouted it to the skies! Contest recognition may be what's needed to set you apart from the many authors clamoring for attention. On a slow news day, just about any award looks like a nugget of gold to a busy editor.

So why are authors so ready to hate contests? Fear of rejection is an easy answer. An article in the revered *Poets & Writers* magazine mentions that writers often consider contests rigged and resent the fees (usually from free to $27 for literary contests and from free to $125 for book awards). The magazine article pointed out that publishers and organizations become dependent on the fees they charge for contests and note that rarely does an unknown author win. I'm not sure the last part isn't sour grapes; the point of many contests is to find delicious new voices that will keep the not-so-voracious appetite of publishers for new material well fed. If it is the truth, we should hone our own skills to approximate those of more established authors.

There are other benefits to contests. Some offer critiques of entries—a value that cannot be overestimated in terms of learning more about the contest-winning process and one's craft. Some publishers sponsor contests to attract submissions of great new manuscripts.

Hint: Some of the most prestigious contests only accept nominations that come directly from publishers. You may need to gently prod your publisher if you know of a contest you think your book is right for.

Here are some guidelines for using contests to gain exposure and expand your credentials:

- Choose contests that fit the size of your pocketbook. No-fee contests work well until you refine your contest IQ. Those include following submission guidelines to the nth degree and selecting contests that suit your material and your voice. Pick contests that impose fees at least as carefully as you might select a tomato from the produce department at your market. Journals that award prizes to the best work submitted for their pages are a good, frugal way to start.

- Choose contests based on the kind of writing you do. Read up on past winners. Examine past winners for genre, voice, length.

- Find contests from a source that lists less popular contests as well as those that have names attached to them like Hemingway, Faulkner, and Pulitzer. Search this chapter for a short list of contest resources. For a list even beginners have a chance of winning, go to howtodoitfrugally.com/contests.htm

- Pay attention to the contest's guidelines, *except* for the one that calls for no simultaneous submissions. This rule is patently unfair to the author. You know it and they know it. It's a rule, not a law. It is a courtesy, however, to notify those contests or journals you have submitted to if your entry wins elsewhere.

- To increase your chances and to keep you from worrying about each entry, submit work to several contests at a time.

- Choose contests that offer career-boosting benefits other than the contest itself. That might be eBooks on writing and marketing for all who enter and critiques from the judges. Many literary journals offer free copies or subscriptions to entrants.

- Though the Submittable.com platform that most journals use these days make bookkeeping fairly easy once you have an account, keep track of entries so you don't submit the same material to the same contest twice.

Hint: Some journals still accept paper manuscripts. Be sure your submissions are pristine and professional.

Find contests that fit your genre and voice on the web, in books, and through organizations. Here are a few leads:

- Use the Deadlines section of *Poets & Writers* magazine to find reputable contests. Most are very competitive and charge fees. Find them at pw.org.
- CRWROPPS announces calls for submissions and contests. To subscribe go to groups.yahoo.com/group/CRWROPPS-B/.
- A fat volume called *Writer's Markets* (bit.ly/Markets4YourWork) publishes an updated edition each year. It lists contests, publishers, agents, and tons more. Buy the book and get online access to updates.
- Check professional organizations like your local Press Women, the National Federation of Press Women, Upper Peninsula Publishers & Authors Association (UPPAA), and the Wisconsin Regional Writers' Association (WRWA), which accepts writers from anywhere.
- Do a Google search on "writing contests" plus your genre.
- Subscribe to *Winning Writers* newsletter at winningwriters.com. I love this one for finding free contests. They also sponsor North Street Book Prize for self-published books.

Once you've won a contest—from finalist to first place—you are newsworthy:

- Add this honor to the Awards page of your media kit. If it's your first award, center it on a page of its own. Oh! And celebrate!
- Write your media release announcing this coup. (See Chapter Eleven to learn to build a targeted media list and Chapter Twelve to learn to write a professional media release.)
- Post your news on media release distribution sites. Find a list of these sites at howtodoitfrugally.com/media_release_disseminators1.htm.
- Notify your professional organizations.
- Notify bookstores' events coordinators. Those where you've signed and where you want to sign.
- Notify your college and high school. Some have press offices. Many publish magazines for alumni and their current students.
- Add this information to the signature feature (see Chapter Twenty) of your email program.

- Add your honor to the bio template you use in media releases—the part that gives an editor background information on you.

- Use this information when you pitch TV or radio producers. It sets you apart from others and defines you as an expert.

- When you win, place, or show, do a web search for "embossed labels." You or your distributor can apply them to the covers of your books. If you win an important award, ask your publisher to redesign your bookcover or dustcover to feature it *a la* the Caldecott medal given for beautifully illustrated children's books. If you don't know this medal, visit your local bookstore and ask to see books given this award. It's one of the most famous and most beautifully designed.

- Put your award front and center on your blog, your website, your social network pages.

- Your award should be evident on everything from your business card to your checks and invoices. I use the footer of my stationery to tout my major awards.

- If your book is published as an eBook only, ask for the contest's official badge or banner to use for promotion. If they don't have one, you can make one of your own using bannerfans.com

- Frame your award certificate and hang it in your office to impress visitors and to inspire yourself to soar even higher!

Robert W. Schaefer, one of the readers of the first edition of *The Frugal Book Promoter*, wrote to tell me that he would appreciate a plan of attack for getting an award for his book. Here's what I told him:

- First and foremost, write a great book. One with great content. One that is organized well. A reminder here. It's almost impossible to do this without some personal guidance, which is why I recommend writers' conferences (see the next section of this chapter), and well-vetted writing classes in your genre.

    Caveat: When you change genres, take a class that focuses on that new genre. Do it even if you have been wildly successful at writing in another genre. Authors who have achieved stature should be *especially* cautious about embarrassing themselves by launching into another arena without knowing all the new stuff they need to know. Poetry is not fiction. Writing a romance requires skills that science fiction does not, and vice versa. Journalists will find that knowing more

- Have your book edited by a professional editor *before* you begin the submission process. Because many publishers have cut their editing budgets, you'll be more assured that the job is done well enough to have it qualify for an award. Read my *The Frugal Editor* (bit.ly/FrugalEditor) to know more about do-it-yourself editing and how to choose a qualified professional.

- If you are self-publishing, hire an excellent book cover artist. Mind you, I didn't say a graphic designer or fine artist. Some artists like Chaz DeSimone (desimonedesign.com) know things about book cover design *and* marketing pitches that many others don't know.

- If you are self-publishing, hire a good formatter or interior book designer, one who knows the intricacies of frontmatter, backmatter, headers, footers, and page numbering.

- If you write nonfiction, learn the art of indexing. It isn't as easy as the word processing programs seem to make it, but I think it's one uphill battle that's worth fighting on your own because no one will know your book—know what you feel is important for your reader to know—like you do. There are, of course, professional indexers who will work closely with you. If your publisher provides an index for you, check it to see if important categories or details have been overlooked.

- Follow the guidelines in this chapter for finding the perfect contest, for *your* book.

- Attack this process with confidence and be willing to make an investment of time and some money.

The more you know about publishing, the better equipped you will be to produce a product you can be proud of (and, hey! Your book *is* a product!). You may even produce a prize-winning book. You wouldn't expect to become a computer programmer without knowing how the hardware worked, now would you?

Writers' Conferences Work If You Work Them Right

. I hear grumblings about writers' conferences all the time, but when I ask, I usually find that authors went to conferences with unreasonable expectations or they selected conferences knowing little about them. Trust me on this, a series of respected writers' conferences may be the near-equivalent of an MFA for a time-starved writer juggling creative aspirations and the requirements of a day job.

Writers' conferences are valuable because they immerse you—albeit for a few short days—into your art. They expose you to a broad array of what you need for success. They tend to make us all aware of how much we don't know and how much we need to know to publish and promote.

Authors often go to writers' conferences hoping they will snag an agent or publisher. The trouble is, they do this before they've been to enough conferences or taken enough classes to polish their craft. After experiences like these, they throw up their hands in horror and decide to self- or subsidy-publish, but if they haven't honed their skills enough to attract an agent or publisher at a conference, it's possible their book is not ready for publishing on their own either. Many times they are frustrated because:

- They attend the wrong conference at the wrong time in their sojourn from first draft to publishing. They may be looking for an agent before their novels are complete or their sample chapters and proposals for their nonfiction book are written.

- They set unrealistic goals for the conference.

- Their expectations for what a conference should provide are too narrow and / or too broad.

When seasoned authors express surprise at how involved they must be in the promotion of their own books, I am convinced anew of the need for conferences. It's difficult to come away from most conferences without getting a handle on what a book requires to make it visible.

Conferences staged by large universities, writers' organizations, writing schools, or well known magazines may give more up-to-date, accurate advice because they vet their presenters and can attract the most experienced writing instructors. That makes them invaluable. Authors should look at the credentials of a conference and its presenters before they register. Even a great conference may not be a match for their genre or their level of expertise.

Aside from the credibility a reputable conference will give to your platform, here is what you'll miss if you never go to one:

- You'll miss a chance to learn about traditional and alternative publishing. If you aren't well-advised, you will doubt your own choices when things go awry (and a few things *always* go awry—it's the way of the world).

- You'll miss all those writing secrets that seminars offer. You can't hear a secret if you aren't in the room.

- You'll miss out on contacts with more publishers, agents, and marketers than you're likely to meet elsewhere in a decade.

- You'll miss the greatest possible critique partners. Conference-goers tend to be excellent critiquers because they care enough to learn about their craft. If you don't already

- You'll miss a chance to corral one of the reputable agents in attendance.
- You'll miss the chance to practice your pitch and may never learn how a good one works.
- If you don't attend a well known conference, you can't add it to your list of achievements in the query letter you send to agents and publishers. Having attended a respected conference is an indication of the investment you have in your career.
- If you don't attend a conference, you'll never know what you missed—the good and the bad. We learn from mistakes as well as successes.

Which Conference is Best for Me?

Choosing a conference can be tricky. Many conferences are expensive. Even free online conferences can take a lot of time. This is one of those occasions when it pays to be picky.

Determine your goals and choose a conference accordingly. Some focus almost exclusively on craft and often call themselves retreats. Some offer seminars in book marketing. Others tend to be entrées to agents and publishers, and some offer information on publishing like the legalities of copyright law. Some do a little of everything.

Study up on conferences. The library has back issues of *Poets & Writers* that include reviews of conferences. Use your networks or Google to get opinions and suggestions from writers who have attended. Here are a few more conference-perfecting ideas:

- Do not choose a conference based on its exotic location unless your first interest is a vacation.
- If you choose a conference that offers critiques of your work by publishers or agents for an additional fee, go for it. If you wait, you may have to kick in another conference fee for the privilege.
- If signing with an agent is your primary goal, wait until your book or proposal is fine-tuned to go to a conference and be sure agents who specialize in your genre will be there by reviewing the conference website. Register early enough to be assured of an audience with your choice.
- Determine the thrust of the conference you will be attending. Because of proximity and prestige, UCLA Extension (uclaextension.edu/writers) has access to Hollywood as a resource.

This makes their conference one of the best for screenwriters. Other conferences have their own specialties.

- If you want to find time to concentrate on your writing, you may prefer a writers' retreat rather than a conference.

- Examine the credentials of the conference presenters. If you write persona poems, you may want to study with a teacher who has had success writing that specific kind of poetry like UCLA's Suzanne Lummis. A person who is interested in writing courtroom dramas will benefit from an instructor who has published in that genre.

- Gotham Writers' Workshop in New York (writingclasses.com) is another bona fide educational institution that offers onsite and web classes. You may find a good one in your town.

- Until you're sure you can utilize an expensive conference to its fullest, select online seminars like Jo Linsdell's PromoDay (jolinsdell.com). It is free, though she very gently suggests her attendees make a small donation to cover her costs. Some years I donate support materials to authors who register. Once you have experienced a conference online, you'll be better equipped to choose an onsite conference. Check the Index for entries on conferences in this book.

Hint: Bring a small pouch of tools with you to conferences. I use a bag I received with an Estée Lauder gift-with-purchase. Toss into it color-coded pens, snub-nosed scissors (sharp ones may not get you through airport security), a small roll of cellophane tape, index tabs and labels, paperclips, strong see-through packing tape (in case you must ship materials books and other materials back home), ChapStick™, hole puncher, breath mints, a tin of aspirin, elastic bands, Band-Aids™, and your personal medication. If you are presenting, throw in a hammer, tacks, razor, a small pair of pliers and a mini measuring tape. Mine even has a spool of very fine wire for hanging large posters. Don't unpack this kit when you get home. You'll need it in the future for other events.

You can use a conference to promote, too.

- Some conferences offer tables where participants can leave promotional handouts for their books or services. Before you leave home, ask your conference coordinator how you might utilize this opportunity.

- Ask the conference coordinator if they publish a newsletter or journal. If so, send the editor media releases as your career moves along.

- Take your business cards to the conference.
- If you have a published book, take your bookmarks to give to others and a few books for influencers you may meet.
- If you have an area of expertise that would interest a conference director, introduce yourself. She may be busy, so keep your pitch very short and follow up later.
- Record the names of fellow conference attendees and presenters who might give you endorsements for your book in the future or be interested in reading your book.

Up next, the does and don'ts for making book tours, book launches, and tradeshows and book fairs work for you.

18 Publishing Dreams vs. Marketing Needs

> The one thing that never disappoints an author is holding a new book in hand. The one thing that pleases authors unexpectedly is how much writing a book forces us to grow.
> ~ CHJ

Other than watching our books hit *The New York Times* bestseller list, what most authors dream about is signing books. You see yourself in bookstores and at book fairs and tradeshows like Book America Expo (BEA). You're at a table signing books with a Franklin Christoph fountain pen and a long line of admiring fans waiting to breathe your essence, touch your ink.

That's a lovely dream, but these venues are not magic. After their first big book tour, some authors decide there are other ways to promote that give them more bang for their buck, more marketing power for the time they take and the stress they create.

I want you to realize your dreams, but I also don't want you to make all the mistakes I made when I started marketing my books. If appearances at book fairs, tradeshows, bookstores, and launches are your dream, go for it. But know that if for any reason you can't do a tour, or an expensive trip to BookCon, all is not lost. There *are* other ways to promote—many more effective. And there are other dreams to catch.

Tradeshows are Not What You Think

Authors don't sell books at tradeshows like BookExpo America (BEA). We give them away. We're selling only in the sense that we're promoting to people who come to tradeshows, people who help us sell them, people like publishers, editors, librarians, and bookstore buyers.

Many tradeshows will not let booth participants sell merchandise directly from the tradeshow floor. Tradeshows are about marketing, though customers may place orders with vendors for future delivery at some of them. It's safe to say that tradeshows exist for every industry. In general, they are huge, busy, creative places. They're also confusing and renting a booth can be too expensive for most authors' budgets.

It confuses many writers that these shows often call themselves book fairs. To keep our terms straight, we'll speak of book fairs as those where readers (and yes, others!) come for a fun day of book-browsing and maybe some buying.

Probably the most famous tradeshows in the world of publishing are BookExpo America, London, and Frankfurt. Library organizations hold regional tradeshows for easy access by librarians; many offer free display and others' booths are quite expensive. To help you see the difference between tradeshows and book fairs, two of the most famous *book fairs* in the U. S. are the one founded by Laura Bush in Washington DC, and the one sponsored by the *LA Times* in Los Angeles.

Authors dream of being part of tradeshows but don't often participate because booths and travel are expensive, access is sometimes closed to independent authors, some publishers don't have a budget that can accommodate them, and few authors know how to get around these restrictions. Keep reading for secrets that may allow you to skirt these constraints and that many don't want you to know!

Services have sprung up to fill the void. Some organizations offer to put your book on display in their booths at these publishing-industry shows for a more reasonable cost than renting a booth on your own. Booths can easily run over $1500. These services are usually around $200 to $500, but your book will get lost among dozens, if not hundreds that they "feature."

The sponsors of these booths often claim to have great success selling the foreign rights to books or pitching self-published books to large publishers. If authors can't be on the premises to show, talk about, and sign their own books, the money spent for these services will almost certainly be wasted. Because the fee is paid up front, booth caretakers might not be invested in the success of the books on display. The sales person in the booth will never have read the book. There is usually no way to hold the organization accountable for lack of *future* successes they didn't promise to begin with.

If you are considering a service like this, ask if they are willing to provide their service and get paid only if they produce results. That they won't is an indication of their effectiveness. When I say "results" I don't mean a list of publishers who have "shown an interest." The lists I was given were either not detailed enough for me to reach the "interested party" or were generic lists given to all their clients. Some of these services do their best, I'm sure. I just think that you might spend your money more effectively.

If you can afford to be in these booths *in person*, here are the advantages:

- Bookstore buyers, acquisition librarians, and the media do attend tradeshows and you might generate interest for your book with some of them.

- Tradeshows can be great learning and networking experiences. Publishers, distributors, warehousers, book-oriented media, foreign rights agents, and publicists will be there. And they expect to be pitched! Most tradeshows even include great education programs taught by the best in the industry, some at no additional charge.

- If you're there on a press pass (and you may be able to get one if you are a bona fide reviewer or writer on matters of publishing for any branch of the media), you will have access to the press room where you can stock their shelves with your media kits and pick up others' kits, too.

- You may someday be a presenter or panelist at one of these shows. If you are an expert on some aspect of publishing and have some speaking credentials, put your expert query letter skills to good use and see what happens.

Caveat: Not all display offers are created equal. Some, like the ones produced by Valerie Allen at AuthorsforAuthors.com can cost as little as $5. per book and they verify what they do by sending images of their displays after the event. When they are inexpensive enough, you might decide that such displays add exposure to an extensive marketing campaign.

Finding tradeshows is easy if you connect with a great list-serve group or forum like the ones sponsored by *Author U* (authoru.org) or find my list of publishing-oriented tradeshows on the Writers' Resources pages of my website at bit.ly/ListTradeshowsFairs. Google this list of library councils for more information:

- American Association of School Libraries
- California Library Association
- Illinois Library Association.
- New England Library Association
- New York Library Association
- New York State Reading Association
- Ohio Library Council
- Pennsylvania Library Association

You may need to show publishing credentials to get into a tradeshow, and, even then, access can be expensive. Those with press badges and those who have rented booths need not pay an entrance fee.

How to Get a Tradeshow Signing Opportunity

Tradeshow signing opportunities are more plentiful than you might think. Here are some backdoor suggestions short of renting an expensive booth of your own:

- When you win an award, the sponsoring organization may invite you to spend signing time in their booth. Before you enter any contest, ask the administrator if they offer this benefit. They may charge for this time to defray their costs and you will probably be *expected* to sign and give away your books rather than sell them.

- If you or your publisher has a distributor or wholesaler, they may extend opportunities (usually for a fee) to sign your book in their booth.

- If your book was published by a large publisher, they may provide you with free booth time.

- Some publishing-oriented organizations like Book Publicists of Southern California or BPSC (bookpublicists.org) or Independent Book Publishers Association or IBPA (ibpa-online.org) may have a cost-sharing booth. As with a display at any tradeshow, to do well you must be *in* the booth, *talking* to people who drop by and use your contact list to let influencers know you will be there.

Sometimes those who have booths at BookExpo America are allowed to apply for one or two signing spots at the back of the hall on the tradeshow floor. These are coveted signing positions, even more prestigious than signing positions in individual booths. Attendees line up to get free books, talk to the authors, have pictures taken with them, and have their books (sometimes ARCs) signed. Back in the day, I got one of these treasured spots for *This Is the Place* through the Small Publishers Association of North America (SPAN) booth. It was a dream come true, even though I had to pay for a spot in SPAN's booth, I felt fortunate to win the draw for the signing positions, and happy to buy and then give away 300 books. A promotion like that is worth the expense and time and much less costly than buying a booth dedicated to a single author. If you promote it right, your appearance gives you credibility in the industry and boosts your book sales. It was a more successful marketing venture than the tradeshow signing I did a few years later out of my distributor's booth or the one I did out of an award booth.

You notice those words, "promote it right." An author doesn't just sign up for a signing, pay the rent for her booth, and hope. This is where those contact lists we talked about in Chapter Eleven come in handy. Let your personal and publishing industry contacts know you'll be there! Of course, you put all the other applicable skills in this book to work for your appearance—media kits, media releases, and query letters, too. I include a sample invitation to one of my BEA booth appearances in the Appendix of this book for you to use as a template for your first tradeshow appearance.

Book Fairs are for the Public

Although Book Fairs naturally attract lots of people in the publishing industry, they also are for readers who might buy your book on the spot! Still, you want to prepare for encounters with the media—producers, directors, bloggers, and others interested in new content. The promotion you do for your book fair appearance isn't only about encouraging people to come buy your book! That promotion you do builds your credentials among general readers and influential people in the entire publishing world.

Like tradeshows, you can do book fairs the expensive way by renting your own booth or the frugal way by sharing with others. The benefits of doing it with others are the same as with any cross-promotion. When all the participants do their own marketing, you all gain exposure from one another's contacts. You also share costs and booth responsibilities.

You can see that like tradeshows and about any other promotion you do, book fairs aren't magic. When authors assume book fairs are about sales rather than exposure and credibility they set themselves up for disappointment. In fact, if you don't use a book fair booth as an opportunity to network, to promote, and to gain credibility for being there, don't do it. Book fairs are like marriage. We love them only when we work hard at them.

> **Hint:** Invitations to every library event planner and acquisition librarian in the vicinity of the book fair venue is one of the best book fair promotions of all.

I once sponsored book fair booths at the *LA Times* Festival of Books. Slowly and at considerable cost—one year at a time—I learned what works and what doesn't. My booth partners and I used tons of value-added promotions including:

- We shared printing and postage costs of catalogs we produced ourselves that featured booth participants' books and an invitation to the fair. With permission, we used the fair logo to give the catalog credibility. We sent our catalog to book buyers, media, and influentials like movie producers (because that fair is in the middle of Hollywood land).

- We produced a video/trailer featuring booth participants that we ran on a large screen in our booth. We charged extra for this service; we figured participants would be more likely to use it for their blogs, websites, and social networks—which was the whole point. Continued exposure for all of our book- fair stars. We also trained these participants in ways to use these videos in their other marketing efforts.

> **Note:** Because CDs can be produced inexpensively in large quantities, we recycled much of the content we developed for

these videos and trailers onto CDs to be given away. A participating author offered our freebies to visitors saying, "A CD for your PC?" Fairgoers rarely declined our offer. Nowadays, CD drives are an optional extra on most new computers so the same idea could be parlayed into distributing custom-printed thumbdrives with your web address on them and ten times the content on board, this is called "Data Preloading" in the biz. A wide variety of innovative packaging types are available including lanyards and keychain attachments, try www.FlashBay.com for ideas. Unlike CDs which eventually get tossed, USB thumbdrives can be recycled by the recipient and your printed message remains on the outside of the drive!

- Books (often overruns or slightly damaged) donated by other authors became gifts-with-purchase of other books from our booth.

- A drawing for a gift basket was successful because it garnered the contact information of many readers. We shared that information with all booth participants.

- We produced totes and bags featuring our bookcover images and our booth number. We gave them to folks to carry the books they had purchased from us. These bags then became advertisements for our booth as our customers carried them around the grounds.

- Some of our booth participants wore T-shirts emblazoned with images of their bookcovers, their website addresses, and our booth number.

- Each participant produced posters that we used to decorate the booth.

- We had mini training sessions for our booth participants in which we urged them to talk up one another's books, guided them through promotion possibilities and display techniques, and gave them resources for promotion materials.

Book fairs are not all equal. Some are right for one title but not another. Some charge $35 and some $1500 for a booth. Book fairs are more valuable tools if you have a connection to the region, if you tie your booth to a local charity, or if the genre of your book fits the theme of the fair or at least the section of the fair your booth is located in.

One way to ensure success at any fair is to be a featured guest or presenter at a fair where the book fair administration promotes you in their advertising campaign. You then double down with your own promotion and end up with a royal flush.

Another is to choose a fair that benefits an organization. Lori Hein, author of *Ribbons of Highway: A Mother-Child Journey Across America* did well at a book fair that benefited her daughter's elementary school. Her signs informed book fair revelers that three dollars would be donated from every book sale and she sold twenty-five books. She says, "Two weeks later I'm still riding the coattails of that one book fair." She did a lot of things right:

- She chose a fair where she had personal ties.
- She chose a fair that was aligned to the title of her book; a school fair and a book about a parent-child relationship were a great team.
- She used good signs.
- She was specific about the amount she intended to donate.
- She passed out fliers and cards complete with a good pitch and contact information to encourage after-fair sales.

Here are other things you can do to increase the effectiveness of your booth and make the experience more enjoyable:

- The *LA Times* offers listings in an advertising section that goes out to their subscribers and other readers before the fair. It seemed expensive at the time, but people who saw my listing in it contacted me six months after the fair and beyond.
- Fair administrators also offer booth extras like electrical hookups and lighting. Lighting is an important part of great retailing and you *are* retailing when you sell books from a book fair booth.
- Be kind to your back. Take a roller board with a pull rope or a handcart.
- Send media releases to local press, TV, libraries, bookstore event coordinators and buyers, and book discussion group leaders.
- Take pictures to use in future promotions and to add to your tweets in the moment.
- Offer a special "fair-only discount" to interested readers.
- Wear a nametag that says "AUTHOR" in large letters the entire day, even when you go to lunch. Use indelible ink on broad satin ribbon, clip it into a swallowtail shape, and hang it from your nametag. Your readers are *there* to see authors. That's you!
- If you are a fair speaker or panelist, use that designation to find an entrée for your book in the booths of participating

bookstores before the fair. They may stock your book after the fair.

- Keep a guestbook; building a contact list should be one of your primary goals at any event you do. Remind guests to *print*.

- Give souvenir buttons to anyone who walks up to your booth. Don't just hand them out. Ask if you may pin them to your customers' shirts; they become your walking billboards and you make a friend. Used like this, buttons are one souvenir that works if you work it right.

- Use specially-designed car magnets and decals and even (less effectively) bumper stickers. The car or truck you bring your books in will be parked at the fair all day.

- If someone from the press visits your booth, your job is to *ask* them for coverage. *Pitch* them ideas. *Help* them get the story they want. Better still, the story they didn't know they were after.

- Be hospitable. Set out a bowl of treats such individually wrapped candies or loose M&Ms™ with a scooper.

- If you'll be standing on the grass wear warm, comfy shoes and socks and bring a mat.

- Bring along a helper, preferably a chatty one.

- Dress the part. Literary authors could consider a scholarly look—perhaps a turtleneck and Harry Potter-style spectacles. As a conversation starter, Kathleen Walls, author of *Ghostly Getaways*, wears a bride dress like the one on the cover of her book.

- Take a kit of essentials including tape, a hammer, pliers, and tacks. Re-supply anything you run out of when you get back to home base. Re-use your kit at the next fair.

- Pack a lunch. Even if you have a friend who can relieve you, you are the star attraction. You're there to meet your public, not disappear into the food zone.

- Take sunscreen and a hat in case your awning doesn't arrive or in case the fair doesn't provide them as part of your rental.

- Consider buying mugs or T-shirts imprinted with your book-cover. You probably won't have much luck selling them, but they make nice gifts if an editor, producer, or director shows an interest in your book. Of course, if the weather turns foul,

- you might actually *sell* lots umbrellas or rain bonnets imprinted with your book cover and web address.

- Make notes on each business card you collect and follow up on leads as quickly as possible.

- Don't forget your thank-you notes. Send them to those who bought your book and to the fair coordinators. Maybe you couldn't be a presenter this time, but if you keep in touch, next time you might be the celebrity *du jour*.

- Did I mention great signs? Use a banner and collapsible stand. They are a bit expensive, but I found my banner proclaiming "Award-Winning Author Now Signing" complete with a photo made a big difference for attracting readers to my table when I was signing.

By now you know you don't need to *sell* your book. It will sell itself if you're marketing it well. Still, at a fair you benefit from tried-and-true sales practices. Stand, don't sit. Practice your pitch and adapt your pitch to your audience. I might say, "*This Is the Place* is a coming-of-age story about a young woman about your age who made it to New York against all odds." to a young adult. I tell older readers how many awards it has won, including the Reviewer's Choice Award.

You can also practice some responses to sales resistance. If a browser says, "I already have too many books on my nightstand," the author doesn't try to sell something they've just told you they don't want. Instead you say, "I know what you mean. However, if you are a member of an organization that could use a presenter, I do those, too," as you hand them a card, flier or even a free book. If a browser says, "I'm writing my own book," the author says, "That's wonderful. I edit books," or "I have a signup sheet for my newsletter. In it are tips and tons of resources for authors!"

Evaluate your fair experience (or any other marketing event) right afterward. I do this so I can refine the procedure the next time 'round, or avoid it altogether. Fairs are a bit like having babies. You are determined to never do it again immediately afterward, but you tend to forget about the pain and are ready to start again in about six months.

> Hint: I often use one idea I found in an old evaluation file: Keep your nametag—the one you used at a fair or presentation—in your glove box or in the box of books you carry in your trunk for sales on the road. If you come across a fair in your travels and decide to stop, wear the tag as you walk the fair. You'll be surprised at how many attendees will want to talk to you about your book.

Book Signings and Bookstore Tours are Like Bathing Suits

Why is this? Because they look better in our dreams than they do in the dressing room. Like itsy-bitsy bikinis or strongmen's tiny suits, cold book signings can be chilly. Until we have a fan base, they are seldom hot, hot, hot!

I witnessed a book signing for Anne Rice at Vroman's Bookstore in Pasadena, CA. People were lined up around the block with her newly purchased books in hand—waiting for her to arrive. I was on the way to a movie next door. When I came out, the line was just as long, but the faces were all new. Heaven (and Vroman's accountants) might be the only entities with a firm take on how many books she signed in two hours or how many more she would sign before her writing hand became too sore to function.

I mention this because signings have their place. That place is just about anywhere if the author is famous. Or if she is a master promoter. If she is not, that place is in the middle of her own little pond.

An emerging author may have more than one pond—a small lake where she works, a puddle of a community where she sleeps, a pool where she was raised—but, unless the author, a publicist, or a publisher has stirred up huge waves in that larger national-book-buying ocean, she may find it discouraging to sign outside an area where she is known.

Someday your signings look like Rice's. Until then, my own signing story may be closer to what you might expect. My launch and the signings I did in my smaller ponds were successful (but by much more humble standards than Rice's!) but still tons of work and not as much fun as the ones in my hometowns where I saw old friends *and* sold lots of books.

Before my first book was published, I spent three decades as a founder and owner of gift stores and worked for a short time as a publicist and journalist. After that many years in the business of selling and PR, and before I ever had a book published, I knew how to plan and work an event and what to expect. Or so I thought. Some authors have experience in related fields, some don't. Some are good at them, some not. Some like promotion and sales, others don't. Even with a strong background in these fields, the major successes I gleaned from book signings was learning what to tell future readers of my how-to books what works well and what doesn't. My greatest pleasure was meeting those who knew my work and came to wish me well.

I've had signings that surprised bookstore event directors. "Wow! Fifty books! And this is your first book. I'm going to call our Van Nuys store and suggest they set something up for you, too!"

And I've had signings where I just wanted to go home, take a hot bath, and bury myself in blankets.

That does not mean I have discarded book signings from my repertoire of promotions. I have, instead, set up rules that fit both my emotional needs and my goals for promotion. Aside from keeping signings within familiar territory, here are some of the guidelines I use:

- I sign only at events where I speak, read, lead a workshop, or serve as a panelist. Do not walk into a bookstore without what is known in the entertainment trade as a warmup.

- I do not think of book sales as the prime purpose for doing book signings—signings are occasions for exposure in person and the press, for branding, learning, networking, and for fun. To have that happen, it is likely the author will need to do lots more than sign up with a dish full of M&Ms and a good pen in hand.

- I want to sign where I have contacts that allow me to get broadcast air and ink space from the event. I want to sign where I can send out invitations to people I know and/or to people a friend of mine in that area knows. Then I know the marketing value of the event will be worth my time—even if the turnout is not.

I only sign for stores that will do their full share of advance publicity. This includes:

- Exposure in their newsletter, in the local media, and on the web.

- Posting signs or distributing fliers or bookmarks in the store before the book signing.

- Utilizing local press and online event calendars. Google's calendar is free. For them. And for you.

You may choose a full-blown book tour of several bookstores across the nation or keep your appearances near home. You do it because a tour fulfills a life's dream or because you believe your book and skill set are suited for tours. If so, take a card from the deck of T.C. Boyle, author-and-promoter extraordinaire. In *Poets & Writers*, Joanna Smith Rakoff says T.C. is "not content with nice reviews and decent book sales... he wants to be a phenomenon." That's how you approach book signings if you choose to take on that assignment. You take the responsibility for making each appearance the very best it can be.

Make Your Book Signing Sizzle

Here are some ideas you can use:

- Coordinate your plans with whoever oversees your bookstore's events. Event planners need to know what you need—for both the setup and the promotion.

- Ask the store manager to occasionally use the store's PA system to introduce you to customers, especially if you are not reading.

- Arrive an hour early to set up. Many stores will not have prepared for your visit even when you previously discussed your needs with them.

- Ask the sales associate at the cash register if you can display a stack of your books on the counter. This area is called "point-of-purchase" by the retail trade—for obvious reasons.

- Although some bookstores stock their own "Autographed Copy" stickers, have some made just in case. Apply them to the covers of the signed copies you leave for the bookstore to sell after the event. Don't worry. You will use all your stickers at your launch and other places you appear. I had my labels printed on gold foil by an address label service I found in my Sunday newspaper throwaway.

- Offer to send autographed bookplates or labels to the bookstore manager when she reorders so she can put them into your books. Many bookstores have special areas with autographed books from past signings on display. Bookplates were originally a way to personalize books in one's library with contact information so that loaned books could be returned easily. They are now available as self-stickers. You can also use mailing labels printed on your computer with your logo or bookcover image. Authors can send signed labels to bookstores as they sell out of the original shipment. It's a great way to stay in touch with buyers and event managers.

- Design knock 'em dead signs to bring with you. Verbiage should have the same level of pizzazz as loglines used for screenplays. Color and images are important. So is quality.

- Put your signs everywhere, including your car parked in front of the bookstore. Perch a 5 x 7 tent card or sign with an easel on top of that stack of your books at the point-of-purchase. Use a small business-card size tent card or Post-it on the shelf where your books are normally displayed. Put signs on your signing table, one in the window, maybe even in the bathroom near a vase of flowers. Send a large poster to the store to use at least one week before the event. Design these signs so they can be recycled for other events. You can print posters at www.ElcoColor.net for a fraction of what you might pay at Fedex/Kinkos or other office stores.

- Display your books face out using plastic or wire display stands or small easels. Find them at craft and art stores.

- Ask the bookstore manager and sales associates to mention you to customers who go through checkout. They could say something like, "By the way, have you stopped to say hello to our award-winning author who's signing books today?" as she points to the pile of books on the counter or to where you are set up.

- Talk to the sales associates. They are the ones who spread the word about books. Give a signed book to a salesperson who is especially interested and ask her if she would recommend it to customers after she reads it.

- Bring something to give to those who buy your book, certainly, but also to those who pause to talk. Everything you hand out should be printed with how-to-order information. Possibilities are:

    o A bookmark.

    o Your promotion/business card.

    o A token souvenir (see "Other Souvenir Items" in Chapter Thirteen).

    o A recipe. Even if your book isn't a cookbook, a recipe from a kitchen scene in your book or related to the region your book is set will be popular; it might include an excerpt or quote from a foody chapter if there is one.

    o Give away a list. An example is "The Year's 10 Best Reads." Include your book and contact information.

    o A flier offering a free eBook. (See Chapter Sixteen's "Write Promotional E-Books.")

    o Snack foods. M&Ms can be custom printed with your title or name. I had "Frugal Editor" and "Frugal Promoter" printed on some for the launch of the second edition of this book.

- Use a guestbook. Encourage people to *print* their email addresses for future promotional purposes. A contest or drawing may persuade them to sign.

- Bring a friend to help. Her duties are to ask people to sign your guestbook, serve as your unofficial photographer, and chat with you when it is slow.

- Take pictures.

- - o   Slip a snapshot into the thank-you notes you send to bookstore personnel after the signing.
  - o   Find out who edits the bookstore's newsletter and send her a print of the crowd.
  - o   Use the photos you take on your website, for signs you make for your next signing, and in your scrapbook. Photos of large crowds can be clinchers for another signing.
  - o   Tuck photos into your query letter or paste into your email queries to other event directors to show how special you make your signings.
- Review your elevator pitch (see "Your Pitches" in Chapter Ten) until it sounds natural. Use it on people who walk by.
- Bring your own fine-tipped markers for signing. Know what message you'll write to personalize your signature. Choose something where the reader's name can easily be dropped in. When you dedicate a book, check the spelling of the recipient's name before you start writing.

Hint: I have a canvas bag with rollers for permanent event storage. It includes my promotion items and a pouch of small tools and a few personal items I won't want to forget.

Book signing Myths Abound

Be especially cautious about information you find on the web. Listen, learn, but consider the source. Many authors and PR "experts" repeat gossip rather than what they know from a reliable source or first-hand experience. Here are some fallacies that run rampant among authors:

Fallacy #1: *You can't have an effective promotional campaign without a book tour.* Most authors today choose to do scattered signings—not complete tours—because most must pay travel expenses themselves.

Fallacy #2: *If you sign books before you leave the bookstore, management can't return them.* I have a big box full of books—some signed, some not—that were returned to my publicist (eventually) after a whirlwind of book-signing gigs. They are proof that bookstores can and do return signed books. And, yes, my publicist did have an agreement with the stores that signed books could *not* be returned. If you are unlucky enough (or unprepared enough) to have a dismal signing, be aware that the store manager will not be thrilled about keeping a half dozen books—signed or unsigned—in her inventory. Even if your book sales went well, follow-up sales may not match that success. A bookstore is in the business of selling books, not stocking them.

Hint: You can help avoid this situation by continuing to promote the bookstore that favored you with a signing so that any leftovers might get snapped up by folks who couldn't get to a signing or new contacts who signed your guest book but didn't buy for whatever reason.

Fallacy #3: *If you take extra books along with you and need to use them, the bookstore will pay you upon delivery or within thirty days.* I still have unpaid invoices from the signings I did in 2001 for *This Is the Place*. Rarely do bookstores pay in less than sixty or ninety days. Rarely will they pay without reminders. Never will they pay unless you provide an invoice. I always ask if a bookstore can pay before I leave the premises and only one, R&K Bookstore in St. George, UT, did so. And they offered before I asked.

Hint: Even with this dismal possibility for getting paid, it is better to provide a few books at a loss rather than inconvenience (or lose!) a reader.

Fallacy #4: *You can ensure success of a signing by running an ad in a local paper or by buying a list of names in that locale.* Lists are important. *Targeted* lists are a whole lot better. Lists you've assembled from your own contacts are pure magic. And one-time ads are rarely effective unless your name is John Grisham.

Fallacy #5: *Bookstores are the only venues for book signings.* There are all kinds of places for you to sign books, places that you have personally supported in the past and that will, now, return the favor. Some nontraditional venues make signing an adventure and possibly more profitable. You will think of your own, but here are some suggestions:

- One critique group of romance and mystery writers sponsors signings at supermarkets that carry mass market books.
- Align yourselves with a charity. Everyone recognizes the extra value. A signing sponsored by Romance Writers of America benefited the Laubach Literacy Programs. Writers can join similar efforts of writing-oriented organizations.
- Museums are possible venues. My first launch benefited the Autry Museum of Western Heritage in Los Angeles. They donated a well-equipped theater, promoted the event, and allowed me to serve a buffet. The Museum kept forty percent of the book sales. Commercial bookstores' pricing policies are about the same. The difference is that booksellers are a profitable venture rather than nonprofit.
- Match nontraditional venues to the genre of your book. Mysteries at a police department as an example. Coffee houses and universities work well for a variety of books.

- My grandson's private school offered to sponsor a signing, at least in part because *This Is the Place* is a coming-of-age story, but also because of our past support, I'm sure.

Try an *Untour* Book Tour

An *untour* is a little like the Mad Hatter's *unbirthday* party. It isn't quite the real thing because it's not a non-stop tour of multiple venues. Untours can be lots less expensive and a lot of fun.

You can plan two kinds of untours. One is a piecemeal tour of bookstores you —a bookstore in one town today, another fifty miles away next month. A more popular model is an online tour, also known as a blog tour or virtual tour. You plan an untour of bookstores when:

- You will regret it if you don't do a tour of real stores rather than blogs and websites.

- You determine that there is no way your publisher is going to foot the bill for a tour as he does for the Stephen Kings in his catalog.

- Your budget is not large enough to duplicate an extensive tour but you still want a taste of a real tour.

- You're willing to spend a lot of time organizing the tour and promoting the tour.

- You don't mind doing your tour in segments, which means, of course, dragging it out over several weeks and months and—possibly—traveling in bits and pieces during that time.

The secret of an untour of bookstores is to piggyback your bookstore appearances onto your other travel needs like trips for pleasure or business. That doesn't necessarily mean only one bookstore appearance a trip, but it might if you can only give one additional day or evening to your book. Here is your plan of attack:

- Each time you leave your home base, the trip becomes an occasion to promote. Juggle your other plans to accommodate your tour. Plan every aspect of it before you go.

- Try to get events at several noncompeting bookstores in the same city or region. Choose widely separated venues only if your other plans take you to each location.

- Choose independent bookstores when possible. Indies are more likely to be interested in your book and will probably expend greater effort to promote your event. After you send your query, follow up with telephone calls to the event directors. A friendly nudge never hurts, especially if you're armed with another reason they would benefit from having you. A valid reason is that you will mention them when you are a guest on a radio show or presenting at a local library.

- If you meet resistance, guarantee sales of books the bookstore purchases for the event. That means that if the store doesn't sell them within a given time, you or your publisher will buy them back. Negotiate. Ask if they will keep a certain number (usually six) signed copies for thirty to ninety days. If they hesitate, offer to pay the return postage on them. Having said that, know that getting paid for your books may require a lot of additional work on your part.

- Show bookstore owners how you can increase their profits with a signing by outlining the support you can give them with contact lists and the publicity you will get for them.

- Plan events that fit the title of your book and your energy level.

- Promote *each* signing *and* the tour as a whole. Use every trick in this book. Feature editors. Weekend calendar sections of the local newspapers. Radio stations. Leave no pebble in place.

- Plan tours in areas where you have a support or where there is special interest in your topic.

- Bookstores aren't the only place to do a signing. If you can't get a bookstore in a specific area to host you, ask a friend to open their home to their reading friends. Ask an organization—perhaps a sister group to one you belong to in your hometown—to let you speak and sign.

- Go on a tour well equipped. That's hard when you fly, but it can be done.

- Expect the unexpected. An unplanned radio interview or an opportunity to add another reading to your agenda might pop up.

- Let friends or relatives help. In fact, choose locations where someone will use their influence, invite their friends, or lend you a car, bed, or relaxing footbath.

- Keep essential information on your iPhone, in your travel journal, or on a calendar you keep at your side. "Essentials" even include directions from your Motel 6 to the bookstore.

- At each stop, make time to drop off promotion packets at libraries and other bookstores and introduce yourself to their staffs. These packets might include an adaptation of your media kit, fliers, small posters to post on bulletin boards, and a copy of your book.

- It might be less expensive overall or more successful in terms of exposure to spend your vacation money and expand an untour into a do-it-on-your-own full tour. Because *This Is the Place* is set in the 50s and features a rusty old Buick convertible, I thought touring Route 66 in a classic car might be a good idea. It didn't pan out, but local TV stations would have loved such a picture-perfect tour.

Hint: If a publisher sponsors your tour, take what you know about promotion from this untour chapter to supplement your publisher's efforts. Your publisher will love you. Your book will, too.

I met a self-published author who decided he didn't care if his budget balanced. His book was his hobby and he was darn well going to enjoy it. He parked a monster vehicle near the Rose Bowl during a University of Southern California vs. UCLA game. It was professionally painted with the image of his nonfiction bookcover, endorsements, his photo, and website address. He had dispensers for fliers specially made to fit on both sides and the back of his venue-on-wheels so people could help themselves to trifold brochures with buy information in them when he wasn't around. This huge vehicle was home, office, and mini museum for artifacts that illustrated the theme of his book. After I talked to him for fifteen minutes, I was exhausted. I walked away shaking my head, pitying the poor publishers who had been short-sighted enough to reject the book of this powerhouse marketer. And, by the way, this might be classified as an untour with this difference: Between separate travel segments, this author's big, bad bus was always on duty.

Your Stay-At-Home Tour (Blog Tours)

These are usually called blog tours or virtual tours. They merely substitute reviews and interviews and the articles you offer at no charge to blogs and websites. You may be a radio show guest using your telephone instead of in-person bookstore signings. That means you can handle everything with your bottom planted firmly in a chair in front of your computer.

These virtual, blog, or stay-at-home tours can be substituted for your untour of bookstores or your real do-it-yourself book tour. They will save you tons of money and effort. You can do blog tours yourself or hire them done.

There are advantages and disadvantages to doing it either way. If you do it yourself, you save money. If you hire it done, you save time and increase your relationships with bloggers and radio hosts—people you might not otherwise find—to use in future promotions. So, if your

The Frugal Book Promoter

budget can take the hit, this is one time that spending a little is worthwhile.

Here are three such virtual tour services, each a little different from the other. Explore them, compare prices, and decide which best fits your goals and title. You may find you can use more than one effectively:

- Denise Cassino helps you achieve bestseller status on Amazon with a tour and viral blast at Mybestsellerlaunch.com.

- Marlan Warren is a publicist and editor who also has an online book tour service. Her website is bookpublicitybymarlan.blogspot.com. Contact her at memoircity@gmail.com.

- Nicki Leigh conducts virtual tours. Learn more at bookpromotionservices.com/tour-prices-2/

When you are touring virtually, don't forget to:

- Use your social networks and newsletter to drive traffic to the blogs and sites that feature your work.

- Put the contact information of those who joined your effort on your media list.

- Send thank-yous.

- Get permission to re-use the reviews and interviews. Once granted, install the best ones on your website and in your media kit and, after a time, rerun them on your own blog. They can be repurposed for your newsletter, too. You can even link to podcasts and videos you used during your launch.

Planning the Ultimate Book Launch

Launches are the best of book signing-related events. If I had my druthers, I'd focus on one large launch per book, perhaps for charity, invite tons of people, and have a party.

Launches are nothing more than glorified book signings. Well, okay. They can be as difficult, expensive, fantastic, and rewarding as a wedding. But you use all the skills in this chapter you'd use for signings and tours—every single one—stir in whatever pizzazz will make your heart zing and go for it. They are almost always held where the author knows the most people and they almost always are the one thing authors do to promote their books that does not disappoint.

In the next section you will find lots of reasons why you are already familiar with many of the marketing basics you will need in the future and how to maximize your success with the new or old versions of marketing magic-makers like interviews, radio, TV, websites… you get the idea. Breakout your highlighter and put your marketing beanie on!

Section V – You and the Media: What's New, Old, and In Between?

> To me anything with a chip is high tech; to my grandson, my limited edition, '85 Apple signed by the Woz himself is an antique despite its chip. ~ CHJ

What we've talked about so far is mostly basic—techniques that have been around forever, like using query letters to get exposure. They are principles that underlie marketing success, old ones *or* new ones. Sometimes they're basics with a new twist. The thing is, media can't be neatly divided between old and new and shouldn't be. Not only do the same principles work everywhere, but most new media is firmly rooted in old media soil. Whether toddlers or seniors, they're all media. They can work together or apart. Together is better.

If we learn one thing from marketing, it may be that discriminating—based on age or anything else— is damaging to our success. Some mediums are better for your title, your talents, and your pocketbook than others, but those are the determiners, not how long they've been around.

So, let's learn how to make the most of every possibility open to you—online or off. Local, national, or international. Old or new. No holds barred.

Section V
You and the World:
What's New, Old, and In Between?

19 Radio and TV: The Ageless Pair

Is radio old or new? I think of it as old, but internet "radio" hosts are out there disagreeing with me thousands of times every day. ~ CHJ

Some authors are frightened by the idea of promoting on media like radio and TV, and others are petrified of anything associated with a computer. But lots of what is accessed through a computer—streaming radio, videos, trailers—grew out of what came before it. When we think about it, the similarities are astounding. Authors can easily avoid whatever media frightens them and concentrate on the media in their comfort zone. I urge them to do just that, especially when it comes to radio, podcasts, and visual media like TV. Once they've had some success with one, it's easy to apply those skills and confidence to others.

Getting Media Interviews

The process is about the same no matter what kind of media host you are pitching. A TV host. A feature writer at *Parade*. Bloggers. Radio hosts of any ilk—"real" air Radio or internet streaming radio like BlogTalkRadio. Bigtime podcasts like Rachel Maddow's *Bag Man*. at major studios. You've already learned how to do that in this book. Apply these time-tested techniques to anything your heart desires.

Use any search engine to find radio, internet radio, bloggers, and TV hosts who are looking for guests. Fran Silverman's *Talk Radio Wants You* (bit.ly/FransRadio) lists radio resources including internet radio programs. To find new resources, compile Twitter lists as you accept followers. You may get ideas for searches within this book or in the Index that would benefit your marketing campaigns—perhaps on topics you haven't been aware of or considered before.

Hint: If you have been writing and recycling articles (see Chapter Sixteen), you have an entrée with those editors and bloggers who may refer you to people looking for guests in other media.

Being interviewed by radio hosts or bloggers with small audiences is a good place to start because you gain experience and expertise with each appearance. Besides, grassroots exposure feels more personal to its audience and often commands more loyalty.

British author Samuel Butler once said, "The advantage of doing one's praising for oneself is that one can lay it on so thick and exactly in the right places." However, for radio and TV, you need to "lay it on" tactfully enough so that you are invited back, invited on other shows, and avoid making yourself laughable before your audience. Here's how you do that:

- Make a list of the points you want to make about your book. The conversation can often be tactfully directed to include them.

- Before the interview, ask your host if she would like you to submit questions or talking points. If she is open to that courtesy, design the content to meet her needs and yours. The sample interview in your media kit will help you with this project. (See Chapter Thirteen.)

- Listen or watch archived shows or arrive early to get a handle on how the host works and what will be expected of you.

- Offer soundbites (clever, memorable ways of saying things) during the interview. Anticipate what an interviewer might ask and come up with some of these golden coins of wisdom; that's easy for you because you're a writer, right?

- Your broadcast may appear on the radio or TV station's website, on iTunes, or YouTube. Ask for a permalink (a link that takes you to the exact page your podcast or video appears on) or HTML code for it. The latter will make your interview appear like magic on your blog or website.

- If possible, linger a while or contact your interviewer by email or phone immediately afterward. It's thank-you time. One way to thank your host is to link to the interview from your website and tweet and blog about it like crazy. Tell your host you are doing it; she needs to see what a valuable guest you are so she'll remember you when you pitch again.

- Give signed copies of your book to anyone who was of special service to you during your interview. It's gracious and these are influencers who will remember your gesture.

- Follow up about four weeks later with a proposal for another interview, one with a different slant than the one you just did. Remind the producer that you would be pleased to serve as an expert should they need one. Talk a bit about your next book, too.

- Don't forget to put the host and producer on your list of media contacts.

Mastering the Interview Performance

Your interview performance will be a success if you have been working on your speaking as suggested in Chapter Seventeen where we talked about speaking skills that are useful in marketing our books—and in life.

If you are still nervous about speaking, radio is a good place to start. It's so much easier to be a relaxed guest on radio than on TV. You already know how to talk on the phone. Most of us are pretty good at that.

After you've prepared talking points with your host, get a glass of water, take a deep breath, and sit back and have a normal conversation. Or better, stand and pace—it helps your voice maintain its energy. If the host forgets to mention your website, blog, or newsletter, do that on your own at the close of the program or when that information feels integral to what you are saying.

Remember, this isn't all about you. It's about the radio audience. You might mention the show's broadcast area or demographic when you are introduced: "Thank you, Sarah. I have been looking forward to meeting your faithful mystery-loving listeners."

TV is easy, once you've perfected radio presentations. You need only add a couple more skills to what you learned with your radio appearances to look professional on TV. Skype has begun to change the time and travel expense drawbacks to appearing on TV so it's often as convenient (and comfortable!) as radio.

Minimize the scare factor by pitching for local TV appearances first, preferably something sponsored by an organization you are associated with or hosted by someone you know.

I was dumfounded when I was accepted for my first TV interview. I walked into Glendale Community College's public information office, told them I had come back to campus to upgrade my computer skills to help with my writing and that my first book had just been published—all in one big, gulpy breath. I hadn't yet asked for an interview when I heard, "We'd love to interview you." This interview aired on local cable TV. It was taped by students who were learning skills needed for the television industry using the school's state-of-the-art studio on campus. I learned a lot about interviews from this experience, but the most important lesson I learned was to muster the courage to ask.

Everyone knows the upside of pictures. It's that "pictures are worth a million words" thing. The downsides of TV are:

- You may be required to travel to be in the studio and that expense is rarely covered by either the TV producer or your publisher.

- Unless you are a celebrity, have written a controversial book, or have a spitfire TV publicist, it is hard to land a national TV spot.

- TV is harsh on those who have not learned its secrets. (Those secrets are coming. Keep reading!) To help you avoid humiliating booboos, review the lists of do's and don'ts in this chapter before each appearance.

Learning new TV skills takes a little courage. Actor Daniel Day Lewis said, "The thing about performance is that it is a celebration of the fact that we do contain within ourselves infinite possibilities." Here's how you prepare for your own TV celebration:

- Breathe deeply before the action countdown. Breathing lowers your voice and relaxes you.
- Beginners should keep their eyes on the interviewer. You don't want the camera to catch a distracted glance.
- As you develop skill, occasionally look into the camera as if it were the person you are talking to. That's your audience. There! In the camera's eye. Watch how TV anchors do it.
- Advanced TV performers learn to watch the camera lights on sets where more than one camera is used. Don't try this without training.
- If you tend to blush when you're excited as I do, tell the makeup artist. She can tone down the amount of rouge she would normally use.
- Bring a copy of your book and keep it in your lap. When you make a point about it, show the cover to the camera with confidence.
- When a woman sits, she crosses her legs at the ankles. Men keep both feet together on the floor.
- Choose clothing in medium or light hues. Avoid white, black, and patterns. Select a fabric that breathes under hot lights.
- Don't wear epaulets or other designs on your shoulders. If they don't stay in place, you'll look as if you're hunching.
- Avoid jewelry that jiggles, clanks, or glares.
- Women should choose neutral-colored fingernail polish. The camera person may take a closeup of your hands holding your book. Very long and brightly-colored nails draw attention from your cover.
- Control exaggerated facial gestures. One author who prefers to remain anonymous says she "rolled my eyes heavenward. I've regretted doing that ever since."

- Be on guard before, during, and after the interview. Even seasoned politicians have found that a live microphone clipped to their lapels can be a lethal weapon.
- The audience and interviewer are friends. Relax.

The bullets above are the TV secrets you can't do without. But there are two more techy ones. Tada!

One is the use of banners of words—still or moving—superimposed on TV screens and the other is the mysterious voiceover. Here is how to handle them:

- Watch for stage dressings. At one interview, the producers had blown up my bookcover and used it as part of the backdrop. If I hadn't noticed, I might have used the book I brought as a prop. Instead, I placed my book on the coffee table that was between my interviewer and me. It looked natural there, but I didn't need to hold it up when I referred to it.
- Messages called chyrons sometimes appear on the screen during your interview. They may include toll-free numbers, website addresses, and your book's title. Ask the producer if they plan to use them and what they will say so you can avoid duplicating those messages and use your on-air time more effectively.
- Similarly, there may be an introduction you don't hear. If there is, it helps to know beforehand what they will say.
- Getting a DVD of your performance can be useful. Bring a blank and a pre-addressed envelope so it will be little trouble for the producer to send you a copy. Your copy can be edited—even made into a montage of interviews—to get future appearances. You may hear these referred to as "reels."
- Send a media release about your appearance to the local press—but not to competing TV stations. If you can, get a photograph of you with the host in front of their prestigious backdrop or sign with a memorable logo—one that says CBS TV, as an example. Send copies to the print media with your release. Use it on your website, too! Tweet it. Put it on Facebook. Try using Instagram to shout out the experience in real time.

Television is a Many-Splendored Thing

Network TV. Local TV. Affiliates. Cable TV. Public-access TV. And, though we don't think of them as TV, videos *a la* YouTube and other online entities. Each provides an author with its own set of opportunities and disadvantages.

Many authors arrange TV interviews in cities where they'll be vacationing. Others try for TV bookings in their home town and then fill in with national radio.

> **Hint:** When pitching TV, be sure the producer "sees" your idea—the possibilities for action, for color, for an interesting setting. Your idea should also fit with current news and the station's audience.

Local TV needs you. You may have a small station in your home town; it may be hiding in a strip mall, at your local community or private college, or in an office building with hardly a sign to identify it. It may be in a dark room with equipment that doesn't look much more sophisticated than the video camera you had when you were ten years old. Hiding or not, that station is there, waiting for you, your ideas, and your book.

These stations look for hometown personalities and people who can speak to local issues—whether they are local or not. There may even be a local program that features authors and books.

> **Hint:** If you are going to appear on TV, contact the most suitable bookstore in that station's broadcast area. Tell the events coordinator or book buyer that when you are on air, you'd like to refer listeners to her store if she has sufficient stock. Do this in plenty of time for her to order books. Offer to do a workshop or a reading at her store after the broadcast.

Network TV is one area where a great publicist with a sizzling Rolodex can help you. When she lands you an appearance, you or your publisher must be prepared to pay your travel expenses. Some stations occasionally use Skype, but usually only for extremely accomplished experts on topics like politics and nuclear physics.

I once was interviewed by Peter Kulevich on CBS TV in Palm Springs. I live within two hours of that resort town, and my author friends who lived there and I had a good ol' time sitting on bar stools at The Chart House watching Peter and me on the evening news. I got the gig because I was participating in an event to promote National Literacy Day—no, not at the library! At Walmart and Sam's Club! I had bombarded the TV studios with my releases—one talked about the "unusual venue" for a literary event, another about the charity tie-in, and another about my traveling all the way from Los Angeles to be in Palm Springs for it. Peter took the trouble to check out my credentials on my website. So, charities good. Bombarding (judicious!), good. Getting out of your usual environment good.

To find locally produced programs (network or otherwise), let your librarian help you find an updated copy of *Bacon's Directory for TV* or guide you to a similar feature at Cision online. They have lists of shows, their producers, their direct phone lines, and addresses. You can pay for lists from folks like American Express, but why do that when your own list may have some local names and Cision is available at your library?

Public-access TV is an opportunity for you to get what you want by doing it yourself. In some markets you can lease a half hour on public-access TV for under the price of lunch for two. A year's programming may cost $2000, cheaper than a single small ad in a metropolitan newspaper. The TV station provides the camera, studio, editing facilities and—if yours is a forward-looking cable provider—may offer free how-to classes in tackling the project.

Federal law requires these stations to offer air time—sometimes for free (if a charity is involved). Some don't like that rule much, so if you are interested in this kind of publicity for your book, you may have to dig—even prod—to get them to admit you as a bona fide show host. This kind of TV is also called *lease access*.

Many who love books have managed to put together public-access programs that showcase publishers, other authors, and themselves. Others start a series that showcases their own expertise. If an author's book tells how to achieve financial security, their TV show carries the same message.

Authors can also produce a one-time special, promote it like crazy, and use clips from it for online video sites.

Connie Martinson loves books and libraries. She started her book show using pure seat-of-the-pants motivation. Her story is an inspiration to those who want to try this method of promotion—that is, start a TV program of your own. To learn from her model or query her for an interview, find her at conniemartinson.com.

Hint: Piggybacking on shows like Connie's rather than the do-it-yourself route may seem more desirable than doing a program of your own. Consider the time such a project requires and goals for your writing and family life against your enthusiasm for it and your well-considered projection for its success.

Public broadcasting systems include radio and TV. Morley Safer once defined National Public Radio as a "never-never land... a haven from commercial considerations, a honeypot for every scholar and every harebrained nut to stick a finger into."

The Public Broadcasting System (PBS) and British Broadcasting Company (BBC) are NPR's close relatives. Safer obviously understands a public figure's need for "a haven from commercial considerations." Maybe he knows a few of us authors, too. These entities are just what we need to give us a foot up.

Hint: Once you've landed an appearance, that experience will help you get other bookings. It's about showcasing your credibility and persistence.

Get an NPR gig by pitching to the host or producer of a specific show like *Fresh Air*. Listen to an assortment of each show's programs so the idea you present to them fits.

Pitch the NPR shows that have the highest ratings first because they may not accept a guest who has appeared on a competitor's show. If one of the biggies features you, however, some lower-rated shows will be pleased to hang onto their coattails.

> **Hint:** Find a sample query letter by Christine Louise Hohlbaum in the Appendices of this book. It got Christine an interview on NPR, and I annotated it so you can see why it was effective.

Online Videos are really nothing more than TV online, right? And they are the hardiest little marketers ever. I have a few video interviews and they were making the rounds on websites about the time I was signing at a book fair. It was about three in the afternoon, hot, and I was getting tired. Suddenly an author walking the fair with her publicist stopped dead in her tracks. "There she is," she squealed. She ran over, told me she had seen my video while she was surfing her iPhone. She decided right then that *The Frugal Book Promoter* was the how-to book she wanted and she determined she would order it even if she found something else at the fair. She was so excited about this serendipity, she bought all my books including my novel and chapbooks of poetry. And so did her publicist. Moral: Videos work anywhere they appear, from iTunes to iPhones, book fairs to bedrooms.

There are all kinds of ways to tackle videos. You can go all out for something that has a chance of going viral, or you can produce simple ones to spruce up your website or blog. You can use humor or an educational format. You can do an interview. You can do one video and reuse it everywhere or do new ones for different events. You can do a series of tutorials or mini how-tos. You can make them yourself or hire them done. They can look like little movies or more like slideshows. Call them what you will, but do them.

If you want to hire someone to help you with visuals, here are some suggestions:

- For trailer-type videos that really market your book, try Reno Lovison at authorsbroadcast.com.
- For slideshows like the ones we used on TV screens in our booths at book fairs, try Joyce Faulkner at katieseyes@aol.com. She is also on Facebook. She is active with a great writer's organization, too, Military Writers Society of America (MWSA). The organization welcomes all writers, but it is an especially good place to be for those who are military or write anything military oriented.

It is always better to choose tech experts familiar with the needs of the publishing industry as well as those with marketing backgrounds.

If you are computer savvy, you are ahead of the game. If not, the next chapter on how similar the internet is to what you've always known will inspire you to use its magical powers to reach more people than we once dared to dream of.

20   The Old Internet

> Pretending anything on the Net is new, new, new and better, better, better is flawed thinking. Even Wikipedia is just an old-style encyclopedia delivered faster using unvetted experts who don't get paid to write it. ~ CHJ

We think that internet developments have brought us new ways to market, but the principles of marketing traveled from pre-web days to the present. Old stuff from the print world or the early days of the internet are not necessarily dated and useless. They may be more effective, not less.

They may be more effective because fewer people are using them now than a mere decade ago. They may be more effective because your audience still responds to old techniques because they are, well... wired that way! They may be more effective because they are easier for you to use and that means you have more time for your writing!

Your Blog Can Be Your Website

Your website might feel old in the newbie world of the internet. New twists and turns keep coming up and some—like the idea that you can use your blog as a website—work well for some authors. But not all authors are created equal. Authors, genres, and even titles within genres may call for different approaches. Commercially successful authors like Scott Turow have their own websites. Some, like Nora Roberts, personalize their sites by writing the copy in first person. Publishers, big and small, are coaxing and commanding their authors to build websites and blogs.

One thing is certain, though. Websites are not an aspect of your promotion campaign that you can dismiss without risk. No matter where you are in the publishing process, now is a good time to set up a website. Doing it early on will give you a handle on your needs. It will give you a chance to explore your branding. To see if you only need something very simple. To understand how your site may grow in order to serve your readers.

Some sites like Authors Den provide beginning authors with a free start and let them graduate to paid levels as their careers grow. Fiction writers may find a site like this continues to fill their needs. Nonfiction writers may eventually need something more elaborate. I continue to use Authors Den (authorsden.com/carolynhowardjohnson) as a backup for when my own site crashes and to do other things with it like distribute my newsletter. It is also an excellent way to network with thousands of other authors. What I don't need to do is drop years of work on my website to use Wordpress no matter how often I hear about its miraculous gadgets that I may never need!

Regardless of where you are in your website trek, here are a few of the most elementary features you will need, features often overlooked by beginners:

- A link so readers, media types, and influencers can reach you. You'd be surprised at how many authors forget this or think their need for privacy precludes using one. Ask your designer. There are ways to maintain privacy and still honor your readers' need to get in touch with you.

- A media room where gatekeepers can download your media kit and high resolution photos of you and your book's cover. Include a place where they can sign up to get your new releases sent directly to their email boxes and a place where you can showcase your coming events and releases.

- Your recent media releases. Because you will add a new release to your site frequently, this page will help your site place higher on search engines, too.

- A special giveaway that lets visitors see what your book is about, encourages them to subscribe to your newsletter, to visit your blog, or to buy your book.

    Hint: Free is and always will be a magic word. Offer something free. See the section in this book on free eBooks and white papers in Chapter Sixteen.

- Mentions of your awards or even a special page to tout your awards and honors. (Learn more about using awards in the Index of this book under "awards.")

- Endorsements galore. I try to use a blurb on every page of my site. See more on blurbs in Chapter Ten.

- Nonfiction writers should include the Contents page from their book. (By the way, fiction doesn't need a Contents page.)

- Authors who have written many books should probably have a website page or section for each of them.

- Include at least one favorable review of your book with permission from the reviewer to reprint it.

- Eventually a page where your readers can buy signed books directly from you.
- Look at your media kit folders. Things in it like your First-Person Essay, your Ten Tips sheet, your Sample Interview can be recycled onto your website, even though they will also be available to those who download your kit.
- Link liberally from one page of your site to another.
- Get a book on *basic* web design. Web design, like so much else surrounding publishing, isn't something you need to know everything about, but the more you know, the more easily you can work with a webmaster to make decisions or to feel equipped to do it yourself.

    Important: Regardless of your website plans, buy your domain name(s) now. I use GoDaddy even though they once had a tacky, sexist advertising campaign. (They have excellent customer service and were smart enough to list to feminists—both men and women—who objected to their advertising!). Nora Roberts writes under pseudonyms. She probably has dibs on domains for all of them as well as her real name. If you lag, you could lose your name in all its iterations to devious folks who scoop them up and then try to sell them back to you at a huge profit.

As you can see, this is a basic list. I don't want to scare beginners off. Sites vary depending on the kind of books an author writes. It is okay to begin piecemeal and add features as you go. Learn enough about building websites to feel confident about adding new content yourself. I found waiting for a webmaster to make every change I needed frustrating and expensive.

I also like the idea of letting an expert—again, someone familiar with the needs of authors—help you build your site and teach you to do it on your own in the process. Someone like that can be your blankie. When your site is ready for public scrutiny, it will look good, do what you need it to do at the stage of publishing you find yourself in, have the potential to grow in any direction your career takes you, and you'll feel able to handle the day-to-day needs of website marketing.

Here are some extras to add as your site grows. They are strongly recommended by most experts:

- How-to author Peter Bowerman notes that most authors' websites don't have a frequently-asked-questions section (FAQ). I don't, but I intend to work on it. If you don't know what those FAQ questions are now, it won't be long before you will.

- A site map will help your visitors navigate your site as it grows larger. They will love you for it.
- Credits and links to the sites of your website designer and photographers.

Your Newsletter

Newsletters are one of those old promotion tools that still work in spite of rumblings that blogs have supplanted them. If I were ranking ways to promote on the web, producing a newsletter would easily be in the top five. Newsletters are discussed in Chapter Sixteen that covers what you can do to promote by doing what you love most (writing!)

Hint: Most nonfiction authors understand newsletter benefits, but newsletters work for fiction writers, too.

Your email Promotions

Email is another promotion tool that—to hear some tell it—is tottering on one leg. But it is the way you communicate with most everyone on the web. There are advantages to reaching people with email:

- Unlike tools like Messenger, your message goes right to people's email boxes. It keeps extra clicks at a minimum.
- Your email signature passively promotes for you every time you send a message

    Hint: If the emails you send require an extra click to get to whatever you want them to see (and that includes the email distribution service you use to distribute your newsletter), examine your process. We web users are getting lazy. An extra click may discourage your audience and increase the chance of a broken link or typo. It is a courtesy to make it as easy on your audience as possible.

The subject line of emails is a sales message for everyone—even for readers who may otherwise not open your mail.

Your email signature needs to be more than just your name. Your contacts want to know more about you, and some *need* to know more about you. Use the automatic signature that most email services provide to give them that information. Once you have your signature set up, it promotes for you—no cost or time required.

To create an autosignature, use the Help menu in your email program. Do a search for "signature" or "signature file." Some email services allow you to include a thumbnail picture of your bookcover or a banner. A banner is a long logo and shouldn't be confused with popup banners on hard-sell websites. See my signature in Appendix Six. Try these ideas, too:

- Change your signature often or at least every time a new promotional idea comes to you.

- Use links to articles about you or by you with a line that says something like, "See what the *Chicago Tribune* said about (your title here)."

- Include a link to your Amazon.com Buy page.

  Caveat: If you use links other than those to pages on your own site, check them frequently to be sure they are live.

- To encourage people to click on your website or blog link or to subscribe to your newsletter, offer something free in your email autosignature.

- Are you an expert? Let 'em know! "Expert on publicity, media relations...."

- Use a brief invitation to upcoming public appearances such as "Visit my booth at the Virginia Book Fair" with a link for more information.

- Design your signature so it blends with your brand. To quote my mother, "You wouldn't wear a polka dot blouse with a plaid skirt, now would you?"

  Caveat: When you send out media releases, queries, or submissions to unknown editors, remove art or photos from your signature. They may render the message unreadable for certain internet servers and editors may not want to risk a virus by opening your mail.

Your other online signatures are important, too. It's only common courtesy to use a signature when you communicate in those little comment windows on blogs or social websites. I know they provide an avatar (logo) and a link to your website automatically, but an email address or link is *not* a signature. You don't send a thank-you note by mail without a signature even if the stationery is imprinted with your name. Your signature is an opportunity to promote your book *and* to serve others by making it easy for them to contact you.

Renting Direct e-Mail Lists

Direct email marketing is not spam. The people on rented lists have given permission in one way or another to distribute certain kinds of information to their email boxes.

An unsubscribe message allows uninterested folks to remove themselves from your list. We only want to reach people who want what we have to give, anyway.

Direct email is not something that works for every book. It is not an easy method of marketing to master, so you either need to be prepared for the grade-fifteen learning slope or hire it done. And that is not cheap.

To learn more about the ins-and-outs of direct marketing, start with Chris Baggott's *Email Marketing by the Numbers: How to Use the World's Greatest Marketing Tool to Take Any Organization to the Next Level* (bit.ly/SuccessfulEmail). Google "direct email services" to get an idea of cost for a *series* of blasts. Notice I said *series*, A single email blast will not work any better than a single ad in a newspaper. It needs to be a whole campaign or nothing.

I like a not-very-commercial, front door approach to email marketing. You send releases, announcements, or personal notes about your new book to your own targeted lists of folks (see Chapter Eleven to learn more about assembling your own lists). Tailor each message to the group you are sending it to so it feels as one-on-one as possible. A businesslike approach is perfect for some groups. For others, chattier may be better.

Autoresponders Increase Results

An autoresponder can make many promotions more effective including anything you do with email. An autoresponder is a techy gadget or website that gets a sample of your writing out to those who request it—all automatically. You are used to getting them yourself. It's an autoresponder that sends you a welcome letter when you subscribe to a newsletter.

You can use autoresponders many ways, but few use them to build interest in their writing. That's a missed opportunity!

These programs also help you collect emails of those interested enough in your title to request information be sent to them. Explore an autoresponder service like sendfree.com to see how they work. After you've posted a provocative excerpt on an autoresponder, you'll be assigned an address that you must promote. I know! Promote it? But it's usually like that: We must promote the promotion to make it effective. Here's how you do that:

- Add your responder address to your email signature.
- Post it on suitable pages on your website. You may eventually need more than one auto-responder address.
- Follow up with a personal note to those who requested information on your autoresponder.
- Add their address to your contact list of readers.
- Put a little pitch for readers to get your first chapter by autoresponder in your letterhead and other stationery and promotion material.

- I used an autoresponder to let people peek at the first chapter of my first novel. Autoresponders are absolutely genre neutral—or all-genre positive!

Electronic Discussion Groups

List-Serves, Yahoo Groups, Google groups, Groups.IO, Facebook groups. It matters not what you call them. They are groups of like-minded folks run by moderators. They are useful tools that aren't being used as much as they once were. There are some where members get off topic, but with a little effort you can find helpful ones that are moderated well. They work well for you because:

- They are targeted. Find groups interested in the subjects you write about. Groups interested in writing. Groups focused on book promotion. Groups that allow you to promote at will. Groups that broadcast opportunities.

- You can choose to receive daily digests or individual posts delivered to your email box so you can work these groups the way it is most convenient for you.

- You build long lasting relationships.

- You can find people interested in cross-promotion—often more quickly than on some of the social networks.

- Depending on the topic of your book, you may find that sponsoring a group is beneficial, too.

- These groups are eager to have you jump into the fray. Ask questions and share your knowledge with fellow members. Notice how others are succeeding. Look for people to review your book, interview you, publish your articles, and publish your next book. Include full contact information in your signature each time you post. Keep your new friends' email addresses.

    Hint: As you read posts on your e-groups, pay attention to other members' signatures. They may include resources you can use in your publishing-related projects such as the names and links of publishers, agents, contests, and blogs.

Most of my readers have been using the web for a long time. By today's fast-moving standards, they don't consider it new. Still, I know many writers who still have not started a blog, for instance, and many more who complain about blogging or keeping up their websites—mostly about how much time it takes. Keep reading. Really. In the next chapter, you may find a few tips that will make your online life easier and more productive.

21 Game Changers

As surely as the greatest artists of history changed the way the world sees artistic pursuits, the web has shaped a new landscape for readers and writers. ~ CHJ

"Game changer" is a label that's over applied to just about every innovation on the web, but it is doubtful many would argue with the idea that blogging and online bookstores have shaken the publishing industry like a nine-point earthquake. Social networks are not far behind.

Myths and Advantages of Blogs

Blogs are often classified as social networks because people can interact with a blogger by leaving comments and because they do interact well with other online networks. Still, most of us think of them as quite different from Twitter, LinkedIn, and others. We see them as more connected to old media or rooted more in print media like periodicals. Not the Pleistocene, but older than some.

Your blogging worries are probably overblown because you've heard the diary myths. That you must post something on your blog every day. That you must expose all your darkest secrets. That blogging doesn't work. That blogging takes too much time. Don't believe the rumors. Blogging is far more connected (read that interactive) with a broader audience than anything we've ever experienced with old media. Blogs are amazing tools that can be shaped to your needs, so put aside preconceived notions.

The advantages of blogging *are many*. Here are the reasons you should blog instead of working at some other promotions that may not be as effective:

- Blogging is creative. It allows you to do what you love most, *write*. I talk about this aspect of blogging in Chapter Sixteen.

- The opportunity to promote is another blogging advantage. Keep reading for ideas on how to do that.

- Blogging is a good way to introduce readers to your voice, promote loyalty, and, in the long run, sell books.

- Blogging helps build name recognition and builds a huge footprint on search engines which makes it easier for readers to find you on the ever-expanding web.

- Blogging helps you network with others in the publishing world, including publishers, agents, other authors, publicists, and other bloggers. Keep reading for ways to connect with others and promote your blog.

Building a blog is easy because some whiz kids designed something called content management service (CMS) for you to use and they often offer it to you free.

If you don't have a website, don't have anyone to help you add a blog to your website, or just want to blog the easy way, start blogging right now using the steps listed below. Guys and gals at Google have made blogging especially easy with blogspot.com (also called blogger.com). It isn't perfect, but it's easy and in spite of occasional glitches, I wouldn't change.

Hint: Blogger/Blogspot is an entity of Google and that is a big reason that material on that blog content service appears so quickly in the Google search engine. It is also why the Google Alerts, a neat research tool that allows authors and others to know what's being said about them on the web, arrives in the email boxes of people using that service so quickly. Many experts like Wordpress for their flexibility.

You can start a blog on Blogger with five (only five!) essential steps. Start with the free Google account you may already have. If you do, the words "My Account" will appear as a link on Google's homepage. It's in blue in the top right corner of the homepage. If not, use a link on that page to set up your account.

1. Once you have an account, you'll find a whole bunch of services that Google offers—also free. Many of them are miracles disguised as links, but right now we're only interested in the little orange icon (or logo) with the "Blogger" link next to it. Click on that link.

2. Find the link that says, "Create a blog." Click.

3. The first prompt will ask you to name your blog. Choose wisely. Go to the Index in this book and look up "branding" before you choose a name for your blog. The name you choose shouldn't limit your focus too severely nor should it be so broad it won't appeal to the audience you seek for your book.

> Hint: For now, ignore the "advanced option" section. Start with these five steps and forget the rest until you feel more comfortable.

4. Next choose a template. Choose something simple. Play with colors that fit your branding campaign and the looks of your book or website. Avoid dark backgrounds. They are hard to read.
5. Your next window says, "Start Blogging." That may be oversimplified, but it's close. Take your time to browse the "Settings" and "Design" tabs.

See how easy that was! Now explore new "Segments" or "Gadgets" a few at a time. They are on your layout or design page. Tweak or start over until you have your blog the way you want it. Nothing is written in stone. It costs you nothing to enjoy the process but the time you might otherwise spend playing online solitaire.

If you are not a freshman computer user and have a website of your own, consider incorporating your blog into your existing site's format. The frequent fresh content of a blog makes the search engines happy. It will make you happy, too, when you see your site move up in the online search-engine ratings. Having your blog or website listed on the first page of often-searched-for keywords is good for your book.

You get to house your blog where you want including your own website. You choose where your blog will live the way you would choose a new home—based on the features you like best. Or you choose Blogspot.com because I told you it is easy, sufficient for most authors' needs, and did I mention free?

> Hint: Blog beginners who want to go all out with WordPress, a blog service with lots of bells and whistles, can get help from Miller Mosaic Social Media Marketing at millermosaicllc.com.

Your blog is pivotal to promotion. We use our blogs to promote, obviously. What isn't so obvious is that the blog itself must be promoted. One of the most important ways to do both things is to integrate it with all the other entities you use for networking on the web. You link to your blog on every suitable promotion you do. Here are a few ways to do that:

- When you post an article on your blog, invite contacts on your other social networks like LinkedIn and Twitter to drop by and comment. Make your invitation into a teaser and include the permalink to your blog. A permalink is the very long address you find in your browser window when you click on the blog's title. It takes visitors to a specific blog post rather than to your most recent post.

- Install an invitation to subscribe to your blog on your website and on your social network profile pages. Tell visitors how they will benefit from doing so.
- Link to your blog from your autosignature.
- Depending on your target audience, use content that keeps them coming back. Freebies. Contests. Games. Breaking news.
- Add social networking widgets / logos to your blog. They do things like let readers easily spread the word about your posts. Don't forget the link or links that lead visitors to your book's Buy page on your favorite online bookstore.
- Partner with other bloggers to help spread the word about your blog. You can trade articles, interviews, and reviews. You can comment on their blogposts and vice versa. You network by using the social networking icons that you both provide on your blogs. And you reciprocally subscribe, too!
- Put your blog on Kindle or iTunes. Readers subscribe to blogs targeted to their interests and buy eBooks that began as blog posts. It's usually a promotion, not a get-rich-quick thing; you get exposure by doing it with your blog and learn a lot by reading the blogged books by other authors you find there. You can also directly subscribe to blogs that focus on your target audience or help you with information you need for your career and that won't cost a thing!
- Stephanie Meyer, author of the famous *Twilight* series, catapulted her book to bestseller lists by visiting blogs targeted to her young adult audience and commenting on the posts. She added something of value to these blog posts, mentioned her own books, and included links to her sales page and to her own blog.
- Trade links with other bloggers. These links go on your blog rolls, the portion of your blogs where you link to related blogs as a service to your readers. You'll find a gadget on Blogger that lets you do this easily.
- Ask people with similar interests to be guests on your blog. You contribute to their blogs, too. Then promote each other's blogs using your social networks.
- Don't forget to "promote the promotion!" Tweet and announce your posts on your active social networks.

Tips for Keeping Your Blogging Time Corralled

Effective blog time-management is easier than you think. There is a rule-of-thumb that you post often because search engines like activity, but there are no blog-frequency cops. Here are six time-saving ways for you to keep an active blog and keep your time expenditure within reason.

- **Using guest bloggers is like spreading love.** Others write one or several guest posts—even a series—on a subject that fits your blog's focus. It's a good way to save time and a good way to network. Your guests may then promote your blog and, by extension, your book.
  Guest-bloggers can submit directly to you and you do the posting, but you can also let them post directly to your blog using the "settings" feature of your blog where you'll find "permissions" which allows the guest to do their own posting. I like the former method because you can better control contents, formatting, and editing.

  Hint: When you guest blog for other bloggers, it gets you, your blog, website, and book in front of other audiences. If you include links in your guest-blogger credits (sometimes called taglines), some people will click on them and be carried back to your other online entities. Some call these active links "incoming links" or "backlinks." Search engines love links that lead to your blog! Google spiders search for these links. These spider-guys think backlinks are so important they raise your blog in the search-engine rankings when they see lots of them pointing to your blog.

- **Get partners for your blog.** Find compatible fellow authors, readers, agents, publishers, or bloggers who agree to write posts regularly. It's like dividing the blogging pie. You write an equivalent number of posts for their blogs. When you combine your talent and time, the power of the project increases incrementally in terms of promoting the blog and in sheer posting power. Search engines love blogs with lots of new content. The drawback is that the spotlight doesn't shine solely on your book and promotions. Children's Author Karen Cioffi-Ventrice's WritersontheMove.com blog is an example of this model.

  Hint: You may still wonder why you'd want to share your blog with a fellow author. Sure, you need to be selective, but maybe you need to review the advantages of "cross-promotion" by looking up that entry in the Index of this book. There are certainly advantages to both sharing and doing it yourself.

- **Recycle articles, tips, bargains,** and anything else you can think of from the other writing and promoting you do. Everything on your blog doesn't have to be new or exclusive. In fact, everything doesn't have to be long or—for that matter—within a specific word count. If you are focused as you should be, most everything you write for your blog may be cycled back to your other promotions. Check Chapter Sixteen on recycling articles.

- **Use the carnival concept.** A carnival is a blog or blog post that lists the best articles or helpful sites related to your blog's focus in the wonderful web world. Put all these links in a single post and include a little synopsis or pitch for each. Carnivals save writing time, but you might spend more time reading to find good content. Some bloggers use carnivals regularly and save up useful links so it requires little effort when they post. You can even include a link back to one of your own favorite posts.

- **Outsource your blogging** to a writer who is familiar with blogs. She might charge per blog or per month for a given number of blog posts. If you choose to do this, your blog won't be free but you'll balance that expense against what blogging space would cost if you were paying for display advertising. Factor in the value of the time you will save, too. You will need to supply the information for each blog until your new freelance helper becomes familiar with the many facets of your books. At that point, she may come up with new ideas for you and thus expand what you could do for yourself. One such writer is Mindy Lawrence (mplcreative1@aol.com).

- *Use videos* to tell your stories if you're a faster talker than writer and if you have a natural skill for presentation or have taken time to develop your speaking skills as I advise in Chapter Seventeen. YouTube has tutorials that tell you how to do this effectively and you can practice by taking videos of yourself and studying them.

Bloggers' Block is a Myth

Writers worry about writers' block but they needn't extend that disability to their blog posts. Reassuringly, there are only a few guidelines and tons of ways to find new content for your blog.

To attract and keep readers, a blog must include practical or entertaining information. It is not that hard and the process of doing it helps a writer focus on the strengths of his or her book to find yet undiscovered aspects of it that help promote it.

Authors often ascribe to the notion that getting ideas for posts is easier for some genres than others, but it's possible for all of them because they all share some qualities by virtue of their being books.

Here are things most authors have in common that are supremely bloggable:

- Yourself. Specifically, the "you" who writes. Your readers may well remember you long after they've forgotten the title of your first book.

- Anything in the news that relates to your book. Nothing is off limits. For a horror writer, the news may be the latest mass murder (isn't there one of those every year?). For a children's story about bunnies, Easter is a blogging opportunity.

- Talk about writing and publishing in general. You think people aren't interested? How many people have said, "Oh, I'd love to write a book!" to you in the last year?

- Every writer knows other writers or soon will. Link to the articles on their blogs and websites. When they're doing something that will interest your audience, blog about it.

- Talk about your promotions, like your latest two-for-one book offer or your Kindle special that gives readers a taste of your writing style.

- Talk about your coming events. Book signings, your launch, your seminars, your speaking gigs.

- How about your opinions. I loved my recent blog that ranted about the confidence-corroding nature of the term "self-promote."

  Hint: Phyllis Zimbler Miller and I wrote an article that shows fiction writers how to use blogs effectively, including blog ideas for different genres of creative writing. Go to fictionmarketing.com.

On others' blogs you may also:

- Review others' books, especially ones that relate to yours in some way.

- Create contests. Let readers submit material for blogs. Make a contest of that, too.

- Interview other authors or experts in fields related to your book. Some bloggers use the same questions for all their guests, but in the interest of more entertaining blog posts, tailor your questions to the interests and accomplishments of the interviewee. Use links to their books and service liberally.

- Quote from blogs and websites with a focus related to yours. Some blogs are nothing more than one inspirational quotation a day. Some blog posts are nothing more than a list of great quotations.

   Hint: Copyright law has a fair-use clause. You may quote excerpts for reviews, essays, and articles and some other purposes at no charge and without permission. Amazon uses quotes of up to twenty-five words in their blurbs. It should be safe to follow their lead; they have an excellent team of lawyers.

Getting unique ideas for your blog is easy. Glean ideas for your blog or any of your other marketing entities as you go about your day—everything from shopping to watching TV. Authors are notorious for taking busman's holidays. We get ideas for our poems, our characters, and our narratives when we travel. We even dream them. Blog ideas come to you the same way. Keep a notebook handy to jot down the best ones.

Hint: Carry a notebook and pencil with you everywhere you go. When I don't have writing equipment, I tear pages and ragged little clippings out of magazines, newspapers, and even junk mail. I put them in my bra so they can remind me to file them when they sprinkle out on the floor at night. They'd get lost in my purse!

Examine your own book for a handle on subjects to blog about, for ideas for future media releases, and for feature ideas you could pitch to editors. A once-a-month search prompts content and marketing ideas for more than just our blogs.

Online Bookstores (Yep! Including Amazon!)

Online bookstores are rooted in tradition. One of the major differences, of course, is that internet thing—connectivity. Brick-and-mortar bookstores encourage browsing. So do online bookstores. You can connect with authors and readers at bookstore readings and seminars. You can connect with authors and readers at online bookstores, too. But at online bookstores that association is less sporadic and readers (and authors!) can review and recommend books almost as if they were bookstore sales associates.

Online bookstores have been game-changers in the blossoming of eBooks and e-readers. They say they contributed to the demise of the several chains of traditional bookstores. Still—just as radio survived TV and TV seems to be surviving the web—the old fashioned printed word on paper and assembled into a book will never disappear. Nor will the indie bookstores that cater to the interests of its customers.

I'm going to be daring. Authors—especially new authors who dream of seeing their books in bookstores—won't like hearing this: You can do without having your book in brick-and-mortar bookstores and still sell lots of books, but no book can reach star status without online stores.

This section on using online bookstores is the most essential advice in this book beyond the need to market in general. Really. Don't let anyone tell you that you can relegate book sales to your own website. Or only to bookstore distribution. Or only to your publisher's website. Not if your goal is to sell books to those outside your mother's sewing circle.

The power of online bookstores is both a blessing and a curse. Your publisher should manage your online bookstore pages, but sometimes publishers don't do it. Or they don't do it in a way that presents your book in its best light. You're tired of hearing this I know, but no one knows your book like you do. No one cares as much about your book as you do. The blessing: Online bookstores—especially Amazon—sell tons of books. The curse: You'll probably have to give your book's online bookstore pages—especially Amazon—all the tending, loving care it needs all by yourself.

Ahh, Amazon. Theodore Roosevelt said, "The mightiest river in the world is the Amazon. It runs from west to east, from the sunset to the sunrise, from the Andes to the Atlantic." The Amazons of mythology were warrior women. Talk about great branding! Amazons, including Amazon.com's bookstore, perform amazing feats. When it comes to book *sales*, Amazon.com strides on the sturdiest of legs. She sells your books here and overseas, print or digital.

Because books from small and large publishers, subsidy- and self-published authors, and other content are found on Amazon's pages, she is a unique buying and selling tool. She also exposes your book to a very important demographic, *readers who are interested in your book, your genre, your topic.* She also offers promotion benefits authors shouldn't ignore. Still, promoting your book on Amazon is like climbing a trellis where thorns grow among the roses; you must read and adhere to the strict guidelines of any Amazon feature you use. And it's best to brace yourself for surprises and a constant learning curve.

Because Amazon is fickle (it's always adding a feature or taking something away, always changing page designs, always changing the names of their features), I can only give you general guidelines to the benefits they offer. Here are a few of my favorites you can access once you have opened an Amazon account:

Authors get a Profile page. You access it through Author Central or Author Connect. Who knows what Amazon calls it this week. It lists your book, an author biography, and coordinates other Amazon features you participate in like writing reviews. Use the magic of Real Simple Syndication (RSS) to install your blog or Twitter stream on this page.

Hint: RSS is a way that anyone (yes, *you*!) can distribute what you do once—maybe your website—to make it appear magically on your blog or your social networks, too. You simply copy and paste either computer code or website addresses. It is a time-saver and effort-expander like none other I can think of.

Amazon's many features contribute to its algorithms. For your book to climb the Amazon ratings and receive other Amazon benefits, those techy formulas must be fed like a mama lion feeds her voracious cubs. Amazon is a search engine and its algorithms are watching what you do on that site! A few things they watch are in this section. Did I tell you their features are always subject to change? Amazon gives and it taketh away.

Hint: Details for choosing the best categories for your book and how to use them to nudge your sales ratings are in my *How to Get Great Book Reviews Frugally and Ethically* (bit.ly/GreatBkReviews). Why are they in a book on getting and using reviews and the endorsements gleaned from them? Because getting book reviews are so important to Amazon ratings. It's part of keeping that hungry algorithm mouth well fed.

Amazon posts sales ratings on each book's Buy page, but they're confusing, I wouldn't be surprised if Jeff Bezos, founder and CEO of Amazon, can't explain how they calculate them. We *do* know that the categories a publisher or author chooses for a book and the reviews posted for that book influence its ratings. Don't believe it when you hear that readers pay attention to them. Most readers don't know or care about ratings. Still, ratings *are* important because they jog algorithms and Amazon cares about algorithms—a lot!

Caveat: Don't let bestseller stardust lead you astray. Author David Vise received bad publicity for allegedly rigging *The New York Times'* bestseller list by buying huge numbers of his own books. It doesn't hurt to Tweet about bestseller successes, but those in the industry are distrustful and rarely fooled or impressed by unethical shenanigans. Don't waste too much of your valuable writing time tracking your ratings, either.

Here's how to (and how not to!) nudge algorithms:

- Amazon's KDP feature lets any independent publisher or author post a book to Amazon. Most subsidy publishers and traditional publishers list their books on Amazon or publish their eBooks on Kindle, but if yours doesn't, get permission from your publisher to do it yourself.

Caveat: Check the contract you have with your publisher and proceed accordingly. If your publisher resists (but your contract doesn't limit you), do it on your own.

- Though readers pay little attention to ratings, many publishing professionals do, and high ratings qualify your book for Amazon's bestseller lists. Making that list qualifies your book for bragging rights, even if a top-ten rating only appeared for a short time.

- The only things you can do to influence those rates is promote like crazy and choose categories (genres, themes, etc.) that have the fewest competing books in them. Denise Cassino (bestsellerservices.com) says, "You can request more effective Amazon categories from either Author Central or Kindle Digital Printing (KDP) using their Contact Us buttons." Denise helped me choose categories for *The Frugal Editor* and it is often a "bestseller" in one of its categories. Do a search on this ever-changing technique for using this Amazon feature on your own or hire someone like Denise or Penny Sansevieri (amarketingexpert.com) to help you with it. But do *not* expect your publisher to do it—or do it effectively.

    Warning: Choose categories with the fewest number of competitors that are still right for your book or you'll lower your *discoverability* on Amazon's search engine.

- Online bookstores are search engines. They can be searched by title, author, or keywords. Be sure you choose keywords *for* your book that lead the right readers *to* your book!

- Amazon offers a "Look Inside" feature. It lets readers sample pages from your book. Some authors disparage this feature, but trust me. It helps sell well-written books. If yours doesn't have this feature, ask Author Connect for it.

Amazon lists both its top reviewers and those it designates as Vine reviewers as headers for each review and each is linked to the author-reviewer's Profile page. Top reviewers are those who have reviewed the most books on Amazon. Vine reviewers are readers Amazon selects and sends books and other products to in exchange for the promise of a review. Use these links to find individual reviewers. Many Amazon reviewers also review for other blogs, journals, and websites. Send query letters only to those reviewers who have reviewed books similar to yours.

Caveat: Occasionally an author tries to become a top reviewer to nudge algorithms to expose their own writing to readers. It may be an impossible goal. Harriet Klausner may have spent every waking hour to read 7,000. It' probably better to write another novel or have a root canal than try to beat that record.

- Online bookstores' review features take on a new importance for authors who write reviews in addition to their books. They can be networking goldmines and they offer wide exposure of their names to *readers*. Authors should be avid readers anyway; it takes little time to add a thoughtful review on sites that allow voluntary posts. Choose a great title. Edit well. Read the submission guidelines.

- You may post videos on your Amazon page and others' pages when you write reviews for others' books. Always put ethics first or you may be banned from the site. See more on writing reviews in Chapter Sixteen.

    Hint: If you can't recommend a book, don't post a review. That doesn't mean that noting a book's weaknesses isn't valid. It's just that there is no point in slashing and burning a book an author has invested herself in. Besides, that kind of review isn't likely to help your branding unless the image you are trying to create is that of a curmudgeon.

Each sales page has buttons near each review for readers to vote "helpful" (or not). Voting encourages readers to peruse the reviews, which is good for the reviewers and good for your book. Encourage your readers to post reviews and vote for content, but don't try to influence their choices. You should vote, too!

Some of the things you can manage yourself through KDP or the Author Connect features are:

- Your blurbs and endorsements. To add an excerpt from a reviewer to the ones your publisher provided, carefully follow fair-use guidelines. "Fair use" is a legal term and worthy of an entire book. To learn more about it, search "copyright," "quotes," and "blurbs" in this book or do a web search.

- Amazon phased out the feature that allows authors (and readers) to post images related to specific books, but they still include images of the back covers of books. Request help through Author Connect or Advantage.

- Amazon's "New and Used" feature lets you sell slightly damaged books and excess stock. A tab on your book's sales page takes you to New and Used. On occasions when spic-and-span copies aren't essential, I can order a book cheaper there and get it more quickly than from my publisher.

- Amazon has widgets that give readers a choice of buying paperback, eBook (or both) of any title. If there is no such link on your book's Buy page even though both are available, contact administration at Author Connect.

- Amazon doesn't delete your book's first edition when you write others. It offers a widget that leads readers from the earlier editions to the latest edition of your book. I'm sure you'd rather have readers buy the updated edition but this widget doesn't appear magically. Author Connection will help.

Amazon myths abound. If you haven't already heard, writers' gossip mills will soon notify you that your writing (like the reviews you post to Amazon) become Amazon's property and cannot be published elsewhere.

I asked Amazon's customer service about their claim to own material posted there. They made it clear that they own only the right to "reuse" what you post, but you may continue to use the material designated as nonexclusive as you see fit. Here is what they said: It applies to any of their disclaimers/guidelines that use the term "nonexclusive."

> "When a customer posts... to our site, the customer is granting us the nonexclusive right to use the [content]. This means that once [material] is submitted to our site, [it] is ours to use as we see fit for as long as we wish. As this license is nonexclusive, the customer who has written the [content] can also use it as he or she sees fit. The [content] can be included in a book or posted on another site."
>
> Nicole L., Amazon.com Customer Service

You will also hear that efforts on Amazon like those I've described do not result in sales. Sales are, indeed, hard to track, but if marketing works, targeted marketing like this works better.

Here's the thing. No marketing campaign works in a vacuum. If you make online bookstores part of a many-speared campaign and cross promote them, your campaign will work. Your marketing will work less well without a smart presence on online bookstores.

Hint: Online bookstores are targets for unethical promotion practices. Please review Chapter Four on the importance of marketing ethics—online or off.

Other Online Bookstores

The other online stores work similarly to Amazon. It seems once your book is doing well on Amazon, online bookstore like Harvard's pick it up. It's nice to have a presence on some of these others, but time doesn't allow us to be personally involved with them all. Furthermore, loyalty counts. Amazon's algorithms are influenced by activity and high activity attracts their attention. I direct my online book sales to them. The more sales you make on a single bookstore, the higher your ratings go. The higher your ratings, the more you get to be seen on that bookstore's bestseller lists (if they have bestseller lists). Here are my favorites:

- **Amazon**—the ones in the US, UK, and Canada—but also the ones in Germany, Japan, Mexico and others where books in English are widely read. I like them because they are so highly trafficked and do so much for authors. They have many others including India and they keep adding more.

- **BN.com**—but don't believe it when you hear that when your book does well on BN.com, it will be more likely to be stocked by the Barnes & Noble brick-and-mortar stores. This company operates as two separate entities.

- **Powell's Bookstore** (powells.com) is known for their selection of used books, their voice, and their assortment of targeted newsletters. They have a brick-and-mortar store in Portland, but they are strong online and encourage online reviews.

As you explore these online bookstores, you may notice that many have so many interactive features they have begun to function like social networks. It so happens that using social networks is the next topic on our agenda. When you can, use the power of these features and apply the social networking skills you'll soon learn (or already know) to these bookstores' sites.

22

Using Social Networks

> Social networks are rooted in the human psyche. We have belonged to them and they to us since homo sapiens first took to caves. ~ CHJ

"Social network" is a term that has recently taken on a whole new meaning. Social networks once included groups like book clubs, service organizations, groups loyal to schools and teams, and our writers' critique groups. Today we think of super-powered social networks on the web first!

Because social networks on the web are new (and so large!), they can be difficult for authors to manage. They can be fun, be useless, or be amazingly effective networking tools. They can also soak up your time. Much depends on how you use them. This chapter explains a simple system I use to manage them as tools for promotion, one that flexes as the sites and my needs change. Whatever system you use, adapt it to your needs and to the networks' frequent innovations.

Simple Social Networking

Basic social networking is essential for authors, but they needn't be conversant with every feature on a network to use it effectively. Knowing the basics usually suffices. Learn the rest on an as-needed basis.

I install a profile page on the networks I am invited to join—when time allows. It doesn't hurt to have that presence. I may occasionally update my profile, but rarely actively participate. I am active on only four and tend to use them differently.

I like Twitter because, at its most basic, it is easy to learn, and it doesn't discourage marketing. I use many of their satellite apps to increase its effectiveness. For years I used a free service and ignored friends' advice to use its powerhouse upgrades. I wish I hadn't waited. Their help with Twitter has cut the time necessary for staying active and involved, and my followers have grown to more than 30,000 without buying names—a process I eschew. I believe in quality, not quantity. To find a good one, ask your Twitter followers for recommendations.

I also use AskDavid.com's free service when I run a Kindle free promotion for my poetry books. David has inexpensive pay-for services, too.

After you have used some of these services, you find ways to make the most of them. David installs his most active participants on his home page. By following and connecting with them, I have found other authors who enjoy retweeting as much as I do.

Hint: Speaking of finding back channels for increasing the effectiveness of your online promotion, here's an example. Twitter tags people (sends them emails when their moniker is used), so if you find room for my @FrugalBookPromo in your author-oriented tweets, I'll get notified and retweet for you!

Choose networks that suit your title and personality. Pinterest is ideal for authors with illustrated books or books that can be illustrated with photos. I promote Pinterest by telling my blog and website visitors that if they save my bookcovers or events, I'll pin theirs. Carolyn Wilhelm sells and gives away many teachers' aids on Pinterest, but she also uses Twitter extensively. Learn from her techniques. Find her on Twitter @wiseowlfactory.

Here is a simple method for making online social networks work for you and your book:

- Sign up. Build a profile. Invite folks you identify as avid readers or with whom you want to build better marketing relationships.

- Accept anyone who wants to connect with you on a network unless they offend your sensibilities. This is business, not social (regardless of the name "social network"). You can't tell who might be interested in reading your book. Even people who are selling something may also read books in your genre.

- Use an avatar (the little identifying logo that most social networks offer their participants). Select one that will help sell your book at a glance. Your bookcover may be a much better avatar choice than your headshot.

- Integrate the networks you use. That is, hook one to the other using Real Simple Syndication (RSS). Some are already integrated in the network's structure for you. Integration is the power of the web in action. One post can be seen by several of your networks.

- Post often. Try for one post a day on each except for Twitter where you can easily do ten a day. Automation and repetition are allowed.

- Let your voice shine through. What you write in your posts should be tailored to your audience and reflect your personality or the book you are promoting.

- Too many social networkers collect names and then rarely use them. The idea is to make friends and call on one another to cross promote or develop projects.

Hint: Try advanced features like Facebook's amazingly targeted (but certainly not very frugal!) advertising opportunities. (See my warning against paid advertising in Chapter Nine.) Or create your own "Pages" (once known as "fan" pages). Their events feature can be effective if you do as I say and "promote the promotion" using the full cross-promotional benefits across social network platforms. Definitely use their "share photos" feature. Mark Zuckerberg, Facebook founder, says that images appeal to folks' most basic inclinations. Most networks have followed their lead and accommodate photos.

Once you have explored some sites, build on them. Search out super social network marketers. I like to watch (and learn from) some master marketer-authors like Shelly Hitz, Penny Sansevieri, Gene Cartwright, and C. Hope Clark.

Note: Many networks have an invitation feature you can use to invite friends to promotional events online or off. They are easy to use when you have only a few friends on these sites, but it can become unmanageable once you have thousands because the sites require you to invite them a few at a time—often around 200. I'm sure the powers-that-be have their reasons, but I find this limitation annoying and downright anti-marketing bigotry.

About those social networks for readers? The ones like GoodReads, (associated with Amazon) and associated sites like LibraryThing? Let's not give them short shrift. In fact, if they interest you as a way to promote (and they should, especially if you write fiction or poetry), follow the simple participation guidelines I've recommended in this chapter for general social networks. But then go a step or two farther.

- Yep. Add reviews of the books you read to these sites. Any old book will do but it will work better if you focus on the books that are related to yours by genre or topic. Include a reference to your book (subtly) in the review, and a credit line—all in accordance with these sites' guidelines. If you decide to do this, go back to Chapter Sixteen and brush up on how to use reviews effectively in my *How to Get Great Reviews Frugally and Ethically* (bit.ly/GreatBkReviews).

- You will find lots of groups—including reading groups—on social networks. Actively participate in a couple associated with your target audience. These groups may provide some Real Simple Syndication features to connect them to other promotions you are doing. We've talked about RSS feeds elsewhere so you know what time-savers they can be. The Index in this book will help you find them. Connect these reader-group sites to your other social network profiles, your blog, and the social media page on your website.

Hint: You can list your books and books related to them on LibraryThing and then use RSS to feed that list to your blog. That keeps your blog fresh because your choices rotate automatically. Amazon's sales "carousels" work in a similar way. Put your own book on these lists and carousels when it's appropriate. It's a great way to let readers know your book is similar to books they have already grown to love. Find carousels and other ways to link to books by finding the Amazon's "affiliate" page.

Social networking needn't be a chore. It can work as relief from hours of writing. It can be as much fun as putting together a puzzle. If it feels threatening, perhaps you are trying to "understand" its advanced features—features you can live without. There are entire books written about utilizing specific networks. If you want to pursue that, go for it. Just know that you can keep it very, very simple—and, yes!—enjoyable.

And speaking of threatening. Read my early experience with Wikipedia in the next chapter. I think you'll see that the online marketing choices are so many—so varied—that you can find a network that's right for you. You can even drop whatever you find annoying and move on.

23
The Dangers of Online Promotion

> When I was a child, I gathered eggs for my grandmother—too many to hold safely in the basket she gave me—and I learned firsthand the meaning of the metaphor "egg on your face" and the aphorism "Never put all your eggs in one basket."
> ~ CHJ

When we think of online danger we tend to think "security." I think our culture manipulates us with fear. Read up on security. Take precautions, by all means, but don't let fear keep you from marketing your book. Security is a topic is for another book, anyway.

I worry more about how—after a huge investment in time and talent—a social network can close your account. Here are my stories. Call them the Ph.D. from the school of hard knocks.

Long, long ago as time is measured by authors, there I was, flipping through the pages of *Time* magazine and there *it* is. A chance to be listed in an encyclopedia called Wikipedia—right up there with Proust and Chekhov. And, I thought, authors (any author, including me!) could see ourselves there before we die!

This article wasn't directed at authors and it didn't suggest anyone who longs for fame get it instantly by adding her biography on what this news magazine's editors call The People's Encyclopedia. But what a fun opportunity for writers! So, I tried it. It took quite a bit of my time.

Naturally, I used the link to my Wiki page a lot. No point of having one if you don't promote it! Then one of my techie newsletter subscribers tells me my page is no longer there. She gives me a link to a very secret, hidden page that discusses *why* I am no longer there.

Wiki operates with free labor, people who consider themselves experts. Many are. But among them are those who relish their power. And some who are so successful they think they are always right. It seems that two of the awards on my page could not be verified online or the award-issuing entity didn't (in their opinion) measure up. Keep in mind, I have a couple hunks of engraved crystal to prove the authenticity of my awards, and the media outlet that apparently wasn't worthy was a long-established local newspaper of a well known Southern California city. They also didn't like that I am self-published, but hadn't bothered to notice the traditional publishing I've done. I decided not to buck this kind of book bigotry. It's not worth it to me.

Another time I was booted from Facebook. They didn't like that I accepted too many invitations to be friends at one time—or wasn't doing it in a way their programs recognized as legitimate. My daughter's Facebook friends thought the whole thing was a hoot. I was not so amused. It only took one letter to get that fixed, but if it had taken me more, I would have happily (well, okay, a little ticked off!) dropped that networking effort, too. The world is full of marketing possibilities. There is no point in making oneself miserable with one, whatever their strengths... or flaws. (It's also a lesson in backing up material, especially on sites that don't belong to you.)

Then there are self-appointed watchdogs who despise abuse of author-friendly websites enough to spend promotion and writing time to report violators, which sometimes causes problems even for the innocent. Isn't that a little like the sick vigilantes of the 1800s?

Others prefer to take the promotion low road by dissing their competitors' work, including writing unfavorable online reviews. If that happens, you can appeal to the powers-that-be on the website in question and they sometimes will remove the offending comments or reviews. Sometimes not. (Please see Chapter Four on ethics.)

Occasionally something goes wrong with a site. It goes out of business or has technical problems, and you lose your great list of loyal readers. Yeah, we should back everything up, but, hey. We're just human!

How does all this affect you? Let's learn from them how *not* to treat your fellow authors. We should support one another, partner, cross promote. The universe is big enough—generous enough—for us all to succeed.

I want you to put your marketing efforts into work that builds on itself. You do that by focusing on the marketing that works for you, but not to the extent that you could lose all your promotion power to the whims of another.

And don't let the nitpickers get to you.

Section VI – Well Traveled, Oft Forgotten

> The noise of the web can be so deafening we don't hear the muted call of good old marketing methods that have worked just fine for decades. ~ CHJ

Most online promotions in this book are extensions of marketing methods that worked well for a very long time. This section, however, is about proven *offline* tools that might be more effective than ever before.

You might ask how anything can be more effective than an online promotion that can reach so many so fast. Because many authors have deserted traditional book promotions for the ease and allure of the web, authors who return to the tried-and-true offline techniques face less competition and their efforts feel more creative and more personal to the recipients.

Though this section is about those old-fashioned methods, isn't it nice we have the web to give any offline promotions a marketing boost! You've seen tags like "As advertised on TV" and "Watch for our brochure in your mailbox." We can add tags like that to our online efforts to draw attention to the marketing we do *offline*. We can even suggest that online readers sign up to receive our offline promotions.

Section VI
Well Traveled, Oft Forgotten

24 Reading Groups

> Writers once sought groups of readers who love the smell of ink and the feel of paper. Now authors who want to share their writing want to find groups who love to read anywhere—online or off. ~ CHJ

Authors can enlarge their circle of fans by using readers' groups. Members read an assigned book then discuss it. Such groups exist everywhere, even in cyberspace. Even on cruise ships. Offline, authors visit such groups, read for them, and sign their books.

If you can locate a group that reads the kind of literature you write, convincing them to choose your book is usually not difficult. They tend to be starved for contact with real live authors. The trick is to offer them more personal service than other writers.

To arrange to sign hard copies for those who belong to online groups, collect real life street addresses from the virtual attendees and send the members well-designed, hand-signed, and dedicated bookplates. These could be sticky labels—either the fancy kind you can buy at bookstores that were traditionally used to specify book ownership or the generic (and frugal!) Avery label variety. They then affix these labels, signed and dedicated by you, to the inside covers of the books they bought to read. Authors of either fiction or nonfiction may also gift their readers with free eBooks that relate to the topic of their books in some way.

Hint: Yes, there are online services that let you sign books digitally, but they are poor substitutes for the real thing.

Real live, in-person reading groups still work best. Faces and handshakes forge relationships. Find reading groups at:

- Your workplace. Check the bulletin board and company newsletter. Lacking a reading group, offer to read from your book at a special lunch or after work. Promise snacks for attendees or free books in exchange for reviews.
- Synagogues, mosques, and church groups.
- Service and social groups and organizations.
- Bookstores.

- Libraries and museums.
- School and parent groups.
- Lists in newspaper and magazine calendar sections.
- Use search engines. My search on "reading groups" reaped resources in the millions including organizations that sponsor reading groups in specific genres.

Once connected, make the event a unique experience. Have a contest. Give away a memento. Do a drawing. Have attendees sign your guestbook. Serve goodies. Stay in touch with members. When you make book club members feel special, word gets around about you and your book.

Next up, catalogs. Catalogs of books seem to evolve daily, but we all remember the ones that got delivered to our mailboxes and every so often contained a book among pages of merchandise somehow suited to the title of that book. My warning is that online book-sale emails come in several iterations including expensive. Keep reading so you know about how some of them might work for you—and how some of them are or can be quite frugal!

25 Catalog Sales

Catalogs are show business. They spotlight a product to sell merchandise, but they also create a buzz, project an image, tell a story, leave an impression. They create celebrity for each of the products within their covers. ~ CHJ

The primary reason for your book to appear on the pages of a retail catalog is sales, but that exposure is also extraordinarily good publicity. I used real paper catalogs for the stores my husband and I once owned. They helped build one little store to five in less than three years!

Your book may be perfect for an email-only catalog issued by businesses, organizations, or retailers. When a travel memoir appears on the pages of *Travelsmith*, it qualifies as publicity because you don't pay for the exposure in it and the image of your cover increases interest among their vetted, targeted audience. The secret is in finding catalogs that match the subject of your book so you can pitch their producers. And it isn't hard to find books-only catalogs; you probably receive at least one in your email box every now and then.

You can also use cross-promotional catalogs published by a group of authors or other organizations. They usually rely on each participating author to distribute the catalog—online or by mail—to achieve mass readership. There is usually a fee for these catalogs to cover the time and expense of putting them together. You could sponsor one yourself and charge others for time required to coordinate and distribute it.

In Chapter Eighteen, review how we used a catalog to make a book fair booth successful. Our catalog promote authors who shared an *LA Times Festival of Books* booth and the books of the participating authors. Jump ahead in this chapter to see how that model—really a kind of case study—might be applied to other situations, too.

Bona Fide Retail Store Catalogs

This category includes everything from catalogs for department stores to boutique clothing stores to gift stores to gadget stores. When you find a fit for your book (such as your nonfiction book on the life of Picasso for a catalog produced by a chain of art galleries) the advantages are:

- The retailer or catalog producer buys your book and features it in their pages. Except for a few, you do not pay for this ad.
- Unlike most bookstores, the catalog company pays the freight for shipping books from you or your distributor to their warehouse.
- Unlike most bookstores, catalog producers do not return what they cannot sell. They probably won't even ask for returns unless you suggest it. And why would you? This is their usual way of doing business. When in Rome, do as the Romans do.

  Hint: These no-return sale terms should be included on both order forms and the sales contract you present to them.
- They reorder just before their stock is depleted.
- They want a title that fits their product mix and sells, though the cover art must appeal to them, too.
- They don't much care if your book is current.
- Most don't require exclusivity.
- They must be sure they have stock to cover their sales, so their orders will be substantial enough to make both you and your publisher smile. Many small-to-medium size publishers have no experience with catalogs, so you may need to show yours *why* they should smile, how to handle billing, and other matters.

Disadvantages are:
- Learning curve ahead! You'll need to expertly pitch your book and negotiate sales to catalog buyers who have different needs and policies from bookstore buyers.
- Because catalogs buy in quantity, they demand a hefty discount. If you or your publisher cannot give fifty percent or more, there is no point in pursuing them. However, if you only break even on catalog sales, it may be worth the trouble for the publicity benefits.
- Some authors and publishers fail to print enough books to supply a catalog's immediate needs. Authors who use print-on-demand technology generally have access to fast turnaround time.
- Nonfiction books are generally—but not always—more suitable for catalogs. Catalog buyers look for books that relate to the needs or interests of the audience they target.

- Here's how to find catalogs that might be interested in your book:

- Do an engine search on "retail catalogs." About 600,000 catalog producers and individual catalogs will appear. Narrow the search to include only catalogs for which your book is a fit.

- Go to a bookstore or library and ask to see their *Catalog of Catalogs*. Find one or more categories that fit your book and... Tada! You've found another way to see your book-cover in print and realize sales at the same time.

- Become familiar with the catalogs that come to your home. Ask your friends to share their catalogs with you. When you find an appropriate one for your book, go for it! Contact information is usually on the inside of the front or back cover.

Hint: If your publisher isn't interested in partnering with you on this project, ask them for a large-quantity price break, stock your own books, and handle the details yourself.

Consider Cooperative Catalogs

Co-op catalogs are cross-promotional efforts that work well for groups of promotion-minded authors. When they are distributed online, people who receive the cooperative catalog and are interested in your book click on a link in the catalog that takes them to the Buy page on your own website. Cooperative catalogs might be distributed by mail, as handouts, or as newspaper inserts.

Some of the authors who participated in the book fair booths I sponsored partnered on a catalog with some Military Writers Society of America authors. Rather than distributing our catalog online exclusively (the inexpensive way to do it), we printed them and sent them third class to lists of media folks, librarians, local directors, and producers, and bookstore buyers provided by the participants.

By using the participants' own contact lists, these catalogs were received by people who might have a special interest because of local subject matter or other connection to a featured author. Participants were asked to drop a postcard to those same people before the catalog was issued asking them to watch for it in their mailboxes. We thought this personal approach would attract more interest than either an online catalog or a catalog received with no pre-promotion fanfare. It's worth repeating: Authors' personal contact lists can be pure gold but only when authors use them.

We used our catalog overrun as handouts to fair visitors—all of whom were readers by definition.

In addition to a small charge for the time it takes someone to design a catalog and administer it, you will probably be expected to promote and distribute any cooperative catalog you participate in—online or off—using your contact list, blogs, and other promotion entities. You handle your own sales and shipping using a mass mailing service or your local USPS office.

When you join and use Help a Reporter Out (HARO), you sometimes receive calls for information on catalog-suitable items—that includes books!— in the daily posts of opportunities HARO sends to your email box. Go to helpareporter.com/.

Corporate sales are another way to sell large quantities of books in one big, book-selling coup! Few authors or publishers use it. It's a shame because if you can target businesses (including charities) that could benefit from what you have written, you have may have the feel-good, win-win experience of your life ahead of you. That's coming in the next chapter.

26 Corporate Sales

> Many companies give presents to clients... such gifts should be kept inexpensive so they are not seen as bribes.
> ~ Amy Vanderbilt

Vanderbilt gave this advice on the niceties of corporate marketing long ago and though the giving of corporate gifts may not be as prevalent today as it was when she wrote her famous books, the practice is still widespread. Often businesses look for gifts that sing less of extravagance and more of long-term benefits. Books are often the answer. Maybe *your* book.

In addition to gifts for social occasions and holidays, large and small companies (including nonprofits) give gifts to their employees as awards or incentives. Sometimes they have training programs (yes, think books!) that help teach their employees and clients subjects they deem vital to their success. Generally they buy in quantity and expect substantial discounts from retail prices. If your book fits the needs of a specific industry, here are ways sell your books to them:

To sell to corporations, you need to put your marketing bonnet on. How does the subject of your book align with a specific business or industry? How might you convince a corporation that it would benefit from utilizing your book? You must know the answers to these questions—preferably answers tailored to the specific business or event—to write an effective pitch.

- If you know someone in a corporation that is a match for your book, ask for their recommendation. Send a thank-you even if your collaboration doesn't work out. Tomorrow is another day and you may be remembered.

- Set up a special page on your own website, and use sites like findgift.com to make it easy for business administrators to find you. Their search engine will lead you to others who have used their corporate gift feature.

- Self-published authors can personalize books to meet the needs of large corporations. As an example, a special edition of *The Frugal Book Promoter* might be titled *John Wiley &*

Sons' Primer: How our authors might contribute to the success of their own books. I could print a separate run that includes an introduction from their marketing department and a dedication page to personalize the book for them. I would set a minimum order requirement to make the process profitable, and I'd need to edit parts so they'd reflect Wiley's policies. You can see the process isn't easy, but there is a big profit potential and publicity value with this kind of sale.

- Contact Jerry Jenkins at specialmarketbooksales.com for corporate book sales representation.

  Caveat: Corporate sales usually work well for gift books, cookbooks, and books with a business or health theme. However, novelists can sometimes come up with ideas beneficial to a business. I can see a book of fiction set in the office of *Vogue* magazine being purchased by a clothing manufacturer to be packaged as part of a swag bag like the ones the Academy Awards committee gives to stars. The book would be fun holiday reading and add a new dimension to bags of jewelry and pink iPhone covers. Try to think outside the box.

Once you have landed a corporate client, ask for their endorsement to help you get similar sales. LinkedIn and Alignable.com have features that make recommendations easy to get.

Traditionally-published authors should check their contracts or negotiate with their publishers before pursuing catalog sales. A book's price structure, speed of production, and reprint and copyright issues may be stumbling blocks. It's worth a try. For the profit. And for the buzz it might create for both you and your book.

You have seen that if we broaden our thinking, there is a whole world of possibilities out there for selling books. The publishing industry limits itself when it thinks only of bookstores or maybe Walmart when it thinks about retailing books. But what about all those other retailers? That's up next!

27 Retail is More than Bookstores

> Bookstores carry more than just books these days and a variety of retailers carry books. Your book is suitable for the merchandise mix of some retailer—from a tire store to a fast food chain. ~ CHJ

A category called "gift books" is a hot commodity in retail circles. Most every store you see in a mall or on the street is ripe for a title that is closely aligned with its image and its customer's needs.

Selling to specialty retailers is a useful way to market books long after the shelf life on a new release has supposedly expired and bookstores have lost interest. As an added benefit, exposure in nontraditional venues creates demand at libraries and bookstores at any stage in the market life of a book.

Unless your publisher specializes in gift books, their wholesaler probably won't approach retailers other than booksellers, but you can make traditional sales calls to local retailers on your own. And you can sell to national and even international retailers using a combination book and business proposal. My booklet *The Great First Impression Book Proposal* (bit.ly/BookProposals) will get you started. To do this kind of selling, you need only adapt the ideas in it and the format it suggests to any category of brick-and-mortar store you think would have a clientele interested in your title.

If you are convinced a particular store could sell a ton of your books, use what is called a "forced sale" technique. Offer the buyer six books in a point-of-purchase display complete with signs (header cards) you have professionally made. The store pays you only if they sell their stock and they don't have to return them if they don't sell; they may use them any way they choose. They agree to place them at their point-of-purchase (near the cash register) in that nifty display you provided for thirty days. They get to try a new product at no risk. They do not have to go to the expense of returning or paying for what doesn't sell. You present the invoice with the conditions on it when you make your sales call.

This sales tool will be ineffective only if you choose a retailer that is unsuited to your book. Even if some books end up not being paid for, they may be read or otherwise make their way into the community. You may have to give away fewer books this way than by sending sample copies to retail outlets one at time, and your sales results might be much better.

Let Retail Sales Representatives Sell Books for You

Once you have a track record selling books as gifts, write up a marketing plan and present it to sales representative groups. You find them in "to-the-trade" buildings like The LA Mart in Los Angeles (lamart.com). Other population centers have them, too. Contact the building's office. Ask for a list of their showrooms, select ones that represent lines that fit with your book's subject matter, and set up an appointment.

When you approach these representatives, sell yourself as well as your book. Offer to do a signing at their next tradeshow, even to give sample books away to the store buyers who frequent their booth or showroom. Suggest they offer one of your workshops as a perk when their accounts buy a minimum number of books. That gives the store owners and buyers (the representatives' customers) a built-in event at no additional cost for the star attraction (yes, that would be *you*!).

Did I mention that when retailers buy from gift-industry sales reps, the merchandise is not returnable? Ahem! That's a huge advantage to both publisher and author.

Attend gift tradeshows and track down a like-minded representative there or advertise for a representative in a for-the-trade magazine like *Gift Shop* (giftshopmag.com).

> **Caveat:** Expect to pay a percentage of sales to representatives, usually ten to fifteen percent of the wholesale price. Also expect to offer retailers a discount of forty to fifty percent from the price printed on your book. To accommodate such a discount, traditionally-published authors may need to cut a deal with their publishers. At the outset, self-published authors must set their price structure to accommodate retail sales (something they need to do anyway if they want to sell books to bookstores—online or off).

Don't give up yet. Keep your alternative-ideas thinking cap on. New authors pass along lots of negative ideas about working with libraries. Adopting short-sighted limited ideas of what libraries can do will severely limit possibilities of having your book read by many but also of selling lots of books.

28 Library Sales

The serious writer would a million times rather see a book sold to a library than to a reader, for it is her wish to have her book read not once by one, but over and over again by many. ~ CHJ

Some authors disparage sales of books to libraries. They believe that if libraries don't have their title in their stacks, a reader will find it necessary to buy a copy. And that would lead to lots more sales, right?

Wrong. The objection voiced against selling to libraries is based on one or more specious arguments. Critics don't stop to think about how often a book sold to an individual may get passed around from friend to friend, given to Goodwill, or sold secondhand. An author does herself a favor if she forgets about how her book might travel once it is purchased. There is nothing she can do about it anyway.

Critics also don't consider how getting your book into libraries helps generate buzz. Ask what your publisher does to alert acquisition librarians so you can supplement those efforts. You can do a better job than your publisher at promoting your book at libraries near your home, but if your book has a regional slant or is of national interest, search for necessary contact information to help your publisher reach them no matter where they are. Or pitch these librarians yourself.

Hint: If your book is of national interest, notify libraries state by state, starting with library systems that would be most interested in the subject matter of your book. Work one state at a time and rewrite your query letter to include benefits for each.

Libraries are workhorses for readers. They labor mightily for authors, especially when we grow our relationships with them. Search for city, college, neighborhood, and university libraries.

- Many—not all—have a policy to buy books written by local authors.
- Contact them to see if you might be scheduled as a featured speaker.

- Get involved by offering to lead a workshop on the subject of your book or by founding a critique group for writers or a book club for readers.
- They may disseminate or post your fliers or bookmarks.
- They may allow you to do a display in their window or on a bulletin board.

   Hint: Go to the Index of this book to find "tradeshows." Also Google "library tradeshows" and "library associations." A few regional conferences and tradeshows sponsored by library associations display our books free.

I once found it necessary to put a book I wanted on a waiting list at my neighborhood library. In the process I learned that the county system for the library had forty-five books on order. So much for the idea that libraries don't buy many books!

29 Postcards

> Because the web is frugal, fast, and interconnected, it has supplanted many stellar methods of promotion that worked before—methods that shouldn't have been discarded. ~ CHJ

Before the web, postcards were the darlings of marketers. We now know the web is faster, more frugal, and more connected, but postcards still make great invitations or announcements for in-person events like launches, signings, and seminars. Here's why:

- Postcards are more likely to get noticed than an email. They feel more personal because they are used less and arrive in folks' mailboxes where they now probably get less junk than they do in their email boxes.
- They're appealing and quick—no stuffing or folding.
- By using the sort function on your computer, you can send only to those within a reasonable traveling distance to your event.
- They are less expensive to mail than other direct-mail means.
- If you send your cards post card rate, USPS returns the ones with invalid addresses to you at no additional charge. A current mailing list can be a huge savings next time around.
- Colorful postcards can mimic your bookcover so your book will be immediately recognizable when your prospective customer shops online or in bookstores.
- They're fast to read.
- Postcards have more staying power than many other forms of communication. People may even post them on their refrigerators.
- Mailing services can handle postcard mailing relatively inexpensively using an author's own contact list, a purchased list from businesses that sell lists like American Express, or they can integrate a combination of the two. That kind of

combination might be quite expensive, but it gives authors a chance to target some readers in selected zip codes and income levels—readers they've never met!

- The response rate to postcards has always been high, perhaps because the perceived value of postcards is higher than that of so much other slush we are inundated with in this information age.

  Hint: Cross-promotion works here, too. Four authors could share a card. Printing huge quantities of cards lowers costs per card; sharing one another's mailing lists exposes books to more readers.

Here's how I designed my postcards so they were more frugal as well as effective.

- On the front (the picture side), place a text box near the image of your bookcover where you can insert your best sales tool—an endorsement or blurb.

  Tip: The newest book in my multi award-winning *HowToDoItFrugally Series* of books (The one you are reading is the third edition of my flagship book!) is *How to Get Great Book Reviews Frugally and Ethically* (bit.ly/GreatBkReviews). It gives you everything you need to know about blurbs including how to legally extract them from reviews and—I guarantee it—more ways to use them than you ever thought possible. Without paying a cent for the reviews.

- On the back (the address side), leave a little less than ½ the width of the card in white space at the right for an address label.

- Print your return address or PO box number on the back so USPS can send undeliverable postcards back to you. The return address goes to the left of the printed bulk mail insignia the post office uses instead of a stamp. Use a very small font size.

- Save the far-left half of the card for details about your book. Leave ¼ inch space along the bottom. The post office prints codes or applies labels there so anything you put there will be obscured.

  My Favorite Money-Saving Hint for Postcards: Leave some space in the block of print on the left to handwrite a message or to apply what I call a target label. This space is for time-limited information like the date, time, and place of your event. By doing this, you can avoid a new print run for each separate occasion. It also allows you to print more cards for your initial order and, as you know, the more you print, the less it costs per card.

Like advertising in general, postcards work well as a sales tool when they are part of a regular and frequent campaign. Quantity discounts encourage you to plan a postcard campaign. That's why I love, love, love the idea of leaving space within the generic information on the left side for handwriting or a label that I mentioned in the hint above.

Postage becomes an issue when your list gets bigger, so choose a card size that meets the USPS bulk mail specifications. The larger cards are more dramatic, but your budget will suffer if you're sending out lots of cards. Guidelines are at USPS.com.

Here are two sources for printing your cards:

- Try Modern Post Card (modernpostcard.com).

- Vistaprint (VistaPrint.com) is popular among authors but you can do better on the price from other suppliers if you are printing large quantities of cards, say more than 1,000. Watch for fluctuating and inflated shipping costs when Vista offers specials or "free" items.

You probably noticed that I repeated how effective quotations (otherwise known as blurbs, endorsements, etc) in this chapter and others are. However, I have barely mentioned quotations of an author's own words. Paying attention to your own memorable tidbits and using available means to get them repeated can be a great—and rarely used way—to broaden exposure in your overall marketing campaign. That's up next!

30   Get Quoted

> In the Academy Award-winning film, *The King's Speech*, Colin Firth says, "I've got a voice." After a meaningful pause, his speech instructor says, "Yes, you do." Our voices are often most heard when what we say is quotable. ~ CHJ

Quotes—or more properly—quotations are pure gold publicity nuggets that work for everyone including mothers. My mom called them "tried-and-true sayings." They certainly worked well for sports figures like John Wooden, the UCLA basketball coach and author who was as famous as his star players. "It's what you learn after you know it all that counts" was so famous it was emblazoned on the cover of a UCLA Extension catalog.

A quotation helped my husband get an endorsement from a famous Asian political figure for his *What Foreigners Need to Know About America from A to Z* (amzn.to/ForeignersAmericaUS). He began his query letter asking for a blurb with this: "Behind an able man there are always other able men." ~ Ancient Chinese Proverb

Being quoted is good branding. A few of my own and those of others are in this book. When you're editing your own work, notice the little nuggets floating around in your copy that are every bit as good as those quoted in *Bartlett's Familiar Quotations*.

Hint: Make your quotations into an alternative tip sheet, perhaps "Seven Quotations to Warm the Hearts of Authors Everywhere."

Reporters who call for submissions with the Help a Reporter Out (HARO) service may be influenced by an author's quotation in their query letter! I tell my clients to subscribe to HARO and build relationships with reporters who write frequently about a topic related to the author's book. That puts them on the go-to list when that reporter needs, well... just about anything on a specific topic. And the author is always credited, usually with a link.

To position yourself to be quoted try:

- Start each of your media releases with a quote.
- Install "Quotable Quotes" page on your website that invite people to use your quotes—credited.

- Include a line about your availability for quotes as part of the last line in your media release, something like, "A media kit, images, and quotations promoting tolerance are available electronically or by post on request or in the author's media room at howtodoitfrugally.com/media_room.htm."

- John Kremer, author of *101 Ways to Market Your Books* (bit.ly/JKremer) advises tweeters that quotes are supremely retweetable. Yes, you can use your own! Put them in quotations marks and initial or fully credit them. There are tons of examples on my Twitter stream, both others' and my own. Scroll a bit on twitter.com/frugalbookpromo.

    Hint: If you need a quotation on anything from marketing to writing to tolerance, ask for my list of quotations or an article at no charge.

So, are you tired? Remember, I told you early on that you don't have to do everything. I mention in this book. That you get to pick and choose marketing techniques that fit your personality, your time limitations, your personality, and your pocketbook. You may also need a little inspiration ....or, mmmm, nudge. You'll find that in the next section of this book. And you'll even get some new marketing ideas—just in case you need a few more to keep your routine fresh. It's successes that keeps you loving the business of writing.

Section VII –
Onward and Upward

> Celebrating helps me acknowledge and enjoy the distance that I have already come along the writing path. By celebrating early and often, I appreciate more of the here and now.
> ~ Bruce Holland Rogers

Many years ago, I happened across advice for my zodiac sign from astrology columnist Joyce Jillson. It doesn't matter what that sign is because it is good for all writers any day of the year:

> "There are plenty of reasons to be proud. Write them down. If you don't celebrate the small wins, you don't have much to build on. It's all about momentum."

31   Success as a Motivator

> Not recognizing our own success is a destructive cycle as old as Greek tragedy because it is part of our psychological makeup.
> ~ CHJ

Our achievements are never enough because success demands more success. Because we are success-myopic, we don't see it when it come along and perches on the bridges of our noses. It's so easy to be infected by negativity—the news about everything from war to the state of publishing is just so dreadful.

If you disparage your own achievements, you are not alone. People who do that have trouble building confidence to try for more or better. Promotion successes kick start a cycle of success only if we put them to use for us psychologically. It's dangerous for your promotion efforts (and your writing) not to nod at your victories—large and small—in the mirror.

An online coaching company for business people who need help with their presentations tells their visitors to "Visualize yourself succeeding." Short, sweet, and fine advice. Rhonda Byrne has become one of the most successful writers around advising people to use techniques that have been known for centuries, things like the law of attraction and manifestation. It's all about attitude. Her attitude certainly helped her book, *The Secret* (bit.ly/RhondasSecrets), succeed.

Sometimes we don't celebrate or visualize success because we don't recognize when we have achieved it. Was "success" that first royalty check? Will "success" only come when our book's name appears on *The Times'* bestseller list? Was it the day we started commanding $5 a word as a freelancer? Or are these all mirages that are expunged by insecurity once we achieve them?

The easiest way to recognize success is to write down goals. Once they're in black and white, more recent expectations can't muss up our perspective. We'll know when we deserve to celebrate. Remember when you thought you'd never get a book written? That day is here. That *is* success.

What if the goal you jot down is "to be just like Danielle Steele?" Study her technique. Take classes. Then tap into your own originality. You may not want to *be* the great D.S., but many of us want to have their voices recognized as hers is. When I feel less than successful, I reread *Word Work* by Bruce Holland Rogers (bit.ly/ThrivingWriter). It's perceptive, witty, perfectly written. Have you heard of him? He won several awards including the Nebula (sfwa.org). He is an example that even if you are big in all the ways that count, your name may not be a household word. So, if your name isn't famous, will you still not feel valued? Probably. Unless you have made a list of those goals and celebrate each time you get to cross one off your list.

32 Book Sales Getting Musty?

> About Publishers: I conducted a study (employing my usual controls) that showed the average shelf life of a trade book to be somewhere between milk and yoghurt. ~ Calvin Trillin, humorist

There is no way to keep your book at the top of the charts forever, but if you keep reviving it, you might make a classic of it. Or your marketing efforts for one book may propel your next one to greater heights.

Fight the *It's-Too-Late* Urge

So your book has been out a year. You're ready to write another book. You don't think your promotion is working. You think you've missed your chance.

Publicity is like the little waves you make when you toss pebbles into a lake. The waves travel, travel, travel and eventually come back to you. If you stop lobbing stones, you lose momentum. I can't tell you how many authors I've seen give up on flinging those little stones into their marketing pond about the time they would have seen results if they had stuck with it.

It's never too late and it's never too early to promote. Rearrange your thinking. Marketing isn't about a single book. It's about building a career. And new books can build on the momentum created by an earlier book if you keep the faith. Review the marketing ideas in this book, rearrange your schedule and priorities a bit, and keep at it.

What if you see an article or newscast that should have used a quote from your book but didn't. Getting lizard-spit green with envy is only useful if it prompts you to act. Call whoever was responsible for the coverage. Introduce yourself as someone who is available as a source next time. Be prepared to offer them a new slant, a new idea on a similar or different subject in which you can be an integral part of the story. Don't stop there:

- Add the editor's email address to your media list.
- Follow up with a letter outlining your ideas or expertise. Put your bookmark in the envelope.

- Watch the medium where you saw this piece. When you see something by the same writer, send a congratulatory note.
- When you land something big, let that editor know about it by sending her a copy of the media release you send to your local press and TV assignment editors. By doing so, you are putting yourself on her radar.

Readership Extending Ideas are All Around You

Here are suggestions for inexpensive battles you might wage with the preservation of your book in mind.

- Run a contest on your website, on Twitter, or in your newsletter. Use your books for prizes or get cross-promotion benefits by asking other authors to donate books or services; many will donate one to you in trade for the exposure. Watch the 99 Cent Stores for suitable favors to go with them.

    Hint: Any promotion you do including a contest is more powerful when you call on your friends to tell their blog visitors or Facebook pals about it.

- Barter your books or your services for exposure on other authors' websites.
- Post your flier, brochure, or business card on bulletin boards everywhere: In grocery stores, coffee shops, laundromats, car washes, and bookstores.
- Offer classes in writing to your local high school, college, or library system. Publicizing them is easy and free. When appropriate, use your own book as suggested reading. The organization you are helping will pitch in by promoting your class. The network you build with them and your students is invaluable. Refer to this experience in your media kit to show you have teaching and presentation skills.
- Slip automailers into each book you sell or give away for publicity. Automailers are envelopes that are pre-stamped, ready to go. Your automailer asks the recipient to recommend your book to someone else. Your mailer includes a brief synopsis of your book, a picture of the cover of your book, your book's ISBN, ordering information, a couple of your most powerful blurbs, and a space for the reader to add her handwritten, personal recommendation. Make it clear in the directions that the reader should fill out the form, address the envelope, and mail it to a friend. You may offer a free item for helping, but don't make getting the freebie too

tough. Proof-of-purchase type schemes discourage your audience from participating.

- Send notes to your friends and readers asking them to recommend your book to others. Or offer them a perk like free shipping, gift wrap, or small gift if they purchase your book for a friend. That's an ideal way to use those contact lists you've been building.

- While you're working on the suggestion above, put on your thinking cap. What directories have you neglected to incorporate into your contact list? Have you joined any new groups since your book was published? Did you ask your grown children for lists of their friends? Did you include lists of old classmates?

- Though it may be more expensive than some ideas in this book, learn more about Google's AdWords and AdSense. Find these opportunities on your Google account page. Many authors of niche nonfiction or fiction that can be identified with often-searched-for keywords find this advertising program effective.

- Check out ad programs like Amazon's Vine review service. You agree to provide a certain number of books to Amazon and pay them a fee for the service. Amazon arranges the reviews for you. It's expensive, but it gets your book exposed to Amazon's select cadre of reviewers who not only write reviews for your Amazon sales page but also may start (or restart!) a buzz about your book.

- Some of your reviews (both others' reviews of your book and reviews you've written about others' books) have begun to age from disuse. Start posting them (with permission from the reviewer) on websites that allow you to do so. Check the guidelines for my free review service blog at TheNewBookReview.blogspot.com.

- Connect and reconnect. Start reading blogs and newsletters you once subscribed to again. Subscribe to a new one. Join a writers' group or organization related to the subject of your book.

- Record a playful message about your book on your voice mail.

- When you ship signed copies of your book, include a coupon for the purchase of another copy for a friend—signed and dedicated—or for one of your other books. Some distributors insert fliers or coupons into your books when they ship them for an additional fee.

- Adjust the idea above to a cross-promotional effort with a friend who writes in the same genre as you. She puts a coupon for your book in her shipments; you do the same for her in yours.

- Donate your book to contests run by other authors. In return they promote your book for you and provide links to your website or blog.

- Explore the opportunities for speaking on cruise ships. Many have cut back on the number of speakers they use and they tend not to be as generous with compensation these days, but your area of expertise may be perfect for one of them. I tried it, but found ship politics a drawback. Still many authors like Allyn Evans who holds top honors in Toastmasters and Erica Miner have used these venues both successfully and happily. For help with the application process from beginning to end, read Daniel Hall's information on the subject at cruisespeaking.com.

Staying in the Promotion Habit

The longer you stick with it the more productive each effort becomes. Try new ideas. At the grocery check-out stand, Janet Elaine Smith, a woman with a saucy sense of humor who wrote fifteen books of fiction, offered the back of her book instead of her driver's license as picture ID. If the checker said there was no number on it, Janet pointed to the ISBN. She said, "If they aren't convinced by the legality of this ploy, I still tell them about my book while I search for my driver's license." She then gave them a bookmark after she had autographed it so they wouldn't throw it away. She was the brassiest of promoters but, as you might guess, none of her many books died inglorious deaths and she mentored new authors along the way, too.

Smith also had a serious side. She set aside a little time every weekday morning to call bookstore buyers. She asked if they had stock on her Irish-themed book for St. Pat's Day. She told them about her newest book. She knew how to build relationships.

Plumb the Web Again

The web is the best tool of all for beginning promoters because it doesn't cost a single copper to learn what's effective and what's not. Here are some free promotion gizmos you can use to extend the reach of your published book:

- Link your website, your blog, your social networks—everything!—to each other and to other like-minded sites.

The Frugal Book Promoter 233

- Get your site listed on as many search engines possible. Go to ineedhits.com and addme.com. These sites lead you through a free-for-all listing spree at no cost.

- Learn a little basic HTML code to help you do more online promotion for yourself. It's faster than waiting for someone else to do it for you. And it's more frugal.

- Learn to use a new web tool like Real Simple Syndication (RSS feeds) that lets you get widgets (little logos or pictures) that take your reader somewhere else on the web with just a click. You often see widgets that let people join or comment on social networks easily. Learn more by searching on "RSS tutorial."

- Use online calendars like Google's to list your events, then feed the HTML code to your website, blogs, and your social networks that accommodate it. That way you need only key in your public events once. When you spend less time to reach more people, you increase your book's chances for success incrementally.

- Emily Bracale, author of the graphic memoir *Our Last Six Months,* contacted all who bought her books online using Paypal when she won Winning Writers' North Street Book Prize. That reminded them of her book's benefits, and several bought another copy as gifts. How'd she do that? She found their email addresses from the receipts Paypal provides. If she had recorded those addresses in her contact list and coded them "Paypal," she might have saved time and used the same addresses in other ways in the interim.

- Add the ability to use quick response codes (QRs) to your battery of techie tools. Some people think they look flowery or like puzzles or computer chips. Or Rorschach tests. They are a kind of barcode, but they can take people with smartphones to a web page or video or even make a call for them—it depends on what the author chooses to put in the code. Use QRs at book fairs, tradeshows, and book signings to let folks with smartphones scan whatever promotional gift or information you want them to have. You can put the codes anywhere: Your business cards, your ads, in your book, or on your printed tote bag. The leading maker of codes is Scanbury. Related to them is a program from Scanlife.com. Get codes made at qrcode.com The example you see here takes you to the Writers' Resources pages on my website.

- Google Alerts has been around a long time, but authors often don't use it or a similar tool. Find Alerts (a little bell icon) on your Google account page. I use it to inform me when my name or titles have appeared anywhere on the web so I can comment and send thanks. It's also useful for those who are doing research for a book by letting them know when pertinent keywords are mentioned.

- Make your book available for e-readers. Many eBook services charge nothing to upload your book. There is a charge only when your book sells. Using Kindle is a shortcut for readers because the free app it offers as soon as a reader clicks "buy" formats their new eBook for the device of their choice.

- Now you have a published book, you are a retailer. Smart retailers take checks, cash, and credit and debit cards. Smart authors want readers to access their books in whatever way they prefer. Get a Square app for credit cards.

- Re-examine the keywords you use when you market on the web. Some work better than others. You may be missing one that doesn't have much competition. That may be the one that puts your blog, website, article, or book at the top of a reader's search page. To find these keyword jewels, use Google's Keyword tool. You'll find it on your Google Account's homepage.

Next up, the Appendices. You do like resources, right?

Appendices

> Appendices were invented by efficient little elves who delight in keeping trade secrets tucked away where only the most curious readers find them. ~ CHJ

Appendices can be full of obscure resources, strict rules, and templates. Mine are not so heavy-handed. It more closely resembles a collection of ideas.

Use the samples in this Appendix as guides so you don't stray into embarrassing territory, but, in the long run, it is *your* voice and the ambience of each circumstance that dictates how these samples should be used.

Hint: I annotated some of the Appendix entries to make it easier for you to see how to apply them to your needs. The annotations are in bold face to set them apart from the query letters themselves.

Appendix 1

Sample Query Letters

When I interviewed literary agents for the chapters on query letters in the second book in my *HowToDoItFrugally Series* of books for writers, *The Frugal Editor* (bit.ly/FrugalEditorKind), Stephanie Kip Rostan, an agent for Levine/Greenberg Literary Agency, Inc., said, "...don't slavishly follow a query letter template.... If you can't write a query letter on your own, I have to be concerned about your ability to write a book. Besides, it's just creepy."

Each book is different. Each occasion that calls for a query—anything from a request for representation to an appeal for a TV appearance—is different. Ditto for each occasion a media release is called for. Thus, I can only suggest.

Because query letters are important for many steps in the publishing and marketing processes, I include several examples for you to use as inspiration, to adapt rather than "slavishly" emulate.

Sample Query for an Agent or Acquisitions Editor

An author must carefully research an agent's or publisher's preferences. The construction of this letter works for most any query, but the tone would not be suitable if an agent represents only nonfiction or speculative fiction.

Dear Agent or Editor: (**Note: You will use a carefully researched name here.**)

> *"Memory is subtle like the caress of a spider's web across one's face or the sweet scent of jasmine in the approaching dusk. It evokes emotion—the sweet, the painful, the frightening—one by one or all at once. Memory is our connection to the souls of others and to our own identity."* Excerpted from *Harkening*

Harkening is a collection of creative nonfiction that evokes the feelings above. It moves through the generations of a single, isolated family living in Utah. It touches on the repression of women, the pain of prejudice, the warmth of family. It moves lineally from the 20s to the present, revealing the lives of a dysfunctional but loving family. (**This is an example of a short soft-sell synopsis.**)

I have a varied background as a writer. I was a staff writer for *The Salt Lake Tribune* and a columnist for the *Pasadena Star News*. My novel, *This Is the Place*, was published by AmErica House in July of 2001, is an award-winning novel, and has received favorable reviews like this one from *Library Journal*: "Howard-Johnson strengthens her novel with behind-the-scenes details of Mormon life and history in a book suitable for all collections, particularly those where... Orson Scott Card's... books are popular." (Here I used **one of those all-important blurbs we talked about in this book.**)

I also have many years' experience as a retailer and, in that capacity, as a speaker at tradeshows and a contributor to industry magazines. (**Note: This letter is a sample from my early writing days. This paragraph shows how to plumb past careers for information about your ability to promote.**)

I am enclosing pertinent information including a brief biography, some promotional material, and my favorite story from *Harkening* based on a childhood experience. (**This letter was sent by USPS. It would offer these materials on request if it had been sent using email.**)

I was impressed by your client list and hope you will consider representing my work. (**It would be better if you can be specific about the authors and titles on that client list.**)

Sincerely,
Carolyn Howard-Johnson

Sample query for a National Public Radio (NPR) interview.

This letter, printed with permission from Christine Louise Hohlbaum, got results! It got her a gig on National Public Radio. Notice the different thrust of this query from the one before. It focuses more on establishing expertise.

> Dear Ashlee: (**Note the friendly opening, the name correctly spelled.**)
> Experts across the board agree that the first four years of a child's life are crucial. These crucial years are a time when the essential groundwork is laid for a child's future: Language acquisition, social skills, and rapid brain development all take place during this time. (**Note that the author sets a professional tone, projects her expertise first thing.**)
> Parents are often so busy juggling career and family they find it challenging to give their children what they need, and sometimes

feel isolated, discouraged, and helpless. **(Here is a suggested consequence if parents don't take advantage of the author's expertise.)**

How can parents nurture their children while still maintaining their work lives? Despite how it may sometimes seem, children do not always need to be with their parents. In fact, they thrive even more when they are with a different number of trustworthy people: daycare workers, relatives, family friends, etc. Exposure to many different settings can enhance a child's growth, not hinder it. **(Here she suggests benefits for those who access her expertise; both benefits and consequences will be important for NPR's own audience.)**

A playgroup is a great way for toddlers to first experience life outside of the home. I'd like to suggest a show about how to develop a toddler/preschooler playgroup as an easy guide for parents and child care workers to follow. **(Ahhh. A specific angle!)**

I have led numerous playgroups over the past few years in several languages. With over 140 published articles on parenting and child-rearing, I have the expertise to discuss parenting issues with authority and clarity. My debut collection of short stories, *Diary of a Mother: Parenting Stories and Other Stuff*, has also been well-received by a breadth of readers. **(Here the author establishes her expertise with concrete credentials.)**

I look forward to hearing from you about my show suggestion, "How to Develop a Toddlers' Playgroup in Five Easy Steps." I will be in Virginia at the end of May for six weeks if you like your guests to appear at the station. **(And here, Hohlbaum takes care of business—everything that her gatekeeper needs to make an interview a reality.)**

Warm regards, (Hohlbaum's close is not overly formal or overly familiar.)

Christine Louise Hohlbaum

Christine Louise Hohlbaum generously allowed me to reprint this query letter for *The Frugal Book Promoter*. She is an American author of *Diary of a Mother: Parenting Stories and Other Stuff* living near Munich, Germany. When she is not writing, teaching, leading toddler playgroups, or wiping up messes, she likes to frolic in the Bavarian countryside. She is presently marketing a book called *The Power of Slow*.

Sample Query for Magazine or Newspaper Feature Stories

This is a letter I wrote that targets media that specialize in senior readers. Most are interested in stories by, about, or of interest to people over fifty-five. It was printed on a letterhead with complete contact information in the header and award logos in the footer.

> The Follies Footlighter (and address)
> Dear Ms. Casteix,
> What you at the Palm Springs Follies started is rather like a film of falling dominoes run in reverse—one domino after the other standing and marching into their older years with pride and gusto. (**Here the letter establishes a connection to the theater's demographic.**)
> I attended your Follies many times when I lived in Palm Springs and owned a business there (Carlan's Fine Gifts in the Palm Desert Mall). In fact, it inspired me to begin writing a novel at the age most are contemplating retirement. (**Here the letter establishes a local connection as well as a connection because of age.**)
> It is amazing to have one's first novel published at sixty-two, but I think my story is typical of aging America in this millennium and I know you agree. We are not aging. We are rarifying.
> Today as we approach fifty, we may have what was once a full lifetime to do something else. Start a new career. Fight intolerance. Help raise a grandchild. You name it. I have done or am planning to do all those things.
> My first novel, *This Is the Place*, is set in Utah. That state is surely in the news. The 2002 Winter Olympics. Polygamy. Bombings on Temple Square. There was even a cover story on genealogy in *Time* magazine last year. My love of genealogy was one of the inspirations for my book. (**Here the letter establishes a connection with current events.**)
> The media find it interesting that I started a new career at an age that many are considering retirement. In February, the *Los Angeles Daily News* ran a story on me and I was also interviewed by a Los Angeles TV station. (**Here the letter establishes credibility.**)
> If you need more information, find a picture, a bio, and the first chapters and prologue to *This Is the Place* by going to: bit.ly/WebPage4TITP
> I am enclosing a first-person essay and a headshot in case you can find room for me on the pages of your *Follies Footlighter*. If I can do anything else to help you or we can work together in some other way, please let me know. (**Here I tell my contact exactly what I want, but appear open to other possibilities.**)
>
> Thank you for your time and consideration.
> Sincerely,
> Carolyn Howard-Johnson

Appendix 2

Sample Media Release

When you send a release by post, use quality 8-½ x 11 inch plain white paper (USA/CAN) or A4 paper (elsewhere). It should be no more than one page. Use Times New Roman font for print and Verdana for releases posted online. When you email a release, use "Media Release: (subject of release here)" in the subject line, not "Press Release," please!

Tailor the title of your release to intrigue the media segment you feel will be most interested in your news.

When you send your release by email, use active links to your resources so your contact can click through to them easily. Because website links won't be active when you send your release by post, underlines are superfluous. Remove them to unclutter your copy.

At the end of your release, insert three pound signs. Your pound sign closure will be followed by a prompt to ask for support materials and will look something like this:

###

Support materials and a media release are available on request.

See several sample releases used for different kinds of promotion on the following pages.

–∞–

Sample media release for an event

MEDIA RELEASE

Library Contact: Chuck Wikes,
Glendale Public Library Event Coordinator
Phone: XX
Email: XX
For Immediate Release

**Lecture Series Offers
Three Faces of Tolerance**

Glendale, CA—Three authors known for their stand against intolerance will be guests of the Friends of the Glendale Public Library Wednesday, March 5, at 7 p.m. at the library's central branch auditorium. The theme for the evening is "Three Faces of Tolerance."

Carolyn Howard-Johnson is the author of two award-winning literary books, *This Is the Place* and *Harkening: A Collection of Stories Remembered*. Both explore the corrosive nature of subtle intolerance. Dr. Alicia Ghiragossian is an internationally known poet who was nominated for the Nobel Prize. Of Armenian descent, she often writes of the Armenian Genocide. Stephen Veres' memoir, *A Light in the Distance*, tells his story of survival and triumph at the beginning of WWII in Budapest, Hungary.

Library Events Coordinator Chuck Wike is pleased that "these three exceptional local authors will discuss the intercultural challenges that face our community." Howard-Johnson and Ghiragossian are residents of Glendale and Veres lives in Burbank.

The event is cosponsored by the Glendale Human Relations Coalition.

Howard-Johnson's poetry and short stories appear frequently in literary journals and anthologies and she has appeared on TV and hundreds of radio stations nationwide. She also teaches classes for UCLA Extension's renowned Writers' Program.

Learn more at http://howtodoitfrugally.com.

###

Media kits, headshots, and other support are
available upon request.

Sample Media Release for the Publication of a Book

With hundreds of thousands of books released each year, it is no longer news that a book has been published. You must hook your releases to the bandwagons of current news—political, technical, business, health, fashion—anything, really, that's being covered by news outlets in the moment. Or you might create news of your own. You might have developed a new genre, founded a critique group for your city's library, or instituted a scholarship for writers.

I am including this sample release because many first-time authors have trouble analyzing their own work for news angles. This one tells little stories about the authors that fit with media interest in globalization, the World Wide Web, and social networking.

> Note: This release is longer than most. Rules are made to be broken, but to fit the one-page rule, this release could be broken into several separate releases—one covering the Smashwords angle, one on the tradition of chapbooks, or one on the idea of small books of poetry as inexpensive greeting cards. These releases with different focuses could then be sent two to four weeks apart.

MEDIA RELEASE
CONTACT: Carolyn Howard-Johnson
Email: HoJoNews@aol.com
Phone: XX

CONTACT: Magdalena Ball
Email: maggieball@compulsivereader.com
Phone: XX
Website: http://howtodoitfrugally.com

For Immediate Release

**Poets Digitize Towards
Deeper Understanding**

World Wide Web—Award-winning poetry partners Carolyn Howard-Johnson and Magdalena Ball live on different continents. In different hemispheres.

That hasn't stopped them from collaborating on a series of poetry chapbooks designed to replace trite greeting cards with real sentiment. With their Celebration Series, the two have developed a new concept for inexpensive seasonal gifts.

Find their other chapbooks of poetry including *Cherished Pulse* (for anyone you love) with artwork from California artist Vicki Thomas at bit.ly/CherishedPulse; *She Wore Emerald Then* (for mothers on your gift list) with photographs by North Carolinian May

Lattanzio at bit.ly/MothersDayKind; *Imagining the Future* (for Father's Day) at bit.ly/Imaginings; *Blooming Red* (a Christmas chapbook) at bit.ly/BloomingRed; and a full book for Earth Day, *Sublime Planet* at bit.ly/SublimePlanet with all proceeds going to the World Wildlife Fund.

Chapbooks have been a tradition in the poetry world since Elizabethan times. The Celebration Series goes beyond the clichéd sentiments in most greeting cards—and does it for about the same price.

Now they're available even less expensively as eBooks on the high profile Smashwords.com site. Smashwords' unique technology allows the work to be available in every format used by millions of new eBook readers flooding the market. Even as hardware and software change, the author's words remain available to readers. This is a revolution for Ball and Howard-Johnson, both of whom started their writing careers when the latest technology was a typewriter and carbon paper for copies.

Magdalena Ball runs the highly respected compulsivereader.com review site. She is the author of the poetry book *Repulsion Thrust*, published in December 2009 to unanimous five-star reviews. Her novel *Sleep Before Evening*, published in 2007, was a Next Generation Indie Book Award finalist.

Carolyn Howard-Johnson's poetry appears frequently in review journals. She is listed in *Poets & Writers* and her chapbook of poetry, *Tracings* (bit.ly/CarolynsTracings), was given the Award of Excellence by the Military Writers Society of America. She is also an award-winning novelist and short story writer and instructor for UCLA Extension Writers' Program.

For more information on any of the chapbooks in this poetry series, contact either author or visit media rooms at howtodoitfrugally.com/poetry_books.htm or magdalenaball.com.

###

Support material available digitally or by post on request.

Appendix 3

Sample Blog Entry

I gave you lots of ideas for blog posts in Chapter Twenty-One on blogging, but here's another one that L. Diane Wolfe, author of *Overcoming Obstacles with Spunk: The Keys to Leadership and Goal Setting*, came up with for Valentine's Day. All blog visitors are readers of one kind or another, so she gave them Valentine gift ideas for storing their hardcopy books and media collections. Of course, she included images and links to where her visitors could buy them. Notice how she editorialized to bring her own personality to the post.

Wood Bookcase / Display Cabinet— The unique design of this bookcase gives you the option of positioning it vertically or horizontally. Is that not cool?

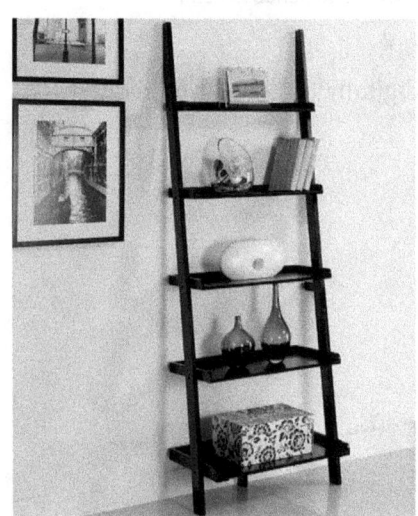

Walnut Five-tier Ladder Shelf— I've always wanted one of these. And a house with that much wall space...

Coffee Bean Book Case/Display Cabinet—This one is just too cute for words! Yes, I have a thing about bookshelves. One can never have too many.

And where's the best place to read but in a comfy hammock. **Hand-woven 'Cool Lagoon' Hammock (Mexico).** I really liked this one. I'll take the house it's in, too!

L. Diane Wolfe has several blogs including circleoffriendsbooks.blogspot.com. She graciously gave me permission to choose at random and reprint selectively from one of her posts.

Appendix 4

Sample Invitation For Tradeshow Appearance

This is the invitation I sent to anyone on my contact list I thought might attend BookExpo America. That included authors, publishers, agents, book publicists, reviewers, those who blog on the publishing industry, librarians, and the media.

USA Book News Awards
cordially invites you to BookExpo America to meet

Carolyn Howard-Johnson
Author of
The Frugal Editor: Put Your Best Book Forward to Avoid Humiliation and Ensure Success

The winner of our 2008 award for
Best Book in the Publishing Category,
she will sign free copies
Friday May 30
from 11 to 11:30
Booth Numbers 835 and 837
PMA Pavilion

Please drop by to chat or to
arrange an interview or event.

The Frugal Editor is also the winner of the
Literary Reviews Award
and the
New Generation Indie Award for Marketing

Make reservations for BEA at: bookexpoamerica.com.
Learn more about the author and her award-winning
HowToDoItFrugally Series of books at
howtodoitfrugally.com.

The Frugal Book Promoter, first in the
HowToDoItFrugally Series, is also a USA Book News
Award winner and a winner of the Irwin Award given for
its outstanding publicity campaign.

Those who came by the USA Book News booth were given copies of participating authors' award-winning books. We also asked visitors to sign our guestbooks. We didn't want to lose a single name because people who attend these tradeshows are publishing industry professionals who can help authors get greater readership for their books.

Appendix 5

Sample Script for Phone Pitch

Here is how Raleigh Pinskey, a seasoned publicity expert, pitches the media by phone. She incorporates elements of a formal, written pitch. It seems long, but if you rehearse Raleigh's script out loud, it moves along so quickly it feels like three or four lines:

> Hello, I'm the author of *101 Ways to Promote Yourself: Tricks of the Trade to Take Charge of Your Own Success.* The book is published by Harper Collins/Quill and has sold close to 100,000 copies. (**Note how she establishes credibility.**)
>
> I show your audience how they can get more than just those fifteen minutes of fame plus money-making tips, and ways they can be a household name, online and offline, locally or globally. (**Here Raleigh lists benefits. Learn more about them by looking up "pitches" in the Index of this book.**)
>
> I've been helping business people to fame and fortune for twenty-five years. I've worked with Sting, McCartney, Blondie, KISS, *Chicken Soup for the Soul*, Fit for Life Solution, and hundreds of mouse and mortar businesses. (**Here she tosses in more credibility plus some razzle-dazzle.**)
>
> My name is Raleigh Pinskey and I would love to be a guest on your show so both of us can help take the members of your audience to their next level of success. (**Notice how she asks for exactly what she wants.**)

Raleigh told me, "I wait until the end to say my name because it's not important until they want to book me. Why take the chance of losing their interest in the beginning with unimportant information and small talk? I go right to the chase."

You may or may not yet have the glitzy platform that Raleigh has. Use what you have and what is appropriate. Some of your credentials may be vocation oriented. You'll gather more as you become more acclaimed.

~Raleigh Pinsky is a well known publicist who regularly books clients on national TV. She gave me permission to share her telephone script with my readers. Learn more about her at PromoteYourself.com.

Appendix 6

Automated E-Mail Signature

Automated email signatures are good little helpmates. Having one saves *you* time and gives your contacts the information they need so they don't waste *their* time. I break some of my own rules about the length of autosignatures because I like to give my readers access to as many of the free resources I provide for writers. I'm also trying to set an example that being shy about accomplishments is counterproductive to the health of your book. This is a signature I used soon after the first edition of this book was published. The banner was a gift from publisher Nancy Cleary who clearly knows the importance of thank-you notes.

> **Hint:** Though it is a function of email services to include the originating email address, I still include it in my signature as a service to those who copy and paste addresses to their contact files. By doing so, I make their copy and paste a one-step process. It is an example of how important it is to do whatever we can to respect the time and needs of our contacts.

> **Caveat:** Some email services and susceptible business put up their little algorithm antennae for spam if you use too many links in your signature, so adjust your signature accordingly for mail to large corporations, universities, law firms and others who may be super cautious about viruses.

I have streamlined my signature in recent years, but here's what my first email signature looked like (see following page):

Carolyn Howard-Johnson
Instructor for the renowned UCLA Extension Writers' Program
Website: http://www.HowToDoItFrugally.com
Amazon Profile: http://bit.ly/CarolynsAmznProfile
Email: HoJoNews@aol.com

Award-winning author of the *HowToDoItFrugally Series* **of Books for writers, including USA Book News award winners**
The Frugal Editor http://bit.ly/FrugalEditorKind
The Frugal Book Promoter http://bit.ly/FrugalBookPromo
The Great First Impression Book Proposal http://bit.ly/BookProposals
Great Little Last-Minute Edits: http://bit.ly/Last-MinuteEdting

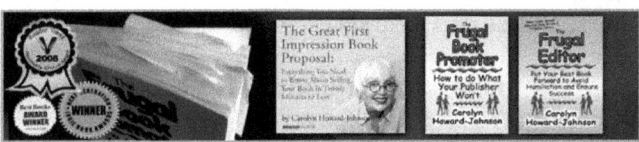

Banner courtesy of Nancy Cleary

Networking:
LinkedIn: http://www.linkedin.com/in/carolynhowardjohnson
Twitter: http://www.twitter.com/frugalbookpromo
Facebook: http://www.facebook.com/carolynhowardjohnson

Blogs for Writers:
http://www.SharingwithWriters.blogspot.com
http://TheNewBookReview.blogspot.com
http://www.TheFrugalEditor.blogspot.com

Long, short, fancy or simple. The choice is yours, but the purposed is to be considerate of your email recipient, to make any further research as easy on him or her as possible.

Appendix 7

Sample Tip Sheet

Tip sheets are one of the items authors include in their media kits to help them get free ink or publicity. See Section III in this book for more on media kits and tip sheets. This tip sheet is a quick list of marketing tips for authors. Notice that a tip sheet can be teaser that doesn't provide all the answers.

One Dozen Publicity No-Nos
or
How to Avoid Being a PR Numbskull

1. Don't assume your publisher will publicize for you.
2. Don't publicize your book. Brand yourself instead.
3. Don't ask an editor, producer, or host for publicity. They are not in business to do favors for you.
4. Don't send a publicity or a news release. Professionals use the term "media release."
5. Don't send material to media professionals who have been dead for over a year or were fired for showing preferential treatment to friends.
6. Don't always avoid controversy. It may be your prescription for getting noticed.
7. Don't discard the word "ethics" from your campaign.
8. Don't pretend those who visit your website are only there to purchase your book.
9. Don't depend only on emails and faxes to get the word out to editors and booksellers.
10. Don't toss your marketing how-to books into your Goodwill bag once your book has been launched. You will need them.
11. Don't treat your writing career as if it were a hobby.
12. Don't believe everything you read on the web about publicizing books (or writing them!). Consider the source and check credentials.

About the Author

Carolyn Howard-Johnson's several careers prepared her for promoting her own and others' books. She was the youngest person ever hired as a staff writer for the *Salt Lake Tribune*—"A Great Pulitzer Prize Winning Newspaper." Writing features for the society page and a column under the name of Debra Paige gave her insight into the needs of editors, the very people authors must work with to get free ink. Being familiar with the way news is handled helps her see how different books fit into different news cycles.

Later, in New York, she was an editorial assistant at *Good Housekeeping* magazine. She also handled accounts for fashion publicist Eleanor Lambert who instituted the first Ten Best Dressed List. There she wrote media releases (then called press releases) for celebrity designers of the day, including Christian Dior, and produced photo shoots for Lambert's clients.

She also worked as columnist, reviewer, and staff writer for *the Pasadena Star-News, Home Décor Buyer*, the *Glendale News-Press* (an affiliate of the *LA Times),* MyShelf.com where she has written a "Back to Literature" column for more than two decades and others. She learned marketing skills both in college (University of Utah, Arizona State University, and University of Southern California) and as founder and operator of a chain of retail stores including the signature gift shop at Santa Anita Racetrack. That shaped her understanding of how authors might best partner with retailers to affect both of their bottom lines.

Carolyn's experience in journalism and as a poet and author of fiction and nonfiction helped the multi award-winning author understand how different genres can be marketed more effectively. She was an instructor for UCLA Extension's renowned Writers' Program for nearly a decade and earned a certificate from that same school's Instructor Development Program. She also studied writing at Cambridge University, United Kingdom; Herzen University in St. Petersburg, Russia; and Charles University in Prague.

She turned her knowledge toward helping other writers with her multi award-winning *HowToDoItFrugally Series* of books for writers, including her flagship book *The Frugal Book Promoter* and her favorite, *How to Get Great Book Reviews Frugally and Ethically*. Her marketing campaign for the second book in that series, *The Frugal Editor* won the Next Generation Indie Best Book Award. She also has a multi award-winning series of *HowToDoItFrugally* books for retailers.

Howard-Johnson was honored as Woman of the Year in Arts and Entertainment by California Legislature members Carol Liu, Dario Frommer, and Jack Scott. She received her community's Character and Ethics award for her work promoting tolerance with her writing and the Diamond Award in Arts and Culture from her community's Library and Arts and Culture Commission. She was named to *Pasadena Weekly's* list of fourteen women of "San Gabriel Valley women who make life happen" and Delta Gamma, a national fraternity of women, honored her with their Oxford Award.

Carolyn is a popular presenter at tradeshows (retail and writing) and writers' conferences and has lost count of her radio show guest spots. She is an actor and has appeared in TV commercials for the likes of Time-Life CDs, Chinet, Blue Shield, Apple, and Disney Cruise Lines (Japan).

Born and raised in Utah, Howard-Johnson raised her own family in sunny Southern California.

Author Photo by Uriah Carr

Bibliography

Sharing Influences and Inspiration with Readers

This bibliography is list of books that have influenced this book in one way or another. It's a list of motivators. A list of influencers. A list of books I love. Because my writing (including this third edition of *The Frugal Book Promoter)* was "researched" by life and experience, the word "references" isn't quite right, and "bibliography" might mislead, too. This book and this list is really the product of life—everything from classes I've taken, the needs and ideas of students I've taught, my job experience, travel and, yes, books that help keep me updated on the publishing industry.

A few of these books are recently published books as one would expect from a bibliography, but most are great oldies. I make no apologies for the latter because, though the publishing industry has grown more quickly than it ever did with the exception of the time after Gutenberg, it is still quite traditional. Some complain that it is reluctant to change in ways that would benefit it most! For me the important thing about writing—the heart of writing—changes barely at all.

That's true of marketing, too. Tried and true techniques get altered and reapplied to new models offered up by new times and technology. Some of my choices for this list have been around a long time, but you may also notice that some reflect a my long journey from early jobs in journalism and publicity, a career in retailing, and an education that spans schools from Utah to California and across oceans and continents. I've taken test runs at teaching everything from middle school to UCLA, too. I am amazed at how many skills in each industry have informed how I approach the publishing industry—everything from copywriting to editing.

The Writing Life

Influential books for writers are often about the writing life, but I am amazed at how few new writers have read one. I never tire of them for inspiration and motivation. You'll see a familiar theme here. They never grow old. Some of my favorites like Carolyn See's is one of those. She was the mother of the talented novelist Lisa See whose *Snow Flower and the Secret Fan* is one of my favorite novels. Here is a short list of "writing life" books including See's:

See, C. (2003). *Making a literary life: Advice for writers and other dreamers.* New York: Random House

Lamott, Anne. 2015. *Bird by bird: some instructions on writing and life*. https://www.amazon.com/dp/0385480016.

King, S. (2014). *On writing: A memoir of the craft*. New York: Scribner.

Berg, E. (2012). *Escaping Into the Open: The Art of Writing True*. New York: HarperCollins.

Craft and Grammar

When my clients and students have trouble with plot structure and characters, I refer them to the master, Joseph Campbell. He is there to help any writer from classicists to playwrights to the most with-it young writers of fantasy and other imaginative genres. Start with *Hero with a Thousand Faces* (bit.ly/JosephWriting) and branch out to everything he has done in print and on TV. "Universal" is the perfect adjective used to describe the help his works give to both writers and readers.

When I found new authors among my clients who needed lots of help with... well, everything, I determined to write a book on dialogue including punctuation, characterization, natural voices... everything associated with that aspect of fiction. I began to research a book *Writer's Digest* featured in their book club for authors. It was so good—so complete—I knew there was no point in reinventing the wheel (by the way, dialogue isn't just for fiction writers these days!)

Campbell, J. (2008). *The hero with a thousand faces*. Novato, Calif: New World Library.

Chiarella, T. 2007. *Writing dialogue*. Cincinnati, Ohio: Story Press (bit.ly/Chiarella).

I also love this book—maybe something Campbell would have written had he lived even longer--for the light it sheds on the activity many of us writers take for granted:

Cron, L. (2013). *Wired for story: The writer's guide to using brain science to hook readers from the very first sentence*. New York: Ten Speed Press (bit.ly/Wired4Story).

Words that Work is, at its core, a lesson in the power of words, but it is also a lesson in avoiding something that may be of value because of bias against some part of creator's life, say race, gender ...or politics.

Luntz, F. I., & Soundview Executive Book Summaries. (2007). *Words that work: It's not what you say, it's what people hear*. Concordville, Pa..: Soundview Executive Book Summaries (bit.ly/FrankLuntz).

I have used this reference for years in a much earlier edition and continue to add notes of my own to available white space when I am traveling or visiting museums:

Grambs, D. (2018). *The describer's dictionary: A treasury of terms and literary quotations.* New York: W.W. Norton and company (bit.ly/DescribersDict).

An entire series of grammar books may change the way you think of language, grammar, and style choice forever more. Here are some starters from June Casagrande:

Casagrande, J. (2014). *The best punctuation book, period: A comprehensive guide for every writer, editor, student, and businessperson.* New York: Ten Speed Press (bit.ly/PunctuationBook).

But to fall in love with June, read this one first:

Casagrande, J. & Frasier, S. (2014). *Grammar snobs are great big meanies: A guide to language for fun & spite.* Penguin. In audio and paperback (bit.ly/GrammarSnobs).

I don't recommend books on grammar that forget language and grammar are flexible and confuse grammar "rules" with "style choices," even unintentionally. Beware. There are a lot of them out there!

Promotion, Marketing

Anderson, C. (2010). *Free: the future of a radical price.* London, Random House Business (bit.ly/RadicalPrice).

Judith Briles often writes books on seldom-covered resources for marketing and publishing books like this one (and click on the link on her name to take you to her Amazon profile that lists all of her books)

Briles, J. (2015). *The CrowdFunding guide for authors & writers: Get free money to finance your book* (bit.ly/BrilesFunding).

I met the author of this book when we were both presenting at one of my favorite writers' conferences, the Erma Bombeck Humor Writers Conference at Dayton University (humorwriters.org), *1001 Ways* was still in its first edition. He called it a "doorstop!" It *is* really fat! Now in its sixth edition, it is a perfect overview of marketing ideas, especially for newly published authors.

Kremer, J. (2006). *1001 ways to market your books: for authors and publishers: includes over 100 special marketing tips just for authors.* Fairfield, Iowa: Open Horizons (bit.ly/JKremer).

Penny Sansevieri is both a writer and publicist. That "writing" part gives her an edge in understanding writers' needs.

Sansevieri, P.C. (2012). *52 ways to sell more books!*. Tucson, AZ: Wheatmark Inc. (bit.ly/Pennys52Ways).

Terry Whalin has a similar edge because he is both an *agent* and writer.

Whalin, T. (2015). *Jumpstart your publishing dreams: insider secrets to skyrocket your success*. New York: Morgan James Publishing.

Publishing

The author of this book is founder and President of Nonfiction Authors Association:

Chandler, S., & Palachuk, K.W. 2018. *The nonfiction book publishing plan: the professional guide to profitable self-publishing* (bit.ly/PubPlan).

I finally stopped telling my clients to read the many wonderful books out there on book proposals as a time- and money-saving way to accommodate agents and publishers because none of them wanted to spend the time required to do it. They preferred to pay me to do it for them. That's when I put together a little booklet that teaches writers to do it themselves in less time than it takes to write a blurb: *The Great First-Impression Book Proposal* is available on Amazon for about $6. and the e-version is free if you are a prime member. (bit.ly/BookProposals). Why should authors write their own when they can afford an expert? Because no one has more passion for their book than the author herself. And no one should have to pay someone else to do it—especially when that someone couldn't possibly do it as well.

Free Press

Once the youngest person hired as a staff writer at *The Salt Lake Tribune*, I am an avid free press, ethical journalism, and separation of church-and-state advocate. The author of this rather esoteric book about free press was one of my fellow high school journalism staff members at the amazing *Olympus High Thunderbolt*!:

Ure, J. W. (2018). *Stop the press: How the Mormon Church tried to silence the Salt Lake Tribune* (bit.ly/StopthePress).

Subscribe to PEN America's free newsletter (PEN.org) to keep you up-do-date on the state of the free press worldwide, a topic that should interest—concern—anyone who writes for fun or profit. This organization "stands at the intersection of literature and human rights to …defend free expression, support persecuted writers, and promote literary culture." Check the grants they offer, too, often with no application fee. C. Hope Clark's fundsforwriters.com is a *Writer's Digest* 100 Top Website that focuses on grants, too.

Teaching, ESL, Immigrant, Tutoring, Accent Reduction, Speaking

Writers in many genres find teaching and speaking one the best ways to supplement their incomes, increase readership, and find more satisfaction as writers. In fact, poets find teaching and public readings the best way to support their careers. UCLA's Writers' Program encourages all their instructors to take advanced classes (at no cost) from their "master instructors." That's how I found my love of speaking, how I was lead to take Pamela Kelly's class on speaking three times, and how I learned to love teaching a lot more on my third attempt than my first.

Kelly, P. G. (2007). *Speak with passion, speak with power!: Transform inexperience and the fear of public speaking into energy, know-how and results!*. Long Beach, CA: Onward and Upward Publishing (bit.ly/PowerfulSpeaking).

I use the English edition of the next book (It is also available in Simplified Chinese and Ukrainian) for my tutoring. It does a great job of introducing acceptable basics of English/American literature and speaks to ESL students in the vernacular:

Johnson, L. (2012). *What foreigners need to know about America from A to Z: Book 2 of 4*. Los Angeles, Calif: A to Z Publishing (amzn.to/ForeignersAmericaUS).

References

Anderson, C. (2010). *Free: The future of a radical price*. London: Random House Business.

Amir, N., & Friedlander, J. (2015). *How to blog a book: Write, publish, and promote your work one post at a time*. Cincinnati, OH: Writer's Digest Books.

Bacon's Information, Inc., & Cision (Firm). (1993). *Bacon's newspaper directory: Directory of daily and weekly newspapers news services syndicates*. Chicago, Ill: Bacon's Information Inc.

Baggott, C. (2015). *Email marketing by the numbers*. New York: John Wiley & Sons.

Ball, M. (2004). *The art of assessment: How to review anything*. Milton, Qld: Mountain Mist Productions.

Casagrande, J. (2010). *It was the best of sentences, it was the worst of sentences: A writer's guide to crafting killer sentences*. Berkeley, CA: Ten Speed Press.

Evans, T. M. (2005). *Literary law guide for authors: Copyright, trademark, and contract in plain language*. Philadelphia, PA: FYOS Entertainment.

Fry, P. L. (2011). *Promote your book: Over 250 proven, low-cost tips and techniques for the enterprising author*. New York: Allworth Press.

King, S. (2014). *On writing: A memoir of the craft*. New York: Scribner.

Kremer, J. (1998). *1001 ways to market your books: For authors and publishers*. Fairfield, IA: Open Horizons.

Levinson, J. C., & Lautenslager, A. (2014). *Guerilla marketing in 30 days*. Irvine, CA: Entrepreneur Press.

Pinskey, R. (2003). *101 ways to promote yourself: Tricks of the trade for taking charge of your own success*. New York: Quill.

Rogers, B. H. (2002). *Word work: Surviving and thriving as a writer*. Montpelier, VT: Invisible Cities Press.

See, C. (2013). *Making a literary life: Advice for writers and other dreamers*. New York: Random House.

Seidman, D. (2002). *The death of 20th century selling: 50 hilarious sales blunders and how you can profit from them*. Barrington, IL: Sales Autopsy Press.

Silverman, F. (2009). *Talk radio wants you*. Jefferson, NC: McFarland and Company Inc.

Thornton, M. (2000). *Fear of writing.* Ranchos de Taos, NM: Word Nerd Press.

Wolfe, L. D. (2009). *Overcoming obstacles with spunk!: The keys to leadership & goal-setting.* Fremont, N.C: Dancing Lemur Press.

Zinsser, W. (2013). *On writing well.* Harper Paperbacks. New York: Harper Hardbacks.

Index

#
#bookbigotry, 108

1
101 Ways to Promote Yourself, 249

9
99 Cent Stores, 230

A
About-the-Author (media kit), 45, 79, 80–81, 86, 92
academia, 5, 9
Academy Awards, 214
adjectives
  avoid, 52, 73, 96
Advance Review (Reader) Copies. *See* ARCs
advances, 14, 20, 63, 99
adverbs, 52
advertising, 13–16, 41–42, 106
  evaluation, 33
  Facebook, 201
  for presenters, 150
  Google Adwords, 231
  LA Times book fair, 151
  vs. blogging, 190
  vs. branding, 37
  vs. publicity, 35
advertorial, 42
AdWords, Google, 231
Aesop (quote), 56
Against All Enemies, 55
agent, 4–8, 14, 27, 31, 72
  and awards, 82
  ARC info, 103
  finding, 137, 140–41, 183, 186
  finding a celebrity via, 47
  pitching, 53–54
  query letter, 95, 236–37
agents
  foreign rights, 147
Alignable.com, 214
Allen, M.A. (author), 127
Amazon. *See* also GoodReads and Kindle
  bestseller status, 163
  blurb limit, 9, 192
  carousels, 202
  KDP for ARCs, 102
  linking, 59, 127, 181
  Matchbook, 126
  publishing with, 128
  reviews, 104, 107, 108
  selling on, 192–97
  unscrupulous behavior, 23
  Vine reviews, 231
Ambrose, S. (author), 5
American Association of School Libraries, 147
American Book Review, 103
American Express lists, 173, 219
Anderson, C. (author), 30, 257
Andrews McMeel Publishing, 122
anecdotes, 86, 116
anonymous, 4, 170
anthologies, 60, 86, 115, 126, 241
  academic, 8
  writing for, 121–22
Antion, T., 132, *See* also Speaking
aoundbites, 49
AP, 116
appearances page (media kit), 82, 85
ARCs, 88, 99–110
  and tradeshows, 148
Arizona State University, 253
article banks, 115
articles, 8, 113
  advertorial, 42
  and platform, 16
  and taglines, 44
  copyright, 115
  free, 73, 114, 117, 162
  nonfiction, 115
  partners, 31

pitching, 55
publishing contacts, 183
recycling, 43, 119, 167, 190
syndication, 116
Asimov, I. (quote), 111
Associated Press, 116
Atlantic Review, 114
attachments, 6
avoiding, 47, 76, 106, 117
Authors Den, 177
Authors Guild, 47
authorsbroadcast.com, 174
autograph
bookmarks, 232
bookplates, 156
stickers, 156
automailers, 230–31
autoresponder, 127, 182–83
autosignature, 180–81, 188, 250,
See also email signature
Autry Museum of Western
Heritage, 159
avatar, 181
defined, 200
Avery label, 207
awards, 62, 135–39, 148, 153, 178,
203
anthologies, 122
as news, 32, 72
logo, 239
awards page (media kit), 79, 82, 92

B

B & N, 107, 120, 198
baby steps, 10–11, 12
back cover, 53, 80, 196
blurbs, 46
teasers, 51
Bacon's Directories, 67, 104, 116,
172
Baggott, C., 182
Ball, M. (author), 15, 59, 120, 242
banners, 49, 138, 153
for email, 180, 250
for websites, 39, 88
barcode, 233
Barnes & Noble. *See* B & N
barter, 7, 114, 230
Bartlett's Familiar Quotations, 223
BEA, 60, 91, 119, 145, 146, 148,
247
beejeebees, 49, 50, 51

benefits, 50, 57, 75
vs. consequences, 50
bestseller lists, 3, 10, 63, 99, 188,
195, 198
bestseller status, 23, 163
Bezos, J. (amazon), 194
biography, 44–45, 71, 80–81, 193,
237
mini, 8
unofficial, 9
Wikipedia, 203
blog, 54–58, 60, 61, 100, 105, 114,
115–18, 119, 120, 128, 168
as website, 177–80
book reviews, 84
interviews, 85
review, 107–8
tour, 105, 160, 162–63
tours, 20
blogger.com, 186
bloggers, 54, 95, 100, 116, 118,
149, 162, 167, 186–92
blogspot.com, 186
BlogTalkRadio, 167
Blooming Red, 243
blurbs, 9, 44–49, 83, 107, 108, 109,
128, 135, 178, 192, 196, 220,
221, 230, 237
book fair, 15, 32, 49, 73, 145, 149–
53, 174, 209, 211
booths, 149
book launch, 10, 32, 56, 58, 67, 74,
131, 163
Book Publicists of Southern
California, 148
bookcover, 31, 39, 48, 88, 90, 92,
108, 132, 138, 150, 152, 156,
162, 171, 180, 200, 211, 219,
220
BookExpo America. *See* BEA
Booklist (ALA), 103
bookmarks, 39, 88, 90, 122, 127,
143, 155, 218
bookpage.com, 104
bookpleasures.com, 104, 120
bookstore, 7, 50, 72, 145, 151,
154–58
brick and mortar, 106
buyers, 99, 107, 146
event directors, 87, 137
online, 4, 9, 23, 119, 188, 192–
97

The Frugal Book Promoter

publicity, 20
signing, 122
boomers, 31
Bowerman, P., 179
Boyle, T.C., 155
Bracale, E., 233
branding, v, vi, 8, 10, 13, 15, 16, 27, 28, 35, 37–40, 44, 49, 58, 81, 95, 114, 122, 155, 177, 186, 187, 193, 196, 223
Brasch, W., 73
British Broadcasting Company (BBC), 173
Brown, M., 32, *See also* contests
Brown, R., 62
budget, vi, 14, 20, 27, 40, 41, 63, 90, 105, 126, 146, 160, 162, 163, 221
bulk mail, 220, 221
bullets, 46, 51
  media release, 74
Bunin, P., 116
Bush, L., 146, *See also* book fair
business card, 37, 48, 53, 58, 88, 122, 138, 153, 157, 230, 233
  media kit, 92
  vs. bookmarks, 90
Butler, S., 168
byline, 8, 45, 84, 86, 87, 114, 117, 118, 119, 120, 123, 124
Byrne, R., 227
Byron (quote), 99

C

CafePress.com, 90
Caldecott medal, 138
calendars, 77, 119, 132, 155, 161, 208, 233
  newspaper, 161
California Library Association, 147
Cambridge University, 253
campaign, 14, 15, 19–22, 23, 24, 27, 41, 42, 46, 51, 57, 58, 59–62, 65, 87, 88, 99, 102, 103, 111, 114, 121, 122, 147, 150, 158, 177, 179, 182, 187, 197, 221, 247, 252, 254
  and relationships, v
Campbell, J., 4, 256
Caram, E.L., 11

career, writing, vii, 3–5, 10, 13–17, 23, 27–28, 38, 43, 65, 79, 80, 136
Carr, U., iii
Cartwright, G., 201
Casagrande, J., 11, 257, 261
Cassino, D., 23, 163, 195
catalogs, 209–12
  Catalog of Catalogs, 211
  cooperative, 149, 211
  gift, 109
CBS. *See* radio and TV
CDs, 149, 254
Celebration Series, 59, 242, 243
charity, 20, 32, 46, 70, 122, 133, 150, 159, 163, 172, 173
Charles University, 253
Cherished Pulse, 59
Chicago Tribune Books, 103
Chicken Soup for the Soul, 249
Christmas Cookies Are for Giving, 74, 75
chyrons, 171
CircleOfFriends blog, 245
Cision, 67, 104, 116, 172, *See also* Bacon's Directories
Citizen, The, 127
Clark, C.H., 118, 201, 259
Clarke, R., 55
classes, v, 4, 11, 15, 40, 60, 132, 133, 138, 140, 142, 227, 230, 241, 255, 259
  how-to, free, 173
Cleary, N., 250, 251
clichés, 81, 243
Clinton, W., 43
clips, 33, 116, 173
  defined, 8
coauthor, 15, 125
Coca-Cola, 28, 38, 39, 49
college public information office, 169
columns, 46, 115–18, 123, 127, 134
CompulsiveReader.com, 104
conferences, writers, 7, 43, 60, 72, 138, 257
  online, 141
conjunctions, 70
consequences, 50–51, 75, 238, *See also* benefits
contact lists, 21, 59, 105, 148, 161, 211, 231

coding, 65–66
content management service (CMS), 186, See also blog
contents page (media kit), 79, 80
contests, 74, 122, 136, 137, 183, 191, 232
   fees, 32, 135
   gift baskets, 89
   literary, 135
   rigged, 135
controversial, 55, 169
Cooking by the Book, 126–28
copyright, 6, 102, 196, 214
   articles, 115
   fair use, 9, 192
   lawyers, 7
   ownership, 80
   poor man's, 6
   reviews, 107
cover letter. See query letter
Cox, B., 61
Crawford, J., iii, 122, 128
credentials, 19, 65, 71, 81, 82, 83, 96, 120, 134, 149, 172, 238, 249
   conference, 140, 142
   contests, 136
   publishing, 147
   speaking, 147
credibility, 14, 44, 66, 84, 107, 114, 116, 121, 131, 140, 148, 149, 173, 239, 249
credit lines, 8, 44, 79, 81, 84, 114, 201
criticism, 120, 134
   fair use, 9
critique groups, iii, 4, 5, 11, 106, 120, 131, 159, 199, 218, 242
critique partners, 100, 140
cross-promotion, 59, 60, 149, 183, 189, 230
CRWROPPS, 137
Cup of Comfort, A, 122

D

Dale Carnegie course, 83
database building, 31, 33, 66
dateline, 70
deadlines, 55, 100, 105, 116
Death of 20th Century Selling, 50
debate team, 83
DeSimone, C., iii, 139
dialogue, 53, 86, 139, 256

Diary of a Mother, 238
Dinyer, E., 122
Dior, C., 253
direct email marketing, 181
direct-mail promotions, 20
discounting books, 15, 91, 133, 151, 210, 213, 216
   Matchbook, 126
   remainders, 27, 50
   series, 127
display stand, 157
distribution of releases, 76–77, 137
distributors, 91, 138, 146, 148, 210, 231
domain name, 179
donate, 142, 151, 230
Doubleday, 108
drawings, 91
Dreyer, C., 99
Drucker, P. (quotation), 1
dustcovers, 44, 56, 57, 80, 81, 138

E

eBook, 59, 106, 136, 138, 188, 192, 234
   Amazon KDP, 194, 197
   anthology, 121
   as galley, 106
   free, 29, 44, 158–60, 133, 157, 178, 207
   Smashwords, 243
editing, 11, 72, 108, 223
   frugal, 139
editors, acquisitions, 135
   pitching, 236
education, programs, 142, 147
Effort and Surrender, 122
eHow.com, 115
ellipses, 48
email, 126, 209, 252
   attachments, 6, 47, 76, 93
   autoresponder, 182
   contacts, 62, 117, 157, 233
   credit line, 8, 44
   etiquette, 61, 168
   links, 72
   media release, 70, 76, 240
   merge, 66
   newsletters, 61
   promotions, 180–83
   query, 47, 95, 97, 106
   renting lists, 181

signature, 39, 48, 53, 137, 250
subject line, 73, 109
vs. postcards, 219
endorsements. *See* blurbs
Entertainment Weekly Magazine, 103
Eric Hoffer Award, 135
Ernest Hemingway First Novel Competition, 45, 136
ethics, 23–24, 252
  journalism, 109
  reviews, 196
evaluate, 33, 153
Evans, A., 232
Evans, M., 7
Evans, T.M., 9
event and program directors, 60, 87
excerpts, 8, 32, 45, 105, 113, 125, 126, 157
  autoresponder, 182
  fair use, 84, 192, 196
  permission, 109
  reading, 83
  reviews, 84
exclusives, 117, 118, 120
expertise, 14, 20, 39, 44, 48, 50, 54, 75, 87, 88, 116, 132, 143, 173, 229, 232, 237
  tip sheet, 80
experts, fellow, 80, 88
e-zines, 30, 61

F

Facebook, 52, 62, 117, 128, 171, 174, 183, 251
  advertising, 201
  banned, 204
  contest promotion, 230
fair use, 196
FAQ, 21, 85, 179
Faulkner, J., iii, 174
Faulkner, W., 45, 136
fax, 56
  media release, 76, 77
fear of marketing, 12
fear of rejection, 10, 135
fear of success, 10
fiction, vi, 52, 96, 103, 123, 124, 128, 139, 177, 201, 207, 214, 232
  and blogging, 191
  proposal, 54

fictionmarketing.com, 191
findgift.com, 213
first person, 85, 177
first person essay (media kit XE "media kits:first person essay"), 85–87
first person essay (media kit), 80
first person essay (media kit), 179
first person essay (media kit), 239
first rights. *See* copyright
First the Raven, 45
fliers, 53, 151, 155, 162, 218, 232
flipchart, 132
Follies Footlighter, 239
followup, 77
foreign rights, 146
Foreword Magazine, 104
forewords. *See* introductions
forewords, writing, 122
formatting, 82, 102, 108, 189
  Kindle, 125
Frankfurt Book Fair, 119, 146
Franklin Christoph fountain pens, 145
free, 29, 42, 44, 88, 120, 125, 136, 142, 178, 186, 199
  air time, 173
  blog, 52
  content, 8
  contest, 32
  ebook, 126–28
  event calendars, 155
  exposure, 16, 29, 79, 99, 109, 115, 117
  publicity, 35, 55
frequency, 33, 42, 72, 189
Frequently Asked Questions. *See* FAQ
Fresh Air (NPR), 174
Frommer, D., 254
Frugal Editor, The, 47, 52, 74, 97, 125, 139, 195, 236, 247, 251, 254
Fry, P., 30
Funds for Writers, 118
Future of a Radical Price, The, 30

G

galleys, 100, 104
Gannon, M., 120
GeBauer, P., iii

genre, 9, 10, 38, 50, 52, 59, 105, 118, 136
Ghiragossian, A., 241
Gibson, J. (photographer), 58
Gift Shop (magazine), 216
gifts (souvenir), 89–90
  logo, 90
  with purchase, 127
Glendale Community College, 169
Glendale Human Relations Coalition, 241
Glendale News-Press, 253
Glendale Public Library, 241
glossy, 57
Glück, L., 10
goals, 114, 118, 141, 152, 155, 173
GoDaddy, 117, 179
Gold, D., iii
Gompertz. R., iii, 35
Good Housekeeping *magazine*, 253
GoodReads, 120, 201
Goodwill stores, 217, 252
Goodwin, D.K., 5, 29
Google
  AdSense, 231
  AdWords, 231
  alerts, 61, 186, 234
  blogger, 186
  calendar, 155, 233
  groups, 52, 183
  keyword tool, 234
graphic designer, 139
grassroots, 1, 100, 117, 167
Great First Impression Book Proposal, The, 54, 215, 251
Great Little Last-Minute Edits, 251
Grisham, J., 159
Guerilla Marketing, iii, 30
guestbooks, 47, 248
Guideposts magazine, 86

H

Hall, D., 232
handouts, 132, 142, 211
  catalogs, 211
  recommenders, 133
  resources, 133
Harkening, 89, 236–37
Hartunian, P., 51
Harvard online bookstore, 197
Harvest Moon, 129
headlines, 33, 49, 70, 73

headshot, 57, 90, 92, 200, 239, *See also* photos
hecklers, 134–35
Heebner, E., iii
Hein, L., 151
Hemingway, E., 45
Herzen University, 253
Hitz, S., 29, 125, 201
hobbies, 71
Hohlbaum, C.L., 174, 237, 238
Home Décor Buyer, 8, 253
Horowitz, S., 118
How to Find the Love of Your Life in 90 Days or Less, 51
HowToDoItFrugally Series, 23, 38, 43, 74, 75, 93, 110, 126, 220, 236, 247, 251, 253, 254
HTML, 118, 168, 233

I

IBPA, 148
Illinois Library Association, 147
image-making. *See* branding
Imagining the Future, 243
imprints, 108
incentives, 213
Independent Book Publishers Association. *See* IBPA
Independent Publisher, 104
indexing, 108, 139
ineedhits.com, 233
instant messaging, 39
instructor. *See* teaching
internet, 177–83
  radio, 167
  website. *See* website
interview (media kit), 21, 80, 85
interviews, 21, 49, 54, 62, 80, 99, 105, 162
  electronic, 183
  getting, 167–68
  performance, 169
  re-use, 163
  television, 172
  trading, 188
introductions, writing, 122
invoices
  bookstores, 159, 215
  custom, 39, 138
Irwin Award, 248
It was the best of sentences, 11
iUniverse, 128

J

James Fellowship, 45
Jenkins, J., 214
Jillson, J., 225
Jobs, S., 40
John Wiley & Sons, 214
Johnson, K.J., 74
Johnson, L.G., iii
journals, 8, 55, 113, 114, 136
   blank, 89
   first rights, 115
   prizes, 136
   review, 100, 104, 106
jpg files, 58
Juvenile Court: A Guide..., 45

K

Karinski, E.M., 129
Karinski. M.K., 129
Keats, 99
Kelley, J., 134
Kelly, P., 132, 259
Kemp, H., vi
keywords, 124, 187, 195, 231, 234
Kindle, 125, 127, 188, 191, 194, 195, 199, 234
King, S., 38, 160
King's Speech, The, 223
Kinko's/FedEx, 48
Kirkus Reviews, 103, 108
Klausner, H., 196
Kleidon, R.A.O., 122
Klein, J., 10, 118
Kremer, J., 31, 61, 224, 257, 261
Krygier, L., iii, 45
Kulevich, P., 172

L

LA Mart, 216
LA Times Festival of Books, 149, 209
Lambert, E., v, 253
Lattanzio, M., 243
Laubach Literacy Programs, 159
launches, book. *See* book launches
Lawrence, M.P., 33
legal, 6, 9–10, 196, *See* also copyright
Leigh, N., 163
Lentz, B., 118
Leonhardt, D., 127
letters-to-the-editor, 119, 124
Levine/Greenberg Literary Agency, 236
Levinson, J.C., iii, 30, 261
Lewis, D.D., 170
library, 30, 87, 141, 173, 211, 230
   acquisition librarians, 21, 146
   appearances, 72, 149, 161, 241
   sales, 217–18
   tradeshows, 146, 147
Library Journal, 99, 103, 237
Library of Congress, 7, 9
LibraryThing, 201, 202
Light in the Distance, 241
Lightning Source, 102
LinkedIn, 52, 185, 187, 214
links, 59, 74, 85, 127, 181
   eBooks, 124
   media kit, 56
   media releases, 72
   vs. signature, 181
List-Serves, 183
Literary Law Guide, 7, 9
Liu, C., 254
local
   libary, 30
   media, 20
   newspapers, 31, 42, 56, 71, 151, 155, 161
   professional organizations, 137
   TV, 162, 169
locale, 56, 159
loglines, 52, 87, 96, 156
   defined, 96
   example, 54
   media release, 71
logos, 38, 39, 61, 88, 156
   in email, 180
   printed items, 90
   using others, 149
Los Angeles Times, 60, 86, 103, 146, 149, 151, 209, 253
Lovison, R., 174
Lulu, 102
Lummis, S., 39, 40, 142

M

M&Ms, 152, 155, 157
Maddow, R., 167
Maguire, K.L., iii
mailing service, 20, 212

Making a Literary Life, 61
manuscripts, 3
  blurbs, 46
  galleys, 101
  plagiarism, 4
  submission, 95, 136
marketing campaign, 19, *See* campaign
  advertorial, 42
marketing tips for authors, 252
Marriott, J.W., 28
Martinson, C., 173
McMullen, T.C., iii
media contacts. *See* lists
media kits, 8, 21, 27, 39, 43–45, 72
  and media release, 69, 76
  assembling, 65–67, 91–94
  endorsements, 48
  first person essay, 85
  mailing, 58
  other items, 88
  photos, 56
  seminars, 88
media releases, 20, 51, 54, 69–77, 95, 107, 133, 148, 178, 223
  and contests, 137
  distribution, 151, 181
  for media kit, 92
media room, 74, 178, 224, 243
mentors, iii, 11, 39
Meyer, S., 188
midlist author, 14
Midwest Book Review, i, 103, 104, 107
Military Writers Society of America. *See* MWSA
Miller Mosaic Social Media Marketing, 187
Miller, P.Z., 191
Miner, E., 232
modernpostcard.com, 221
momentum, 225, 229
motivation, 10, 173, 255
museums, 208, 257
MWSA, 174, 211, 243
MyShelf.com, 32, 104, 120, 253
myths, 4
  blogging, 185–88
  book signing, 158–60

N

nametag, 151, 153

National Federation of Press Women, 137
National Literacy Day, 172
National Public Radio. *See* NPR
networking, v, 31, 122, 146, 155, 196
New Book Review, 105, 120
New England Library Association, 147
New York Library Association, 147
New York Times, 33, 81, 100, 103, 134, 145, 194
newsletters, 29, 30, 46, 60, 61, 106–7, 117, 118, 121, 132, 137, 142, 158
  editors, 73
  your, 107, 115, 118–19, 125, 163, 178
Newsweek, 99
Next Generation award, 243, 254
Nike, 4
Nobel, 4, 241
nom de plume. *See* pseudonyms
nonfiction, vi, 33, 37, 38, 54, 86, 139, 177, 180, 207
  articles, 115
  catalogs, 209
  consequences, 51
  proposals, 54
  tip sheets, 123
novel, vi, 8, 10, 19, 30, 52, 81, 96, 123, 125, 139, 183
  locale, 56
NPR, 173, 237–38

O

Ohio Library Council, 147
Olympic Games, 30, 51, 128, 239
On Writing, 38
On Writing Well, 85
online danger, 203–4
op-ed, 44, 81, 116, 124
opposing views, 73
out of print, 27

P

Packer, ZZ, 37
panelist, 32, 83, 147, 151, 155
Parade, 167
parentheses, 48
Pasadena Star-News, 116, 253

The Frugal Book Promoter 271

Pasadena Weekly, 254
Patterson, J., 8, 125
Pay It Forward, 53
Pennsylvania Library Association, 147
People Magazine, 85
permalinks, 117, 121, 168, 187
permission, 9, 58, 80, 81, 86, 88, 101, 149
  blogs, 189
  fair use, 84
  to email, 181
  to reprint review, 80, 83, 85, 106, 107, 163, 178, 192
photo, 37, 40, 56–58, 72, 76, 92, 103, 153, 158, 171, 178, 200, *See also* headshots
Pinskey, R., 56, 249, 261
Pinterest, 200
plagiarism, 9–10
plagiarism, 4–7
platform, 1, 3, 7, 10, 14, 27, 37, 60, 104, 113–17, 121, 140
  defined, 15
Plutarch, 12
POD, 104, 108, 210
  galleys, 101
podcasts, 56, 163, 167, 168
poetry, vi, 7, 38, 39, 44, 59, 81, 121, 126, 135, 142, 174, 199, 201, 241, 242, 243
Poets & Writers, 37, 120, 135, 137, 141, 155, 243
point-of-purchase, 156, 215
  defined, 156
postcards, 62, 219–21
posters, 48, 53, 142, 150, 156, 162
pound signs, 72, 240
Powell's Bookstore, 198
PowerPoint, 132
Poynter, D., 7, 9, 107
praise, 48, 79, 83, 84, *See also* blurbs
  media kit, 108
present tense, 52
presenter, 50, 147, 150, 153, 254
press badges, 147
press pass, 120, 147
press release. *See* media releases
press room, 147
Press Women, 137

previously published material. *See* copyright
Primary Colors, 10
print-on-demand. *See* POD
Priority Mail, 109
prizes, 4, 89, 91, 136, 230
professional organizations, 20, 133, 137
profile pages, 193, 195, 199
program directors, 60, 87, *See also* conferences
Promote Your Book, 30, 261
promotion, v, 13, 14, 15
promotion gifts. *See* gifts
promotion tools, 180–82
pseudonyms, 10, 38, 179
public relations, v, vi, 9, 13–17, 21, 29, 35, 60, 61
publicists, iii, 19, 20, 22, 33, 131, 147, 186, 247
publicity, 25–42
publicity commandments, 29–34
Publicity Hound newsletter, 119
Publishers Weekly, 21, 103
Pulitzer, 73, 135, 136, 253

Q

QR code, 233–34
query letters, 14, 20, 21, 46–49, 51, 53, 74, 76, 97, 99, 107, 135, 148, 165, 195, 236
  sample, 236
quick response codes. *See* QR codes
quotation marks, 75
quotations as promotion, 9, 46, 107, 123, 223
quotes, i, 46, 73, 123, 192, 196, 223, 224

R

R&K Bookstore, 159
Radio and TV, 76, 82
  internet radio, 167
  interviews, 167–69
  live microphone, 171
  local TV, 172
  network TV, 172–73
  public access, 173
  public broadcasting, 173
Rakoff, J.S., 155
Random House, 108, 255, 257, 261

reading groups, 201, 207, 208
Really Simple Syndication. *See* RSS
recycling articles, 190
Red Sky Press Award, 122
references, iv, 21, 255
referrals, 7, 12
relationships, iii, v, vi, 16, 28, 33, 54, 62, 105, 114, 162, 183, 200, 207, 217, 223, 232
release dates, 101, 102, 103
remainder tables, 27, 50
Repulsion Thrust, 243
research, 79, 87, 234
response rate, 73, 220
résumés, 3, 7, 8, 15, 27, 82, 83, 131
retail, 30, 50, 91, 151
   catalog, 209, 211
   retail price, 213
   retail sales, 215–16
retail price, 103
reviews, 23, 61, 84, 99–110, 207, 220
   Amazon Vine, 231
   credibility, 84
   writing, 188, 196, 201
   writing reviews, 119–21
Rice, A., 154
Robb, J.D., 10
Roberts, N., 32, 177, 179
Rogers, B.H., 225
Romance Writers of America, 159
Rooney, A., 116
Roosevelt, F.D., 4
Roosevelt, T., 193
Rosen, J., 21
Rostan, S.K., 236
royalties, 6, 63, 99
RSS feed, 194, 200, 202, 233
Ruminator Review, 104

S

Safer, M., 173
sales
   associates, 157, 192
   catalog, 209–12
   corporate, 213–14
   forced sale, 215–16
   library, 217–18
   sales page, 59, 105, 108, 188, 196, 231
Salt Lake Tribune, v, 237, 253, 258
Sansevieri, P., 46, 61, 195, 201, 258

Scanbury, 233
Scanlife.com, 233
Schaefer, R.W., 138
scholarships, 32
Scott, J., 254
Screen Actors Guild, 46
screenplay, 49, 156
search engine
   Amazon, 195
search engines, 61, 106, 114
   Amazon, 194
   findgift.com, 213
   finding hosts, 167
   rank, 119, 178, 185–90, 233
Secret, The, 227
See, C., 61, 255
Seidman, D., 50
self-improvement, 134
self-mailer, 133
self-published, 7, 101, 104, 108, 137, 146, 162, 193, 203, 216
self-syndicate, 117
sell sheets, 102
seminar topics, 43, 87
seminars page, 88, *See also* media kit
seniors, 55
sequels, 125
Shakespeare, 4
SharingWithWriters blog, 29
SharingwithWriters newsletter, 33, 61, 73, 107, 128
She Wore Emerald Then, 242
Shifrin, E.B., 87
shipping (promotion), 231
short stories, 113, 238, 241
shy writers, 250
sidebars, 115
signature line, 117, *See also* autosignature
signed book copies, 157
signs, 48, 151, 153, 155, 156
Silverman, F., 167, 261
site map, 180
Skype, 169, 172
slideshows, 174
Small Press Review, 103
Small Publishers Association of North America. *See* SPAN
smartphone, 233
Smashwords, 242, 243
Smith, D.L., 29

The Frugal Book Promoter

Smith, J.E., 232
Smith, Liz, 116
social networking, 99, 120, 188, 198, 199, 242, *See also* profile pages
soundbites, 49, 80, 168
souvenir, 89–90
spam, 30, 72, 73, 181, 250
SPAN, 148
speaking, 20, 87, 131–35
 credentials, 81
 cruise ships, 207
 expenses, 35
special editions, 213
spell and grammar checker, 74
stationery, 38, 39, 48, 53, 70, 92, 108, 138, 181, 182
statistics, 15, 28, 123
Steele, D., 227
Stewart, J., 35, 119, 128
subhead. *See* decks
subject line, 61, 73, 97, 107, 109, 117, 123, 180, 240
submissions, 11, 44, 104, 114, 115, 121, 135, 136, 137, 181, 223
 simultaneous, 136
Submittable.com, 136
subsidy-published. *See* self-published
Swan, L., 60
syndication, 116, 117
synopsis, 1, 47, 54, 55, 71, 84, 96, 106, 190, 230, 237
Szerman, M., 30

T

Table of Contents. *See* contents
taglines, 14, 44, 45, 53, 114, 119, 124, 189
Talk Radio Wants You, 167
talking points, 85, 168, 169
target audience, 188, 201
tear sheets, 8
Ten Best Dressed List, 123, 253
testimonials. *See* blurbs
thank-yous, iii, 16, 31, 48, 61–62, 89, 90, 93, 96, 114, 121, 153, 158, 168, 181, 213, 250
This Is the Place, 19, 30, 38, 51, 52, 72, 89, 123, 128, 148, 153, 159, 160, 162, 237, 239, 241
Thomas, V., 242

Thornton, M., 11
Thurber, J., 85
Time magazine, 118, 123, 203, 239
tip sheets, 123, 252
Toastmasters, 83, 132, 232
Tracings, 243
trade magazines, 30, 216
tradeshows, 49, 60, 87, 91, 119, 143, 145–48, 216, 218, 233, 237, 248, 254
trailers, 150, 167
translate, 128
Treisman, J., 53
Trillin, C., 229
trim size, 103
Trombley, L.S., v
Turow, S., 177
TV. *See* Radio and TV
Twain, M., v, 40
Twitter, 35, 117, 128, 167, 185, 187, 194, 199, 200, 224, 230, 251
typos, 74, 118, 134

U

UCLA Extension Writers' Program, 11, 126, 243, 251
Union Leader, The, 127
University of Akron, 122
University of Southern California (USC), 60, 162, 253
University of Utah, 253
USA Book News award, 247, 248, 251
USA Today, 134
USC Marshall School of Business, 15

V

Vanderbilt, A., 213
verbs, 52, 70, 74
Veres, S., 241
videos, 74, 119, 131, 149, 150, 163, 167, 171, 174, 190, 196
Vine reviewers, 195, 231
violation notice, 102, 103
Virginia Book Fair, 181
Vise, D., 194
Vistaprint, 221
Vogue magazine, 214
voice, 33, 75, 81, 114, 136, 169

voice mail, 231
voiceover, 171
Volkman, V., iii
voting online, 196
Vroman's Bookstore, 154

W

Walls, K., 126
Walmart, 122, 172, 214
warehousers, 146
Warren, L., 21
website, 177–80
What Foreigners Need to Know About America from A to Z, iii
When She Sleeps, i, 45
wholesale, 148, 215, 216
widgets, 188, 197, 233
Wikes, C., 241
Wikipedia, 6, 177, 202, 203
Wilde, O., 82
William Faulkner Writing Competition, 136
Winning Writers newsletter, 137
Wisconsin Regional Writers' Association, 137
Wolfe, L.D., 244, 245, 262

Wooden, J., 131
Word Works, 10
word-of-mouth, 6, 125
Writer's Digest, i, 135, 256, 259
Writer's Markets, 137
Writer's Weekly, 128
Writers Guild of America, 6
writers' conference. *See* conferences
WritersOnTheMove.com, 189

X

Xerox, 6

Y

YahooGroups.com, 52
Your Blog, Your Business, vi, 51
YouTube, 35, 74, 128, 168, 171, 190

Z

Zinsser, W., 85, 86, 262
Zuckerberg, M., 201

ZAQdesigns

Book covers and interiors that **STAND OUT!**

www.zaqdesigns.com

Writing for Bliss **is most fundamentally about reflection, truth, and freedom.**

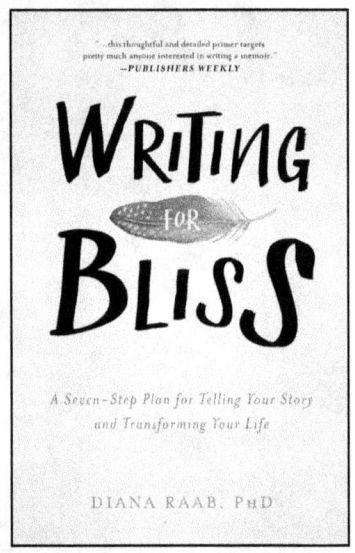

With techniques and prompts for both the seasoned and novice writer, it will lead you to
- tap into your creativity through storytelling and poetry,
- examine how life-changing experiences can inspire writing,
- pursue self-examination and self-discovery through the written word, and,
- understand how published writers have been transformed by writing.

"Part writing guide, part memoir, and part love letter to the craft of writing, Diana Raab's *Writing for Bliss* is a caring and motivational guide. Raab's love of words and her belief in the power of story shine through. With its hypnotic and personal stories, interviews with other authors, and many useful writing prompts, *Writing for Bliss* will find a valued spot on the bookshelves of those seeking greater understanding."

--ANGELA WOLTMAN, *FOREWORD REVIEWS*

Poet and memoirist Raab (*Lust*) credits her lifelong love of writing and its therapeutic effects with inspiring her to write this thoughtful and detailed primer that targets pretty much anyone interested in writing a memoir. Most compelling here is Raab's willingness to share her intimate stories (e.g., the loss of a relative, ongoing struggles with cancer, a difficult relationship with her mother). Her revelations are encouraging to writers who feel they need "permission to take... a voyage of self-discovery." The book's seven-step plan includes plenty of guidance, including on learning to "read like a writer," and on addressing readers as if "seated across the table ." Raab covers big topics such as the "art and power of storytelling" and small details such as choosing pens and notebooks that you enjoy using.

--*PUBLISHER'S WEEKLY*

Paperback * Hardcover * Audiobook * eBook * Workbook Editions

Learn more at www.DianaRaab.com

From Modern History Press

How Dare We! Write: a multicultural creative writing discourse offers a much needed corrective to the usual dry and uninspired creative writing pedagogy. The collection asks us to consider questions, such as "What does it mean to work through resistance from supposed mentors, to face rejection from publishers and classmates, and to stand against traditions that silence you?" and "How can writers and teachers even begin to make diversity matter in meaningful ways on the page, in the classroom, and on our bookshelves?"

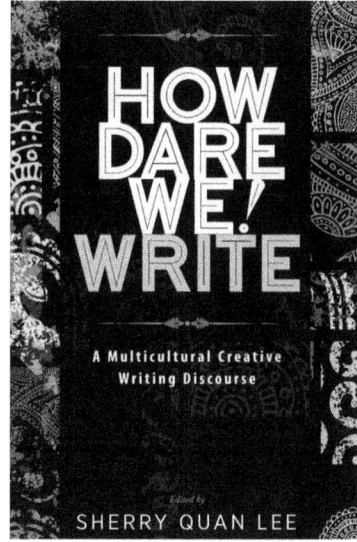

How Dare We! Write is an inspiring collection of intellectually rigorous lyric essays and innovative writing exercises; it opens up a path for inquiry, reflection, understanding, and creativity that is ultimately healing. The testimonies provide a hard won context for their innovative paired writing experiments that are, by their very nature, generative.

-- Cherise A. Pollard, PhD, Professor of English,
West Chester University of Pennsylvania

So-called "creative writing" classes are highly politicized spaces, but no one says so; to acknowledge this obvious fact would be to up-end the aesthetics, cultural politics (ideology) and economics on which most educational institutions are founded. *How Dare We! Write*, a brilliant interventive anthology of essays, breaks this silence.

-- Maria Damon, Pratt Institute of Art;
co-editor of *Poetry and Cultural Studies: A Reader*

How Dare We! Write a collection of brave voices calling out to writers of color everywhere: no matter how lonely, you are not alone; you are one in a sea of change, swimming against the currents.

-- Kao Kalia Yang, author of *The Latehomecomer: A Hmong Family Memoir*, and *The Song Poet*, a Minnesota Book Award winner

Paperback * Hardcover * eBook Editions

Learn more at www.SherryQuanLee.com

From Modern History Press

www.ingramcontent.com/pod-product-compliance
Lightning Source LLC
Chambersburg PA
CBHW071659160426
43195CB00012B/1519